PROGRESS IN LANGUAGE

AMSTERDAM STUDIES IN THE THEORY AND HISTORY OF LINGUISTIC SCIENCE

General Editor
E. F. KONRAD KOERNER
(University of Ottawa)

Series I - AMSTERDAM CLASSICS IN LINGUISTICS, 1800-1925

Advisory Editorial Board

Sheila Embleton (Toronto); Kurt R. Jankowsky (Washington, D.C.)
Brian D. Joseph (Columbus, Ohio); Winfred P. Lehmann (Austin, Tex.)
James D. McCawley (Chicago); Sergej A. Romaschko (Moscow)
Terence H. Wilbur (Los Angeles)

Volume 17

Otto Jespersen

*Progress in Language,
with special reference to English*

OTTO JESPERSEN

PROGRESS IN LANGUAGE
WITH SPECIAL REFERENCE TO ENGLISH

New Edition
with an Introduction
by

JAMES D. McCAWLEY
University of Chicago

JOHN BENJAMINS PUBLISHING COMPANY
AMSTERDAM/PHILADELPHIA

1993

Library of Congress Cataloging-in-Publication Data

Jespersen, Otto, 1860-1943.
   Progress in language : with special reference to English / Otto Jespersen. -- new ed. with an introd. / by James D. McCawley.
           p.   cm. -- (Amsterdam studies in the theory and history of linguistic science. Series I, Amsterdam classics in linguistics, 1800-1925, ISSN 0304-0712; v. 17)
Includes index.
1. Historical linguistics. 2. English language--Grammar, Historical. I. McCawley, James D. II. Title. III. Series.
P140.J46   1993
417'.7--dc20   93-36955
ISBN 90 272 1992 3 (Eur.) / 1-55619-314-9 (US) (alk. paper)   CIP

© Copyright 1993 - John Benjamins B.V.
No part of this book may be reproduced in any form, by print, photoprint, microfilm, or any other means, without written permission from the publisher.

John Benjamins Publishing Co. · P.O. Box 75577 · 1070 AN Amsterdam · Netherlands
John Benjamins North America · 821 Bethlehem Pike · Philadelphia, PA 19118 · USA

CONTENTS

Foreword by *E. F. K. Koerner*   vii
Photograph of Otto Jespersen   viii
Introduction by *James D. Mc. Cawley*   ix

Progress of Language, with special Reference to English

FOREWORD

1993 is the fiftieth anniversary of the death of one of the greatest 20th-century scholars in the language sciences, Otto Jespersen. On 29–30 April this year, the Department of English Philology at the University of Copenhagen will hold an international symposium to mark the hundredth anniversary of Jespersen's appointment to the first chair of English language in Denmark. It seems that there is hardly a better year — 'anniversary compulsion' (Peter Aykroyd) aside — for a reprint of Jespersen's *Progress in Language; with special reference to English*, which he wrote during the first year of his Copenhagen professorship, publishing it in the following year in London and New York, for, as Hans F. Nielsen has recently shown,[1] Jespersen maintained the essentials of his argument against the prevailing mode of 19th-century linguistic thought until the end of his long life and scholarly career.

While Jespersen was publishing the first volume of his monumental *Modern English Grammar on Historical Principles* (1909-1949), *Progress in Language* appeared, as the imprint tells us, in a "Second edition — practically without changes" (London: Swan Sonnenschein, 1909). Jespersen's 1941 study *Efficiency in Linguistic Change* still harks back to his original position, modified in parts as could be expected. His thesis has been that languages do not develop 'downwards' — Schleicher's *Verfall* comes to mind — as was the majority view in 19th-century linguistics, but toward a higher degree of communicative efficiency with the most economical grammatical means.[2]

I would like to thank James D. McCawley, Andrew McLeish Distinguished Service Professor in the Departments of Linguistics and of East Asian Languages & Civilizations of the University of Chicago, for kindly providing a splendid introduction to the present reissue of *Progress in Language*.

Les Jardins du Château, Hull, Québec   E. F. K. Koerner
5 February 1993

---

[1] See his paper, "On Otto Jespersen's View of Language Evolution", in *Otto Jespersen: Facets of his life and work* ed. by Arne Juul & Hans F. Nielsen (Amsterdam & Philadelphia: John Benjamins, 1989), 61-78.
[2] This 1941 essay was reprinted in *Selected Writings of Otto Jespersen* (London: George Allen & Unwin; Tokyo: Senjo Publ. Co., n.d. [c.1960]), 346-426.

Otto Jespersen (1887). By courtesy of the Royal Library, Copenhagen.

INTRODUCTION

Progress in Language, while dating from fairly early in Otto Jespersen's (1860-1943) academic career (it appeared in 1894), is preceded by 67 other publications of his, and is a long way from being his first book: he had already published school textbooks of English and French, a French reader in phonetic transcription, a monograph on Danish phonology, coauthored with Verner Dahlerup (1859–1938), a monograph on articulatory phonetics in which he develops his 'analphabetic' system of transcription, his Ph.D. thesis on the history of English cases (which was reworked into chapters III-VII of *Progress in Language*), an edition of Stevenson's *Treasure Island* for use in Danish middle schools (the original had been published only 11 years earlier), a monograph on the phonetics of colloquial English (coauthored with E. Th. True), and monographs on Robert Browning and Chaucer. It is nonetheless much earlier than the books through which he is best known in the late 20th century (*Growth and Structure of the English Language*, 1905; *Modern English Grammar on Historical Principles*, 7 vols., 1909-1949; *Language*, 1922; *The Philosophy of Grammar*, 1924; *Mankind, Nation, and Individual from a linguistic point of view*, 1925; *Essentials of English Grammar*, 1933; *Analytic Syntax*, 1937), and is certainly the earliest of his books that is of sufficient inherent interest to late 20th century readers to warrant its reprinting.

The inventory of topics covered in *Progress in Language* is somewhat peculiar. While more than half the book (chapters VI-VIII, comprising 190 pages) is devoted to the history of English, there is also a chapter on "The History of Chinese and of Word-Order", one on "Primitive Grammar" [sic], of which half is devoted to Bantu languages, and a final chapter on "Origin of Language". However, relative to Jespersen's goals, the anticipated reactions of his presumed audience, and the knowledge that he possessed at the time, the choice of topics in fact made considerable sense. Jespersen wished to divorce the notion of 'progress' in linguistic change from the at that time highly influential division (by August Schleicher and his followers) of languages into 'isolating', 'agglutinating', and 'flexional', categories that were supposed to correspond to successively more advanced stages of development. From the point of view of Schleicher's scheme, English had already achieved flexional status at the time of its earliest attestations and then rapidly degenerated to a status approaching that of a mere isolating language. Jespersen, however, regarded Schleicher's categories as of dubious value even as a framework for typology, and rejected Schleicher's invidious comparisons of isolating with flexional languages as preposterous: for Jespersen, inflexional morphology is more of an obstacle than an aid to efficient communication, and the changes that English has undergone over the last millenium have worked to the advantage of its speakers by broadening the range of things that they can say at all and increasing the amount of utility that they can derive from given linguistic machinery.

The most valuable parts of *Progress in Language* are clearly the three chapters on the history of English, in which Jespersen documents in great detail the loss of the case system in nouns, the massive restructuring of the case system in pronouns, and the development of *-s* from a genitive marker on one class of nouns into an adjunct to whole noun phrases that is no longer strictly speaking an inflectional element.[1] In the process, he asked and answered important questions that had largely been ignored, such as why the spread of genitive *-s* and the spread of plural *-s* yielded such different results (*the Queen of England's crown* but *the Queens of England* and not **the Queen of Englands* ; voicing of the spirant in *wives* but not in *wife's*). In arguing that "the cause of the decay of the Old English apparatus of declensions lay in its manifold incongruities" (p.176) and that contact with Norman French played only the role of accelerating changes that were already in progress, he happily parted company with the venerable Jacob Grimm[2] and argued that the fine details of the changes that took place in the 11th–14th centuries were vastly dif-

---

[1] Jespersen saw this even though his terminology did not provide any way of saying "noun phrase" (see McCawley [1992b:6] for respects in which Jespersen's lack of a terminological distinction between 'noun' and 'noun phrase' occasionally brought him to grief) and he in fact states the right generalization with the wrong word: "The *s* is always wedged in between the two words [sic] it serves to connect" (p.313). He noted correctly that it is wedged in between the two things that it serves to connect and incorrectly spoke as if those things had to be words, even though his argument gives much prominence to combinations in which the things connected are entities larger than words.

[2] In the overview of the history of linguistics in *Language*, Jespersen presents a very unflattering picture of Grimm: Grimm appropriated from earlier work by Rasmus Rask the ideas in historical linguistics that Grimm is most famous for, namely the consonant correspondences between the Germanic languages and between the major branches of Indo-European, but fudged the terminology (through systematic equivocation over the term 'aspirate') so as to create the illusion of a cyclic permutation of three categories of sounds and thereby pander to 19th-century German intellectual fashion, in which ternary groupings and cyclic changes held favor. What Jespersen regarded as most valuable in Grimm's output was the massive body of examples that Grimm found of the various sound correspondences and Grimm's work on historical syntax.

ferent from what one would expect if French influence were a significant factor, e.g., genitive -*s* spread more rapidly than plural -*s*, even though it was only the latter for which French provided any model, and plural -*s* spread faster in the north, where little French was spoken, than in the south, where French influence was the strongest. By leaping from an extended quotation of Grimm's purple prose, with its statement that "According to a universal and natural law, where two different tongues come in collision, grammatical forms are lost", to a realistic description of the sociolinguistic situation in Norman-ruled England, in which the English vastly outnumbered the Normans and presumably treated borrowings from the court language the same way that modern Frenchmen and Englishmen treat borrowings from each other's languages, Jespersen amusingly but effectively accuses the whole German historical linguistic establishment of failing to give appropriate consideration to what should be central to discussions of linguistic change, namely the dynamics of the communities within which the changes take place. He was later (1922, Chap.11) to stress the importance of distinguishing the kinds of situations in which languages are in contact and the linguistic effects that normally result from the different kinds of contact. Interestingly, for Jespersen, the kind of contact that is most likely to cause loss of morphological distinctions is not that in which, as in the Grimm quotation, the languages differ greatly in their vocabularies, but that in which (as in the contact between Danes and English in northeastern England) the languages had such a high degree of mutual intelligibility that speakers of one could treat the other as a different form of their own language.

There are several ways in which one can dispute Schleicher's view of his flexional type as the pinnacle of linguistic evolution. In the 20th century, the most common response to that view has been to dispute that there is any pinnacle to linguistic evolution and to hold that there is no particular direction to linguistic evolution, with languages of any of Schleicher's types being able to develop in the direction of either of the other types. Jespersen, however, adopted a very different response, claiming that languages normally evolved in the direction of Schleicher's 'isolating' type. This response was in sharp conflict with the then almost universally accepted belief that the earliest human languages must have been 'simple', with no morphology or syntactic irregularity and with a small inventory of phonological segments and a small vocabulary consisting of short words. The chapter on Chinese is included so that Jespersen can disabuse his readers of the then common belief, endorsed by Schleicher himself, that Chinese had preserved a type of linguistic structure that had existed in the earliest days of human language and had changed little, aside from substantially enlarging its vocabulary.[3] Jespersen cites evidence that many Chinese monosyllables have evolved from earlier disyllabic words[4] and quotes an argument (unfortunately, a rather bad argument) that Chinese must have had an ancestor with an inflectional system for it to be possible for it and the flexionless Tibeto-Burman languages to have a common ancestor but still have different word orders.

Jespersen in fact rejected the then nearly universally accepted belief that morphologically complex words normally arise through the fusion of independent words; his view was rather that inflectional and derivational morphemes much more commonly arise through the fission of polysyllabic words into pieces that acquire their meanings through the fission, as in the reinterpretation of *oxen*, in which the *n* was originally part of the noun stem, as *ox* + *-en*, with *-en* taking on the function of a plural ending. He found particularly congenial Brugmann's (1888) account of Indo-European gender, according to which the genders had arisen through chance similarities in the endings of words that could be interpreted as representing a gender category, and those endings were reinterpreted as signs of membership in such categories not only when the meanings were appropriate to a gender category but even when they were not. The chapter on "Primitive Grammar" takes seriously the (by now thoroughly discredited) idea that the languages of more 'primitive' cultures are themselves more primitive, in the sense of preserving features of early human languages that have been lost as high cultures have developed and their languages have developed with them. The importance of this chapter lies mainly in the contribution that it makes to Jespersen's case against the view of linguistic complexity as having developed through the fusion of short, simple linguistic elements: he argues that the Bantu class-prefix and agreement system arose the way that Brugmann took the Indo-European gender system to have arisen and that the prevalent direction of change in Bantu languages is towards simplification of

---

[3] Jespersen's information on Chinese comes primarily from Gabelentz's 1881 *Chinesische Grammatik*. Gabelentz applies to the variety of Chinese that he describes the term *kuan hoa*, which normally implies what is now called "Mandarin"; however, the forms in the *Chinesische Grammatik* are phonologically much closer to Cantonese than to Mandarin (e.g., all six final consonants /p t k m n ng/ are retained, whereas Mandarin has lost final /p t k/ and changed final /m/ into /n/). Gabelentz does give lists of words in which he contrasts *kuan hoa* with Cantonese, though the differences that he notes are mainly in the vowels. Jespersen accepts uncritically Gabelentz's statements to the effect that, for instance, Chinese had no part of speech distinctions.

[4] De Francis (1984, Chap.11) points out that a significant number of apparent compounds in Chinese have always been disyllabic and that the popular belief that they consist of two morphemes owes its existence solely to the writing system, in which there is a separate character for each syllable.

the system of classes. The most entertaining parts of this chapter are the long quotations from authors such as Whitney, interrupted by bracketed heckles from Jespersen calling attention to the circularity of their arguments for complexity as arising from fusion of simple units.

While the chapters on English are the ones that make the most substantial contribution to linguistics as it is usually practised today, the most strikingly original chapter in the book is the final one, on the origins of human language. The chapter is included, in all probability, to defuse an argument that many readers were sure to throw at Jespersen: if linguistic change is predominantly in the direction of languages with short words, little inflection, and great regularity, does that not commit one to the absurdity that the earliest human languages, in every sense the most 'primitive' languages that have ever been spoken, were highly complex?

Jespersen argues that the supposed absurdity is not so absurd after all, and in the process he concocts a scenario for the origins of human language that is both the most ingenious and the most sophisticated that I have ever encountered and shows him to have mastered ideas of evolutionary biology that even the biologists of his time rarely appreciated fully. Jespersen separates the question of the origin of language from the question of the origin of words and argues that the elements that first took on the function of words must have existed long before they functioned as words and long before there was a language for them to be part of. He suggests that a language could not develop until a community already had a large body of conventionalized sound-meaning pairings that it could split up and recombine so as to enlarge the previous finite set of 'messages'. He holds that the many so-called theories of the origins of language (the 'bow-wow theory', 'ding-dong theory', etc.) all are in a sense right, since all of them identify sources of vocabulary that may have played a role in the earliest human languages, but that all of them are wrong in giving special significance to one particular source of vocabulary, and none of them is really a theory of the origin of language, since none of them gives any plausible way of getting from the particular type of vocabulary that it regards as having a special status to anything like a language: "Each one of the theories [...] is able to explain *parts of language*, but still only parts, and not even the most important parts — the main body of language they hardly seem even to touch" (p.331).

This chapter provides most of the material that Jespersen used in the final chapter of his 1922 book *Language*, the main difference between it and the 1922 reworking of it being that in the latter version Jespersen tied his conjectures about the origins of language together with his subsequent research on language acquisition[5] by attributing to early humans the same tendency towards gratuitous segmentation of meaningful sound that he found to be widespread among children and which is exhibited in adult language in folk etymology and in innovative morphology such as the creation of novel words ending in a suffix *-teria* that arose through segmentation of the word *cafeteria*. Thus, when members of prehistoric human communities took a major step towards real language by breaking up polysyllables (such as the syllables of songs associated with specific events) into parts to which they assigned meanings, they were doing something that human beings have been doing naturally for millenia. Jespersen's suggestion of song as a major source of proto-vocabulary is a particularly brilliant idea, since the social functions of songs (in courtship, ritual, and whatnot) allow fairly specific and often complex meanings to be associated with what are at the outset 'nonsense syllables' and make it likely that these complex sound-meaning pairings will be learned by all members of the community and will persist over long periods of time.[6]

Jespersen accompanies his scenario for the origins of language with comments in which he pokes fun at the simple-mindedness of most 19th-century scholars' ideas about how language might have originated. He finds the allusion to dogs in the name 'bow-wow theory' particularly inappropriate, "for naturalists maintain that dogs did not learn to bark till after their domestication", and he quotes with approval Renan's remark that according to that 'theory', "first the lower animals are original enough to cry and roar; and then comes man, making a language for himself by imitating his inferiors". One of his biggest criticisms of his predecessors is that they "tacitly assume that up to the creation of language man had remained mute or silent" (p.332). For Jespersen, the question of how our distant ancestors created words is silly unless one purges it of that assumption and breaks it into two much more sensible questions: what uses did those ancestors make of the sounds that their vocal organs could produce, and how could they have adapted their full repertoire of vocal sounds and associated functions into words? He is amused at the way that scholars such as Madvig and Whitney seem to "imagine our primitive an-

---

[5] Jespersen had in fact been actively engaged in research on language acquisition since very early in his academic career, as can be seen from his astute deployment of observations of child language in one of his earliest papers (Jespersen 1886). While he does bring child language into his 1894 account of origins of language (e.g., p.334), it is only in the 1922 version that he provides any substance to the idea that the steps by which the earliest human languages developed included things that modern children do in acquiring their first language.

[6] Jespersen could well have also pointed out that the proto-vocabulary posited by the earlier 'theories' does not lend itself to useful segmentation: even if one were to analyze the concept 'dog' into two parts, one expressed by *bow* and the other by *wow*, it is unlikely that one would have much occasion to recombine those parts with anything else.

cestors after their own image as serious and well-meaning men endowed with a large share of common sense" (p.356) and as "sedate alderman-like citizens with a prominent sense for the purely business and matter-of-fact side of life" (p.357). He contrasts with such a position his own view that "the genesis of language is not to be sought in the prosaic, but in the poetic side of life; the source of speech is not gloomy seriousness, but merry play and youthful hilarity".

Among the few authors that Jespersen quotes with approval in his final chapter are Charles Darwin and Herbert Spencer. He chides his fellow linguists for having overlooked Darwin's *The Expression of the Emotions*, in which Darwin identifies physiological responses to surprise, pain, etc. as causing the production of sounds that in many languages have been conventionalized as interjections. One striking characteristic of *Progress in Language* is the skill with which Jespersen adapts the central ideas of Darwinian evolutionary biology to questions of linguistics. Throughout chapters VI-VIII, his accounts of the various developments in English are in terms of variation, selection, and multiple functions of the various forms whose survival is at stake. A particularly large role in Jespersen's thinking is played by Darwin's idea of *preadaptation*, that is, the exploitation of existing structures to serve functions that need not bear any relation to the functions that have allowed them to survive so far, as in the development of the mammalian inner ear from bones that were originally segments of the lower jaw and whose secondary function of transmitting external vibrations to the nervous system becomes primary after they have ceased to function as parts of the jaw. In such changes there is always a change in figure-ground relationships, and Jespersen was particularly keen at noticing figure-ground changes in linguistic units, as in his treatment of English possessive -'s as having changed from the status of a case-marker in a noun to that of the linking element in a *NP's N* construction. Other signs of Jespersen's familiarity with the cutting edge of late 19th-century biological thought are his paraphrase of Haeckel's Law (commonly given as "Ontogeny recapitulates philogeny", pp.334-335) and his intransigently uniformitarian views on language change, as where he opposes Schleicher's view of periods of progress and of retrogression with the assertion that "the moment of a nation's entering into history is of no consequence at all for the direction of linguistic change, which goes on in an essentially identical manner now and in the days of old" (p.136).[7]

---

[7] See McCawley (1992a) for further discussion of biological ideas in Jespersen's writings on language.

The parts of *Progress in Language* that I, as an admirer of Jespersen, find embarrassing are those in which he speaks like a typical 19th-century imperialist about 'savages', 'barbaric peoples', and 'primitive people' and seems all too willing to attribute intellectual inferiority to 'savages', as where he treats "the frequent emphasising of a negation by seemingly redundant repetitions" as a tendency of "undeveloped minds" (p.38) and uncritically accepts the conclusions of various (largely unidentified) authors that a savage's "power of abstraction is not sufficiently developed" to conceive of the notion 'knife' as opposed to notions relating to doing various things with knives (p.348).[8] In some of his references to 'savages' and 'primitive languages', however, Jespersen, whose well-honed wit is apparent at many places in this book, may have been indulging in the sort of humor that has been the basis of unwarranted accusations of racism that have been directed against H. L. Mencken: his seemingly racist descriptions of languages such as Zulu and of their speakers often serve to introduce comparisons of these low-prestige languages with prestigious older Indo-European languages such as Latin, in which some of the characteristics that contributed to the high prestige of the latter (such as the rich agreement system) are seen to differ little from characteristics that had been offered as rationales for the low prestige of the former.

Much of the fascination of reading this long out-of-print classic lies in seeing its relationship to Jespersen's long and distinguished subsequent career: seeing how much importance he already attached to variation in language, how tightly his views on linguistic change were already integrated with his views on synchronic grammar, how intransigently sociolinguistic his thinking about language change was (in the sense that he never lost sight of the communities in which the various stages of languages were spoken and regarded his hypotheses about language change as hypotheses about the dynamics of those communities), and how vast a collection he had already amassed of English examples illustrating even very subtle details of phonology, morphology, syntax, and semantics. Leaving aside his occasional uncritical parroting of

---

[8] Actually, the examples that Jespersen cites are in many cases poor illustrations of the supposed generalization. Languages that "have no word for *brother*, but only for 'elder brother' and 'younger brother'" operate in terms of highly 'abstract' kinship notions but simply use a semantic dimension in their kin terminology that European languages do not use. Languages that "can only express 'hand' as being either 'my hand' or 'your hand' or 'his hand,' and so on" make explicit a distinction that functions at least covertly in all languages, namely that between alienably and inalienably possessed entities, and need not differ at all from European languages in the range of abstractness in their thinking about hands. The passages in which Jespersen makes generalizations about "the languages of savages" are among the few places where he writes about matters of which he is grossly ignorant, and here the usually high intellectual level of his writing drops precipitously.

fairy tales about Chinese and about primitive people who lack powers of abstraction, *Progress in Language* is linguistics on the same striking level of sophistication that characterized nearly all of his later work and which perhaps no other linguist save Edward Sapir achieved so consistently. While it was aimed at an audience whose concerns and assumptions overlap little with those of modern readers, *Progress in Language* can be appreciated more fully by modern readers than it could be by Jespersen's contemporaries, because Jespersen's own concerns and assumptions are closer to those of his successors than of his contemporaries. I am proud to have an opportunity to play a role in making Jespersen's first large-scale linguistic study once again available to linguists.

Chicago, December 1992   James D. McCawley

REFERENCES[†]

Brugmann, Karl. 1888. "Das Nominalgeschlecht in den indogermanischen Sprachen". (Friedrich Techmer's) *Internationale Zeitschrift für Allgemeine Sprachwissenschaft* 4.100-109. (Repr., Amsterdam: Benjamins, 1973.)
Darwin, Charles. 1872. *The Expression of Emotions in Man and Animals*. London: John Murray.
De Francis, John. 1984. *The Chinese language: Fact and fantasy*. Honolulu: Univ. of Hawaii Press.
Gabelentz, Georg von der. 1881. *Chinesische Grammatik*. Leipzig: T. O. Weigel. (Repr., Berlin: Deutscher Verlag der Wissenschaften, 1953.)
Madvig, Johan Nikolai. 1875. *Kleine philologische Schriften*. Leipzig: B. G. Teubner. (Repr., Hildesheim: Georg Olms, 1966.)
McCawley, James D. 1992a. "The Biological Side of Otto Jespersen's Linguistic Thought". *Historiographia Linguistica* 19:1.97-110.
----------. 1992b. "Introduction". Reprint of Jespersen, *The Philosophy of Grammar*, 1-9. Chicago: Univ. of Chicago Press.
Renan, Ernest. 1848. *De l'origine du langage*. Paris: M. Lévy frères. (4th ed., 1863.)
Schleicher, August. 1850. *Die Sprachen Europas in systematischer Übersicht*. Bonn: H. B. König. (Repr., with an introd. by Konrad Koerner, Amsterdam & Philadelphia: John Benjamins, 1983.)
Whitney, William Dwight. 1875. *Life and Growth of Language: An outline of linguistic science*. New York: D. Appleton & Co.; London: H. S. King. (Repr., with a foreword by Charles F. Hockett, New York: Dover, 1979.)

[†] For references to Jespersen's writings, see Select Bibliography (overleaf).

SELECT BIBLIOGRAPHY OF JESPERSEN'S WRITINGS[*]

1887 [1886]. "Zur Lautgesetzfrage". (Friedrich Techmer's) *Internationale Zeitschrift für Allgemeine Sprachwissenschaft* 3.188-217. (Repr. in Jespersen 1933.160-192.) [Translation by Christian Sarauw of "Til spörgsmålet om lydlove", *Nordisk Tidskrift for Filologi*, new series, 7.207-245 (1886).]

1894. *Progress in Language, with special reference to English*. London: Swan Sonnenschein; New York: Macmillan. (Repr., together with an introd. by James D. McCawley, Amsterdam & Philadelphia: John Benjamins, 1993.)

1904a. *Lehrbuch der Phonetik*. Authorized translation from the Danish by Hermann Davidson. Leipzig & Berlin: B. G. Teubner. (2nd ed., 1913; 3rd ed., 1920.)

1904b. *How to Teach a Foreign Language*. New York: Macmillan.

1905. *Growth and Structure of the English Language*. Leipzig: B. G. Teubner.(9th ed., 1938; 10th unchanged ed., with a foreword by Randolph Quirk, Oxford: Basil Blackwell, 1982.)

1909–1949. *Modern English Grammar on Historical Principles*. 7 vols. London: Allen & Unwin; Copenhagen: Einar Munksgaard.

1914. "Energetik der Sprache". *Scientia* 16.255ff. (Repr. in Jespersen 1933b: 98-108.)

1917. Review of Ferdinand de Saussure, *Cours de linguistique générale* ed. by Charles Bally & Albert Sechehaye, with the collaboration of Albert Riedlinger (Lausanne & Paris: Payot, 1916). *Norsk Tidsskrift for Filologi*, 4th series 6.37-41. (French transl., by Adigard de Gautrie, in Jespersen 1933b: 109-115.) [Written Nov. 1916.]

1922. *Language: Its nature, development and origin*. London: Allen & Unwin. (Repr., New York: W. W. Norton, 1964.)

1924. *The Philosophy of Grammar*. London: Allen & Unwin; New York: Henry Holt & Co. (Repr., with an introd. by James D. McCawley, Chicago: Univ. of Chicago Press, 1992.)

1925. *Mankind, Nation and Individual; from a linguistic point of view*. Oslo: H. Aschehoug & Co.; Paris: H. Champion; Cambridge, Mass.: Harvard Univ. Press.

1933a. *Essentials of English Grammar*. London: Allen & Unwin.

1933b. *Linguistica: Selected papers in English, French and German*. Copenhagen: Levin & Munksgaard. (Repr., 1970.)

1937. *Analytic Syntax*. London: Allen & Unwin. (Repr., with an introduction by James D. McCawley, Chicago: Univ. of Chicago Press, 1984.)

1941. *Efficiency in Linguistic Change*. Copenhagen: Einar Munksgaard.

---

[*] A full bibliography of Jespersen's writings up to 1930, compiled by C. A. Bodelsen, appears in *A Grammatical Miscellany Offered to Otto Jespersen on His 70th Birthday* (Copenhagen: Einar Munksgaard, 1930), pp.433-457; it is supplemented by a list of Jespersen's subsequent work, compiled by Niels Haislund, that is appended as the final six pages of Louis Lenor Hammerich's (1892-1975) obituary for Jespersen in *Oversigt over det kgl. danske Videnskabernes Selskabs Forhandlinger* 1944.41-63.

PROGRESS IN LANGUAGE

WITH SPECIAL REFERENCE TO ENGLISH

BY

OTTO JESPERSEN, Ph. Dr.

PROFESSOR OF ENGLISH IN THE UNIVERSITY OF COPENHAGEN
AUTHOR OF "THE ARTICULATIONS OF SPEECH SOUNDS"
"CHAUCER'S LIV OG DIGHTNING," ETC.

LONDON
SWAN SONNENSCHEIN & CO.
NEW YORK: MACMILLAN & CO.
1894

PREFACE.

THIS volume is to a certain extent an English translation of my *Studier over Engelske Kasus, med en Indledning: Fremskridt i Sproget*, which was submitted to the University of Copenhagen in February, 1891, as a dissertation for the Ph. D. degree, and appeared in print in April of that year. In preparing this English edition I have, however, altered my book so materially as to make it in many respects an entirely new work.[1] In the first place, what was originally only an introductory essay has been enlarged and made the principal part of the book, as already indicated by the altered title. Consequently, I could only retain those chapters of the special investigation on the history of English cases which had some bearing on the central idea of "Progress in Language," *viz.*, chs. vi. and vii. (formerly i. and ii., on "the English Case-Systems" and on "Case-Shiftings in the Pronouns"), while the last chapter, dealing with the history of voiced and voiceless consonants, was of too special a nature to be inserted in this volume. I shall probably find an opportunity of reprinting part of this investigation in the introduction to the edition of Hart's *Orthographie*, which I am preparing for the Early English Text Society; and I may here provisionally refer the readers to Dr. Sweet's *New English Grammar*, §§ 731, 861, 862, 863 (cf. also §§ 810, 813, 997, 999, 1001), where I am glad to say that the eminent author has accepted even those of my results which run counter to his own previous views.[1] By leaving out this chapter I have found place for the last two chapters of the present volume, of which one (viii. "The English Group Genitive") is entirely new; while the other, on the "Origin of Language," was read in a somewhat shorter form before the Philological Congress in Copenhagen, on the 21st of July, 1892, and printed in the Danish periodical *Tilskueren*, in October of the same year.

---

[1] The small numbers in parentheses refer to the paragraphs of the Danish book; they will enable the reader to judge of the changes made in revising the work for this edition.

[1] §§ 1076-87 of the same Grammar will be found to cover nearly the same ground as my ch. vii. (ii. in the Danish edition).

Secondly, I have left out whatever seemed to me little likely to present any interest to English readers, especially the numerous instances of Danish developments parallel to those mentioned in chapter vii.; in the new chapter viii. I have refrained from giving such parallel cases, but I hope some day to find an opportunity of publishing my Danish collections separately.

Thirdly, I have taken due notice of those reviews of my Danish book in which reasons were given for dissenting from my views; I must especially thank Professors Herman Möller and Arwid Johannson for opening my eyes to some weak points in my arguments, even if I have not been able to make their opinions mine; on the contrary, a consideration of their objections has only strengthened my belief in the progressive tendency of languages at large. In the linguistic literature which has appeared since my *Studier*, I have found little to learn with regard to my own subject; if G. von der Gabelentz's *Die Sprachwissenschaft* (Leipzig, 1891) had appeared before instead of after my *Studier*, it would probably have influenced my exposition, as I should have been able from that admirable work to draw many arguments in favour of my hypothesis; but as it is, I have thought it the wisest plan to leave the main structure of my work as it was, and only once for all refer the reader to Gabelentz's great work, which no one can read without great profit. My attention was not drawn to Misteli's *Charakteristik der hauptsächlichsten Typen des Sprachbaues* (Berlin, 1893) till nearly the whole of my book was ready for print in its English shape; the reader will there find good, if somewhat abstruse and rather too "philosophical" summaries of the distinguishing features of many languages.

Such of my readers as are not specially interested in the history of the English language will perhaps do well to read of chapters vi.-viii. only those sections which deal with problems of a more general character (§§ 138-150, 209-215, 216-218, and 240-247); I myself look upon these three chapters as specimens of the manner in which I hope, by-and-by, to treat the most important points in the development of the English language; a few more chapters of the same description are nearly ready, dealing chiefly with the relations

PREFACE.

between adjectives and nouns (or first parts of compounds) and those between nouns and verbs (cf. § 65).

As the term "Old English" is still sometimes used in different senses by different authors, it is not superfluous to remark that throughout this book it means the English language till about 1150, called by many scholars "Anglo-Saxon". In the very few places where I have used a phonetic transcription, the sign · indicates that the preceding vowel is long.

I shall conclude this Preface by mentioning the difficulty I have often felt in expressing my thoughts adequately in a language which is not my own; if my English is not too awkward and clumsy, this is to a great extent due to my friend G. C. Moore Smith, M.A., of St. John's College, Cambridge, who has been kind enough to read my manuscript very carefully and to emend my style in not a few points; I seize this opportunity of thanking him most heartily for his extremely valuable assistance. I must also thank Cand. E. Lennholm, of this city, who translated most of chapter vi. for me from the Danish original.

OTTO JESPERSEN.

CONTRACTIONS

USED IN THE QUOTATIONS IN CHAPTERS VI.-VIII.

Alford, *Queen's Engl.* = *The Queen's English*, 8th edit., London, 1889.

Ancr. R. or *A. R.* = The *Ancren Riwle*, edited by Morton (Camden Society, 1853); cf. also Kölbing's collation in *Jahrbücher für Romanische und Englische Literatur*, vol. xv.

Bale, *Three L.* = *A Comedy concerning Three Lawes* (1538), edited by Schröer in *Anglia*, vol. v.

Beitr. = *Beiträge zur Geschichte der Deutschen Sprache und Literatur* (Halle).

Blanch. or *Blanchard.* = Caxton's *Blanchardyn*, ed. by Kellner (Early Engl. T. Soc.).

Carlyle, *Her.* = *Heroes and Hero-Worship*; *Sart.* or *S. R.* = *Sartor Resartus* (London, Chapman & Hall).

Ch. or Chauc. = Chaucer; Morr. or M. = the Aldine edition, by R. Morris; the *Canterbury Tales* (C. T. or *Cant.*) are generally quoted according to Furnivall's groups (A, B, C, etc.); Skeat's editions in the Clarendon Press Series have generally been used; *M. P.* = *Minor Poems*, edit. by Skeat, 1888; *Hous of F.* = *The Hous of Fame*, in the same edition; *L. G. W.* = *The Legend of Good Women*, edit. by Skeat, 1889.

Chron. = *The Anglo-Saxon Chronicle* (edit. by Plummer, 1889 and 1892).

Cura P. = King Alfred's Version of Gregory's *Pastoral Care*, edit. by H. Sweet, 1871.

Dickens, *M. Ch.* = *Martin Chuzzlewit* (the Charles Dickens edition, Chapman & Hall); *Christm. Books* = *Christmas Books* (Macmillan).

CONTRACTIONS.

Einenkel, *Streifz.* = *Streifzüge durch die mittelenglische Syntax* (Münster, 1887).
G. Eliot, *Mill* = *The Mill on the Floss* (T.); *Life* = *Life of G. E.*, by W. Cross (T.).
Ellis, *E. E. P.* = *On Early English Pronunciation*, i.-v., 1869-89.
Engl. St. = *Englische Studien*, herausg v. E. Kölbing.
Fielding (Field.), *T. J.* = *Tom Jones*, i.-iv. (London, 1782).
Greene, *Friar B.* = *Friar Bacon and Friar Bungay*, edit. by A. W. Ward (1887).
Lay. = Layamon's *Brut*, edit. by Madden.
Malory (Mal.) = *Le Morte Darthur*, edit. by O. Sommer (1889).
Marlowe (Marl.), *Jew* = *Jew of Malta*; *Tamb.* = *Tamburlaine*, edit. by A. Wagner (Heilbronn, 1889 and 1885).
M. E. = Middle English (ab. 1150-1500).
Meredith, *Trag. Com.* = *The Tragic Comedians* (T.); *Eg.* = *The Egoist* (1 vol), Chapman & Hall).
Milton, *P. L.* = *Paradise Lost*; *S. A.* = *Samson Agonistes*.
Murray, *Dial.* = *The Dialect of the Southern Counties of Scotland* (1873).
N. E. D. = *A New English Dictionary*, by J. A. H. Murray and H. Bradley.
O. E. = Old English (before 1150).
Oros. = King Alfred's *Orosius*; L. = the Lauderdale MS., edit. by H. Sweet (1883); C. = the Cotton MS, edit. by Bosworth (1859).
Orig. Engl. = *Very Original English*, by H. Barker (Lond., 1889).
Roister = (Udall, ?) *Roister Doister*, Arber's reprint.
Ruskin, *Sel.* = *Selections from the Writings of John Ruskin*, i.-ii. (G. Allen, 1893).
Sh. or Shak. = Shakespeare, quoted in the spelling of the first folio (1623); the acts, scenes, and lines, numbered as in the Globe edition; for *Romeo and Juliet* (*Rom.* or *Ro.*), Th. Mommsen's edition has been used, in which the lines of the second quarto are numbered continuously; the abbreviations of the titles of the plays will be easily understood; *All's*, *As*, *Ant*, *Cor*, *Cymb*, *L. L. L.* = *Love's Labour's Lost*, etc., *Mcb.* = *Macbeth* (the numbering of the lines according to A. Wagner's edition, Halle, 1890); 1 *H. IV.* = *First Part of King Henry the Fourth*.
Shelley, *Poet. W.*, Macmillan's one-volume edition.
Sheridan, *Dr. W.* = *Dramatic Works* (T.).
Spec. = *Specimens of Early English*, by (Morris and) Skeat, i.-iii.
Spectator, H. Morley's edition (Routledge).
Storm, *E. Phil.* = *Englische Philologie* (Heilbronn, 1881).
Sweet, *H. E. S.* = *History of English Sounds* (1888); *N. E. G.* = *New English Grammar* (1892).
Tennyson, *Poetical Works*, Macmillan's one-volume edit, supplemented by Tauchnitz ed.
Thc. or Thack. = Thackeray, *V. F.* = *Vanity Fair* (in the Minerva Library); *P.* or *Pend.* = *Pendennis* (T.); *Esmond* (T.).
Thanks awf'lly, Sketches in Cockney (Field & Tuer, 1890).
The other abbreviations require no explanation; the works of W. Black, Robert Browning, Byron, Conan Doyle, Miss Muloch, R. L. Stevenson, Swift, Trollope (Troll.) and Mrs. Humphrey Ward are quoted from the Tauchnitz edition (T.), but in all other cases I have used editions printed in England.

TABLE OF CONTENTS.

CHAP.		PAGE
I.	Introduction,	1
II.	Ancient and Modern Languages,	18
III.	Primitive Grammar,	40
IV.	The History of Chinese and of Word-Order,	80
V.	The Development of Language,	112
VI.	English Case-Systems, Old and Modern,	138
VII.	Case-Shiftings in the Pronouns,	182
VIII.	The English Group Genitive,	279
	Appendix.—"Bill Stumps *his* Mark," etc.,	318
IX.	Origin of Language,	328
	I. Method,	328
	II. Sounds,	338
	III. Grammar,	345
	IV. Vocabulary,	350
	V. Conclusion,	354

CHAPTER I.

INTRODUCTION.

1. (1) No language is better suited than English to the purposes of the student who wishes, by means of historical investigation, to form an independent opinion on the life and development of language in general. In English we have an almost uninterrupted series of written and printed works, extending over a period of more than a thousand years; and, if we are not contented with the results to be obtained from these sources, comparative philology comes in, drawing its conclusions from all the cognate tongues, and showing us, with no little degree of certainty, the nature of the language spoken by the old Germans at the time when the differentiation of the several tribes had as yet scarcely begun. The scientific investigations of our century go still further back: they have brought together Greek and Latin, German, Slavonic, Lithuanian, Celtic, Indian and Persian, as one indissoluble unity; through a long succession of parallelisms they have pointed out what is common to all these languages, and have made it possible to some extent to reconstruct the unwritten language used in intercourse by the ancestral people several centuries before the era of any languages historically accessible to us. If we do not know where the original Arian (or, as it is often termed, Indo-European or Indo-Germanic) people lived, we know much about the structure of their speech.

2. (1) During the course of the ages the language of the Arians has changed in a multiplicity of ways in the mouths of different nations; but nowhere has the original type been more radically modified than in England. The amount and thoroughness of these modifications will perhaps be perceived most clearly if we take some recognised definition of the most essential features characterising Arian speech, in opposition to the motley crowd of other tongues. We shall find that scarcely one of those features is characteristic of present-day English. FRIEDERICH MÜLLER thus describes the distinguishing traits of the languages of the Arian type:[1] "In the Indo-Germanic languages root, stem and word are rigorously discriminated". In English words such as *man* or *wish* no one is able to make any such separation. "The two categories of noun and verb are kept clearly from each other." Not so in English: *e.g.*, *man* is generally a noun, but it is used as a verb when we say, "*Man the ship*"; compare also *I wish* and *my wish*. "Nouns belong

[1] *Grundriss der Sprachwissenschaft*, iii., 2, p. 420.

to one of three genders, masculine, feminine, or neuter." From English grammatical gender has disappeared. "The distinction between the several grammatico-logical categories is here carried out strictly." This is not the case in English, where, to mention only one point, nouns and adverbs may be used as adjectives.

3. (2) But if the old order has thus changed, yielding place to new, the question naturally arises: Which of these two is the better order? Is the sum of those infinitesimal modifications which have led our language so far away from the original state to be termed evolution or dissolution, growth or decay? Are languages as a rule progressive or regressive? And, specially, is modern English superior or inferior to primitive Arian?

If I am right in my interpretation of the tendencies of recent philology, the answer cannot be doubtful; but there is as little doubt that this answer will be the exact opposite of what an older generation of linguists would have given as their verdict. It may therefore be of some interest to examine more closely the linguistic philosophy of the age that is now going out. How did the leading men of some thirty years ago classify and estimate different types of speech, and what place did they assign to such languages as modern English?

It would scarcely be possible to find any one man better suited to represent typically the views here referred to than AUGUST SCHLEICHER. In a series

of highly important works[1] he has dealt with problems of classification of languages and linguistic development in general: by his exceptional knowledge of a number of languages and as being the first master builder of that lofty structure, the Arian "ursprache," he stands out pre-eminently among his contemporaries, and exercises a vast influence down to our own day: in spite of all apparent difference, it is his ideas that form the basis alike of MAX MÜLLER'S brilliant paradoxes and of WHITNEY'S sober reasonings: he is rightly to be considered the spiritual father of every comparative philologist of our own times, notwithstanding the gulf separating his views from those of some of the younger generation. Let us, therefore, try to give a short account of his leading ideas and the manner in which he arrived at them: our investigation will show the curious spectacle of a classification and a theory completely outliving the basis of reasoning on which they were founded.

4. (3) From the outset Schleicher was a sworn adherent of Hegel's philosophy: this is a fact well worth remembering, for not even the Darwinian

---

[1] *Sprachvergleichende Untersuchungen*: I. *Zur vergl. Sprachengeschichte*, 1848; II. *Die Sprachen Europas*, 1850.—*Zur Morphologie der Sprache*, St. Petersburg. Acad. Impér., 1859.—*Die Deutsche Sprache*, 1860: 2te ausg., 1869.—*Die Darwinsche Theorie und die Sprachwissenschaft*, 1863.—*Die Unterscheidung von Nomen u. Verbum* (Sächs. Gesellsch. d. Wissensch.), 1865.—*Ueber die Bedeutung der Sprache für die Naturgeschichte des Menschen*, 1865.

sympathies and views of which he was a champion towards the end of his career, made him alter the doctrines of his youth. The introduction to his first book is entirely Hegelian: it is true that he professes himself a follower of Wilhelm von Humboldt with regard to the division of languages; but, as a matter of fact, this is what he is not. Humboldt has four classes: an Hegelian wants neither more nor less than three, and is therefore obliged to tack together Humboldt's "incorporating" and "agglutinating" classes. Then everything is in order, and we are enabled philosophically to deduce the tripartition. For Language consists in *meaning* (bedeutung; matter, contents, root), and *relation* (beziehung; form); tertium non datur. As it would be a sheer impossibility for a language to express form only, we obtain three classes:—

Class I. Here meaning is the only thing indicated by sound; relation is merely suggested by word-position; this is the case in monosyllabic languages, or, as they are also termed, *isolating or root languages*, such as Chinese.

Class II. Both meaning and relation are expressed by sound, but the formal elements are visibly tacked on to the root which is itself invariable: *agglutinating languages*, *e.g.*, Finnic; and

Class III. The elements of meaning and of relation are fused together or absorbed into a higher unity, the root being susceptible of inward modifications as well as of affixes to denote form: *flexional languages*,

represented by the two families of speech which have played the most important parts in the history of the world: Semitic and Arian.[1]

5. (4) According to Schleicher, the three classes of languages are not only found simultaneously in

[1] I hope I shall be forgiven for not translating the following bit of Hegelian philosophy: "War das erste die differenzlose identität von beziehung und bedeutung, das reine ansich der beziehung, das zweite die differenziirung in beziehungs- und bedeutungslaute—das heraustreten der beziehung in ein gesondertes, lautliches dasein für sich—so ist das dritte das aufheben jener differenz, das sich zusammenschliessen derselben, die rückkehr zur einheit, aber zu einer unendlich höheren einheit, weil sie aus der differenz erwachsen, diese zu ihrer voraussetzung hat und als aufgehoben in sich befasst" (*Sprachvgl. Unters.*, i., 10). Schleicher is neither the first nor the only author who has divided languages into three groups: his classification is nearest akin to those of FRIEDRICH SCHLEGEL (non-inflexional;—affixing (including among the rest Semitic);—inflexional) and of A. W. SCHLEGEL (les langues sans aucune structure grammaticale[!];—les langues qui emploient des affixes;—les langues à inflexions). Besides these we have BOPP: languages consisting of monosyllabic roots but without power of composition; —languages of monosyllabic roots susceptible of composition, among others the "Sanskritic," *i.e.*, Arian languages;—languages of dissyllabic roots susceptible of inner modification (Semitic); GRIMM: non-flexional;—flexional;—analytic; POTT: normal [flexional];—intranormal [isolating and agglutinating];—transnormal [incorporating]; MAX MÜLLER: family languages (juxtaposition);—nomad languages (agglutination);—state languages (amalgamation). It will be seen that the only thing really common to these systems is the number three. Of the various trinities Schleicher's has been the most widely accepted.

the tongues of our own day, but they represent three stages of linguistic development; "to the *nebeneinander* of the system corresponds the *nacheinander* of history". Beyond the flexional stage no language can attain; the symbolic denotation of relation by flexion is the highest accomplishment of language; speech has here effectually realised its object, which is to give a faithful phonetic image of thought. But before a language can become flexional it must have passed through an isolating and an agglutinating period. Is this theory borne out by historical facts? Can we trace back any of the existing flexional languages to agglutination and isolation? Schleicher himself answers this question in the negative: the earliest Chinese with which we are acquainted is as monosyllabic as the Chinese of to-day, and the earliest Latin was of as good a flexional type as are the modern Romance languages. This would seem a sort of contradiction in terms; but the Hegelian is ready with an answer to any objection; he has the word of his master that History cannot begin till the human spirit becomes "conscious of its own freedom," and this consciousness is only possible after the complete development of *Language*. The formation of Language and History are accordingly successive stages of human activity.[1] Moreover, as history and historiography, *i.e.*, literature, come into existence simultaneously, Schleicher is enabled to express the same idea in a way that is "only seemingly para-

[1] *Sprachvergl. Unters.*, i., 16; *Deutsche Spr.*, 35.

doxical,"[1] namely, that the development of language is brought to a conclusion as soon as literature makes its appearance; this is a crisis after which language remains fixed; language has now become a means, instead of being the aim, of intellectual activity (*Sprachvergl. Unters.*, i., 24). We never meet with any language that is developing or that has become more perfect (*ibid.*, 13); in historical times all languages move only downhill; this is not to be disputed ("das ist ausgemachte wahrheit," *ibid.*, 14); linguistic history means decay of languages as such, subjugated as they are through the gradual evolution of the mind to greater freedom (*ibid.*, 17).

6. (4) This doctrine of an antagonism between language and history is a pet theory which Schleicher never abandons; in his first book (ii., p. 134) he speaks of "die geschichte, jene feindin der sprache"; and in his Darwinian period he puts it in this way: "The origin and development of language is previous to history, properly and strictly speaking.... History shows us nothing but the aging of languages according to fixed laws. The idioms spoken by ourselves, as well as those of all historically important nations,

[1] *Sprachvergl. Unters.*, i., 20. This "seeming paradox" has, however, been subsequently modified by Schleicher; see *Deutsche Spr.*, 47, where he says: "People did not apply themselves to writing or literature immediately after the acquisition of language; writing requires no small degree of culture, and consequently presupposes some historical development".

are senile relics" (*Die Bedeut. d. Spr.*, 27; cf. *Die Darwinsche Theorie*, 27; *D. Spr.*, 37).[1]

7. (5) According to Schleicher, then, we witness nothing but retrogression and decay; but as the same view is found as early as Bopp, and as it is the fundamental belief, more or less pronounced, of many other linguistic speculators, we are justified in supposing that with Schleicher the theory is not really due to the Hegelian train of argument, but that here, as not unfrequently, reasoning is summoned to arms in defence of results arrived at by instinct. And the feeling underlying this instinct, what is it but a grammar-school admiration, a Renaissance love of the two classical languages and their literatures? People were taught to look down upon modern languages as mere dialects, and to worship Greek and Latin; the richness and fulness of forms found in those languages came naturally to be considered the very *beau idéal* of linguistic structure. To men fresh from the ordinary grammar-school training no language would seem respectable that had not four or five distinct cases and three genders, or that had less than five tenses and as many moods in its verbs. Accordingly, such poor languages as had either lost much of their original richness in grammatical forms (*e.g.*, French, English, or Danish), or had never had any (*e.g.*, Chinese), were naturally looked upon with something like the pity bestowed on relatives in reduced circumstances, or the contempt felt for foreign paupers.

8. (6) Comparative philologists had one more reason for adopting this manner of estimating languages. To what had the great victories won by their science been due? Whence had they got the material for that magnificent edifice which had proved spacious enough to hold Hindus and Persians, Lithuanians and Slavs, Greeks, Romans, Germans, and Celts? Surely it was neither from Modern English nor Modern Dutch, but from the oldest stages of each linguistic group. The older a linguistic document was, the more valuable it was to the first generation of comparative philologists. An English word like *had* was of no great use, but Gothic *habai dâdeima* was easily picked to pieces, and each of its several elements lent itself capitally to comparison with Sanskrit, Lithuanian and Greek. The philologist was chiefly dependent for his material on the old and

---

[1] A peculiar form of the downhill theory with special reference to Romance languages is found in an early work of GASTON PARIS's (*Rôle de l'Accent Latin*, 1862). In the primitive era we find language in process of formation, and regularity; next comes the period of literary languages, in which the genius of the language goes astray on account of the imperfect knowledge of the educated classes, while the uneducated lose the proper linguistic tact, and corrupt the language; finally [the holy number of three once more!] after the literary language is forgotten and the vulgar tongue has prevailed, a longer or shorter period of depravation is followed by a second formation of new languages;—"mais comme, au lieu de se créer de première main, ils n'auront eu pour se construire que des matériaux déjà incohérents et dégradés, ils seront inférieurs en beauté et en logique aux langues précédentes".

archaic languages; his interest centred round their fuller forms; what wonder then if in his opinion they were superior to all others? What wonder if by comparing *had* and *habaidêdeima* he came to regard the English word as a mutilated and worn-out relic of a splendid original? or if in noting the change from the old to the modern form he used strong language and spoke of degeneration, corruption, depravation, decline, phonetic decay, etc., or even adopted for himself Schleicher's noble simile? "Our words, as contrasted with Gothic words, are like a statue that has been rolling for a long time in the bed of a river till its beautiful limbs have been worn off, so that now scarcely anything remains but a polished stone cylinder with faint indications of what once it was" (*Deutsche Spr.*, 34).

9. (6) Suppose, however, that it would be quite out of the question to place the statue on a pedestal to be admired; what if, on the one hand, it was not ornamental enough as a work of art, and if, on the other, human well-being was at stake if it was not serviceable in a rolling-mill: which would then be the better,—a rugged and unwieldy statue, making difficulties at every rotation, or an even, smooth, easy-going and well-oiled roller?

10. (7) Schleicher does not explain by what test he estimates the comparative merits of languages; the whole tenor of his linguistic philosophy hinders him from getting at the only one that really is of any value: the practical interests of the speaking (or talking) community. Schleicher emphatically repeats on every occasion that linguistics is a natural science; he never wearies of insisting upon the distinction between linguistics (or glottics, as he himself terms it) and the purely historical science of the scholar ("philology" in the broad or German sense of the word). Language is to Schleicher a natural object, just as much as a plant is. And if you object that language is nothing but human action and has no material existence, he will answer[1] by defining language in an entirely materialistic way as the result, perceptible through the ear, of the action of a complex of material substances in the structure of the brain and of the organs of speech with their nerves, bones, muscles, etc. Anatomists, however, have not yet been able to demonstrate differences in the structures of these organs corresponding to differences of nationality,—to discriminate, that is, the organs of a Frenchman (quâ Frenchman) from those of a German (quâ German). Accordingly, as the chemist can only arrive at the elements which compose the sun by examining the light which it emits, while the source of that light remains inaccessible to him, so we must be content to study the nature of languages not in their material antecedents but in their audible manifestations. It makes no great difference, however; for "the two things stand to each other as cause and effect, as substance and phenomenon: a philosopher would say that they are identical".

[1] Cf. *Die Bedeutung*, etc., 7-11.

11. (7) I, for one, fail to understand how this can be, what Schleicher believes it, "a refutation of the objection that language is nothing but a consequence of the activity of these organs". The sun exists independently of any human observer; but there could be no such thing as language if there was not besides the speaker a listener who might become a speaker in his turn. However this may be, it is certain that Schleicher never succeeds in establishing a rational basis for determining the relative value or merit of different languages.[1]

But this is quite easy if we take for our guide an idea expressed long ago and with considerable emphasis by WILHELM VON HUMBOLDT, that language means speaking, and that speaking means action on the part of a human being to make himself understood by somebody else. Then it becomes evident that that language ranks highest which goes farthest in the art of accomplishing much with little means, or, in other words, which is able to express the greatest amount of meaning with the simplest mechanism.

[1] As a rule Schleicher seems to take the morphological classification as the starting-point for his estimates of languages; but this is not the case when, in *Zur Morph. der Spr.*, p. 7, he says that perfection in language is dependent on the function of the sounds (cf. p. 11, *ibid.*, on Chinese). In *Die Deutsche Spr.*, 34, he seems to establish a duality of phonetic decay and progress in function and syntax; and in the same work, p. 60, we find one isolated expression that sounds quite modern: "The old wealth of forms is now thrown aside as a dispensable burden".

12. (7) RASK says[1] that "an elaborate linguistic structure with a variety of endings in declensions and conjugations has certain advantages . . . but it may be that the advantages of the opposite simplicity are still greater". MADVIG defends our modern analytical languages with great vigour. He says that they are just as good as the old synthetic ones, for thoughts can be expressed in both with equal clearness; poverty in grammatical forms is no drawback to a language. I shall try to show that we are justified in going still further than these two eminent men, and saying the fewer and shorter the forms, the better; the analytic structure of modern European languages is so far from being a drawback to them that it gives them an unimpeachable superiority over the earlier stages of the same languages. The so-called full and rich forms of the ancient languages are not a beauty but a deformity.

13. (8) In putting forward these propositions, I am not treading on entirely new ground. In JACOB GRIMM'S singularly clever (though nebulous) essay on the *Origin of Language* (1851), I find such passages as the following: "Language in its earliest form was melodious, but diffuse and straggling (*weitschweifig und haltlos*); in its middle form it was full of intense poetical vigour; in our own day it seeks to remedy the diminution of beauty by the harmony of the whole, and is more effective though it has inferior means", he arrives at the result that "human

[1] *Samlede Afhandlinger*, i., 191.

language is retrogressive only apparently and in particular points, but looked upon as a whole it is progressive, and its intrinsic force is continually increasing". The enthusiastic panegyric on the English language with which he concludes his essay forms a striking contrast to Schleicher's opinion that English shows "how rapidly the language of a nation important both in history and literature can sink".[1]

14. In recent linguistic literature indications of a reaction against the prevailing manner of estimating languages are also found, though the reaction is only of a sporadic and rather timid character. Thus KRÄUTER[2] says: "The dying out of forms and sounds is looked upon by the etymologists with painful feelings; but no unprejudiced judge will be able to see in it anything but a progressive victory over lifeless material.[3] Among several tools performing equally good work, that is the best which is simplest and most handy; this illustration has some significance for the subject under discussion. . . . That decay is consistent with clearness and precision, is shown by French; that it is not fatal to poetry, is seen in the language of Shakespeare."

OSTHOFF says: "We should avoid a one-sided depreciation of the language of Lessing and Goethe

[1] *Sprachvergl. Unt.*, ii, 231.
[2] In Herrig's *Archiv f. das Studium neuerer Sprachen*, 57, 204.
[3] Compare Schleicher's expression, "the subjugation of language through the evolution of the mind," quoted above, § 5.

in favour of those of Wulfila or Otfried, or *vice versâ*. A language possesses an inestimable charm if its phonetic system remains unimpaired and its etymologies are transparent; but pliancy of the material of language and flexibility to express ideas is really no less an advantage. Everything depends on the point of view: the student of architecture has one point of view, the people who are to live in the house another."[1]

E. TEGNÉR gives as the conclusion of an interesting disquisition that "so far from being more perfect than both the other groups [agglutinating and isolating] the flexional languages are radically inferior to them because they impede liberty of thought".[2]

15. (8) As such utterances are, however, comparatively isolated, and as the authors quoted, as well as the great majority of living linguists, are in many respects still in the toils of Schleicher's system, I hope that the following attempt to apply consistently the principle laid down in § 11, and to draw some further conclusions from the results obtained by comparison of the older and younger stages of Arian languages, will have some interest for linguistic students. My design being principally to gain in-

[1] "Schriftsprache und Volksmundart," in *Sammlung gemeinverstl. Vorträge*, 1883, p. 13.
[2] "Språkets makt öfver tanken," 1880, pp. 46-65. SAYCE is also an admirer of agglutination in preference to flexion, cf. below, § 99.

sight into historical developments, it will be noticed, firstly, that I do not attempt to fix the comparative value of languages that are not closely related to each other; and, secondly, that the examples I take are not isolated facts, but typical and characteristic of the total structures of the languages I am dealing with.

CHAPTER II.

ANCIENT AND MODERN LANGUAGES.

16. (9) First, let us look at Schleicher's example: English *had* and Gothic *habaidēdeima*. The English form is preferable, on the principle that any one who has to choose between walking one mile or four miles will, other things being equal, prefer the shorter cut. It is true that if we take words to be self-existing natural objects, *habaidēdeima* has the air of a giant, and *had* (like most other words which have been exposed to phonetic changes carried on through a long succession of ages) is left a mere pigmy. If, however, we remember the fact that what we call a word is really and primarily the combined action of human muscles to produce an audible effect, we see that the shortening of a form means a diminution of effort and a saving of time in the communication of our thoughts. If *had* has suffered from wear and tear in the long course of time, this means that the wear and tear of people now using this form in their speech is less than if they were still encumbered with the old giant *habaidēdeima* (comp. below, § 92, footnote).

17. (10) But it is not only in regard to economy of

(18)

muscular exertion that the English *had* carries the day over the Gothic form. *Had* corresponds not only to *habaidêdeima*, but it unites in one short form everything expressed by the Gothic *habaida, habaidês, habaida, habaidêdum, habaidêduts, habaidêdêduþ, habaidêdun, habaidêdjau, habaidêdeis, habaidêdi, habaidêdeiwa, habaidêdeits, habaidêdeima, habaidêdeiþ, habaidêdeina*,—separate forms for two or three persons in three numbers in two distinct moods! It is clear, therefore, that the English form saves a considerable amount of brain work to all English-speaking people, and especially to every child learning the language. Some one will, perhaps, say that on the other hand English people are obliged always to join personal pronouns to their verbal forms, and that this is a drawback counterbalancing the advantage, so that the net result is six of one and half a dozen of the other. This is, however, not entirely the case. In the first place, the personal pronouns are the same for all tenses and moods, but the endings are not. Secondly, the possession of endings does not exempt the Goths from having separate personal pronouns; and whenever these are used, the verbal endings which indicate persons are superfluous. They are no less superfluous in those extremely numerous cases in which the subject is either separately expressed by a noun or is understood from the preceding proposition. So that, altogether, the numerous endings of the older languages must be considered uneconomical.

18. (12) If I have shown that the older Arian languages burden the memory by the number of their flexional endings, they do so no less by the many irregularities in the formation of these endings. Irregularity may be termed a consequence of flexion—not, indeed, a logical consequence of any definition of flexion, for we might very well imagine some language of the Volapük kind in which all flexions were completely regular; but, as a matter of fact, such a language never existed. In Latin, in Greek, in Sanskrit, in Gothic, in all existing flexional languages of the same type, anomaly and flexion invariably go together. If the accidence of Modern English nouns can be set forth in a few pages, this is not exclusively due to the fewness of the cases, but also to the fact that nearly all nouns are declined in pretty much the same way: but the further back we go in the history of English or any other cognate language, the greater is the number of exceptions and anomalies of every description which we shall encounter. This will become especially clear when the facts of grammar are arranged as I have arranged them below (chapter vi.). And it is not only the forms themselves that are irregular in the early languages, but also their uses: logical simplicity prevails much more in Modern English syntax than in either Old English or Latin or Greek. But I need hardly point out that growing regularity in a language means a considerable gain to all those who learn it or speak it.

19. (12) Let me here quote an interesting remark made by FRIEDRICH MÜLLER in speaking of a totally different language:[1] "Even if the Hottentot," says he, "distinguishes 'he,' 'she,' and 'it,' and strictly separates the singular from the plural number, yet by his expressing 'he' and 'she' by one sound in the third person, and by another in the second, and by his denoting the plural differently according to person and gender, he manifests that he has no perception at all of our two grammatical categories of gender and number, and consequently those elements of his language that run parallel to our signs of gender and number must be of an entirely different nature". Fr. Müller certainly goes too far in this glorification of the speech of his own countrymen, on account of its superiority to that of the poor Hottentots; for could not the very same thing which he objects to the Hottentot language be predicated of his own? "As the Germans express the plural number in different manners in words like *gott—götter, hand—hände, vater—väter, frau—frauen*, etc., they must be entirely lacking in the sense of the category of number!" Or let us take such a language as Latin; there is nothing to show that *dominus* bears the same relation to *domini* as *verbum* to *verba, urbs* to *urbes, mensis* to *menses, cornu* to *cornua, fructus* to *fructûs*, etc.; even in the same word the idea of plurality is not expressed by the same method for all the cases, as is shown by a comparison of *dominus—domini, dominum—dominos, domino—dominis, domini—dominorum*. Fr. Müller is no doubt

[1] *Grundriss der Sprachwiss.*, i., 2, 7.

wrong in saying that such anomalies preclude the speakers of the language from conceiving the notion of plurality; but, on the other hand, it seems evident that a language in which a difference so simple even to the understanding of very young children as that between one and more than one, can only be expressed by a complicated apparatus, must rank lower than another language in which this difference has a single expression for all cases in which it occurs. In this respect, also, Modern English stands higher than Latin, Hottentot, or the oldest English.

20. I must pause here a moment to reply to some objections that have been made to my manner of viewing these points. It has been said[1] that the difficulties experienced by a grown-up person in learning a foreign language are not felt by a child picking up its mother tongue: children will learn an inflexional language with the same ease as one which is analytical; the real difficulties in learning a foreign language are "those thousands of chicanes caused by that tyrannical, capricious, utterly incalculable thing 'idiomatic usage,' but this gives little or no trouble to children learning to talk". I think, however, that if any one will listen attentively to children talking, he will soon perceive that they make a great number of mistakes, not only in inflecting strong verbs like regular verbs, etc, etc., but also in arranging the words of a sentence in a wrong order,

[1] HERMAN MÖLLER, *Nord. Tidskrift for Filologi*, n. r. x. See esp. p. 295.

giving unusual significations to words, using the wrong prepositions, and, in fact, violating usage in every possible way. In all this I see evidence of the labour involved in learning a language, a labour that is not to be underrated even when the language is learnt under the most favourable circumstances possible. And I think there can be no doubt that the exertion must be greater in the case of highly complicated linguistic structures with many rules and still more exceptions from the rules, than in languages constructed simply and regularly. It is, of course, impossible actually to prove that it is easier for an English child to learn to speak English than it was for a Gothic or Anglo-Saxon child to learn those languages; but it seems highly probable.

21. Nor is the difficulty of correct speech confined to the first mastering of the language. Even to the native who has spoken the same language from a child, its daily use involves no small amount of exertion. Under ordinary circumstances he is not conscious of any exertion in speaking; but such a want of conscious feeling is no proof that the exertion is absent. And it is a strong argument to the contrary that it is next to impossible for you to speak correctly if you are suffering from excessive mental work; you will constantly make slips in grammar and idiom as well as in pronunciation; you have not the same command of language as under normal conditions. If you have to speak on a difficult and unfamiliar subject on which you would not like to say anything but what was to the point or strictly justifiable, you will sometimes find that the thoughts themselves claim so much mental energy that there is none left for speaking with elegance or even with complete regard to grammar: to your own vexation you will have a feeling that your phrases are confused and your language incorrect. A pianist may practise a difficult piece of music so as to have it "at his fingers' ends"; under ordinary circumstances he will be able to play it quite mechanically without ever becoming conscious of effort; but, nevertheless, the effort is there. How great the effort is appears when some day or other the musician is "out of humour," that is, when his brain is at work on other subjects or is not in its usual working order. At once his execution will be stumbling and faulty.

22. (11) To return to *had* and *habaidēdeima*. If we look at the meaning of these forms we perceive that the English word has made a great advance on the road from the concrete to the abstract. It is a well-known law in psychology that the power of grasping abstract notions is of comparatively late growth in the individual as well as in the race. The development in language of grammatical forms of a more abstract character constitutes a great advance upon the earlier state when there was little beyond concrete terms. The notion that was formerly expressed by one inseparable word is now often expressed by means of a group of pronouns, auxiliary verbs, prepositions, and other little words, each with a comparatively abstract signification. It is one of the consequences of this change that it has become considerably easier to express certain minute shades of thought by laying extra stress on some particular element in the speech-group. The Latin *cantaveram* amalgamates three ideas into one indissoluble whole; but in the English *I had sung* the elements are analysed, so that you can at will accentuate the personal element, the time element, or the action. Now, it is possible (who can affirm and who can deny it?) that the Romans could, if necessary, make some difference in speech between *cántaveram* (non saltaveram), "I had *sung*," and *cantaverám* (non cantabam), "I *had* sung"; but even then if it was the personal element which was to be emphasised, an *ego* had to be added. Even the possibility of laying stress on the temporal element broke down in forms like *scripsi, minui, sum, audiam*, and innumerable others. It seems obvious that the freedom of Latin in this respect must have been far inferior to that of English. Moreover, in English the three elements, "I," "had," and "sung," can in certain cases be arranged in a different order, and other words can be inserted between them in order to modify and qualify the meaning of the phrase. Note also the conciseness of such answers as "Who had sung?" "I had"; "What have you done?" "Sung." And contrast the Latin "cantaveram et saltaveram et luseram et riseram," with the English "I had sung and danced and played and laughed".

23. (II) In language, analysis means suppleness, and synthesis means rigidity; in analytic languages you have the power of kaleidoscopically arranging and re-arranging the elements that in synthetic forms like *cantaveram* are in rigid connexion and lead a Siamese twin sort of existence. The synthetic forms of Latin verbs remind us of those languages of South America in which we are told that there is no word for "head," or "eye," but only for "my head," "your head," "his eye," etc.[1] In one language the verbal idea (in the finite moods), in the other the nominal idea is necessarily fused with the personal idea. And if Latin *pater* has the advantage over the American words that it is not always limited to "my father," or somebody else's father, it is limited in other ways: it is one definite number, one definite sex, one definite case. It is more restricted in its use, more concrete than necessary; and such a restriction is, or, under certain circumstances, may be, a hindrance to freedom or precision of thought. In Swedish *make*, "mate," is masculine, and *maka* feminine; and TEGNER expressly regrets this distinction, saying: "On account of the impossibility of separating the stem *mak-* from the 'organically' coalesced endings *-e* of the masculine and *-a* of the feminine, we cannot give such a form to the sentence 'sin make må man ej svika' as to make it perfectly clear that the admonition is

---

[1] So also in other languages. "The Hottentot cannot use a noun without a pronominal suffix, indicating not only gender and case, but also person as well, except as a predicate" Sayce, *Introduction*, i., 379; Fr. Müller, *Grundriss*, i., 2, p. 2).

applicable to both husband and wife"[1]. In this case the Danes have advanced beyond their neighbours by abolishing the distinction and using *mage* for both sexes.

24. Most English pronouns make no distinction of sex: *I, you, we, they, who, somebody*, etc. And yet, when we hear that Magyar, and, indeed, the great majority of languages outside the Arian and Semitic world, have no separate forms for the masculine and feminine pronouns of the third person, that is, make no distinction between *he* and *she*, our first thought is one of astonishment; we fail to see how it is possible to do without this distinction. But if we look more closely we shall see it is at times a great inconvenience to be obliged to specify the sex of the person spoken about. I remember once reading in some English paper a proposal to use the word *thon* as a personal pronoun of common gender; if it was substituted for *he* in such a proposition as this: "It would be interesting if each of the leading poets would tell us what he considers his best work," ladies would be spared the disparaging implication that the leading poets were all men.

Now, *thon* has no great chance of becoming popular, and the proposal has hardly any significance except as showing that the want of a genderless pronoun is sometimes felt. And it is curious to see the different ways out of the difficulty resorted to in the language of daily life. First the cumbrous use of "he or she,"

[1] *Språkets Makt*, 50.

as in the following sentences: "Everybody to do just as he or she likes" | Fielding, *Tom Jones*, i., 174, "the reader's heart (if he or she have any)" | Thackeray, *Pendennis*, iii., 294, "every woman and man in this kingdom who has sold her or himself" | G. Eliot, *Mill on the Floss*, i., 54, "each was satisfied with him or herself" | Miss Muloch, *John Halifax, Gentleman*, ii., 128, "each one made his or her comment" | C. Doyle, *Study in Scarlet*, 66, "the murderer has written it with his or her own blood".[1] In many cases *he* will be used alone in spite of the inaccuracy which results: compare, for instance: "If anybody behaves in such and such a manner he will be punished," with, "Whoever behaves in such and such a manner will be punished".

But in many cases these two expedients will be found not to answer the purpose. If you try to put the phrase, "Does anybody prevent you?" in another way, beginning with "Nobody prevents you," and then adding the interrogatory formula, you will perceive that "does he" is too definite, and "does he or she" too clumsy; and you will therefore say (as

[1] Dr. O. SIEBBYE has kindly sent me the following examples of this ungainly repetition in the Latin of the Roman Law (*Digest*. iv, 5, 2): "*Qui quave ... capite diminuti diminutæ esse dicentur, in eos easve ... iudicium dabo*" | (xliii., 30): "*Qui quave in potestate Lucii Titii est, si is eave apud te est, dolove malo tuo factum est quominus apud te esset, ita eum eamve exhibeas*" | (xi, 3): "*Qui servum servam alienum alienam recepisse persuasisseve quid ei dicitur dolo malo, quo eum eam deteriorem faceret, in eum, quanti ea res erit, in duplum iudicium dabo*".

Thackeray does, *Pendennis*, ii, 260), "Nobody prevents you, do they?" although, of course, *nobody* is of the singular number and ought to be represented by a singular pronoun. In the same manner Shakespeare writes (*Lucr.*, 125): "Everybody to rest themselves betake". The substitution of the plural for the singular is not wholly illogical; for *everybody* is much the same thing as "all men," and *nobody* is the negation of "all men"; but the phenomenon is extended to cases where this explanation will not hold good. As this curious use of the plural pronoun to supply the missing genderless singular is not mentioned in English grammars, as far as I know, I subjoin the examples I have found of it:—

Fielding, *Tom Jones*, ii, 160, "*every one* in the house were in *their* beds" | *ibid.*, ii., 184, "she never willingly suffered *any one* to depart from her house without inquiring into *their* names, family, and fortunes" | *ibid.*, ii., 248, "*everybody* fell a-laughing, as how could *they* help it?" | *ibid.*, iii, 66, "the two parties proceeded three full miles together before *any one* offered again to open *their* mouths" | G. Eliot, *Mill*, i., 12, "if *everybody* was what *they* should be" | *ibid.*, i., 75, "it was not *everybody* who could afford to cry so much about *their* neighbours" | *ibid.*, i., 310, "I never refuse to help *anybody*, if *they've* a mind to do themselves justice" | *ibid.*, ii., 304, "I shouldn't like to punish *any one*, even if

they'd done me wrong" | Thackeray, *Vanity Fair*, 338, "*a person* can't help *their* birth" | Ruskin, *Selections*, i. 305, "all that can possibly be done for *any one* who wants ears of wheat is to show *them* where to find grains of wheat, and how to sow them" | Anstey, *Vice Versâ*, 174, "no one but children invited, and *everybody* to do exactly what *they* like" | Mrs. H. Ward, *David Grieve*, i., 325, "*Somebody* will see us!' she cried in a fever, 'and tell father.' 'Not *they*; I'll keep a look-out.'" | *Cambridge Trifles*, 79, "*Everybody* will forget *themselves*" | Sketchley, *Cleop. Needle*, 27, "as if it was easy for *any one* to find *their* own needle" | Sweet, *Elementarbuch*, 40, "I don't know what's become of my umbrella. *Some one* must have taken it by mistake, instead of *their* own" | Murray, *Dial. South. Scotl.*, 192, "*wad a buodie* hurt *thersel*, yf *they* faell owre theare?"

25. English *who* is not, like the *quis* or *quæ* of the Romans, limited to one sex and one number, so that our question "Who did it?" to be rendered exactly in Latin would require a combination of the four: *Quis hoc fecit? Quæ hoc fecit? Qui hoc fecerunt? Quæ hoc fecerunt?* or rather, the abstract nature of *who* (and of *did*) makes it possible to express such a question more indefinitely in English than in any highly flexional language; and indefiniteness in many cases means greater precision, or a closer correspondence between thought and expression.

26. (11) The doing away with the old case distinctions in English has facilitated many extremely convenient idioms unknown in the older synthetic languages, such as: "The girl was given a book" | "the lad was spoken highly of" | "I love, and am loved by, my wife" | "these laws my readers, whom I consider as my subjects, are bound to believe in and to obey" (Fielding, *Tom Jones*, i., 60) | "he was heathenishly inclined to believe in, or to worship, the goddess Nemesis" (*ibid*, ii., 165) | "he rather rejoiced in, than regretted, his bruise" (*ibid*, iii., 121) | "many a dun had she talked to, and turned away from her father's door" (Thackeray, *Vanity Fair*, 9) | "their earthly abode, which has seen, and seemed almost to sympathise in, all their honour" (Ruskin, *Selections*, i., 441).[1] Another advantage is derived from the giving up of the distinctive forms of the singular and plural in adjectives and adjectival pronouns, as is seen from a comparison of the English "*my* wife and children" with the French "*ma* femme et *mes* enfants," or of "*the local* press and committees" and "*la* presse *locale* et *les* comités *locaux*". Try to translate exactly into French and Latin such a sentence as this: "What are the present state and wants of mankind?" (Ruskin, *loc. cit.*, 405). In nouns, on the other hand, the two numbers are kept apart in English, except in a very few words (deer, sheep, series, cf. § 130). Danish has a somewhat greater number of words that are alike in singular and plural; but the advantage of having everywhere the same indifference to number as is seen in English adjectives or in Chinese nouns will appear from the words that a Dane or an Englishman editing a text would use to express the same idea: "et (singular) eller (or) flere (plural) ord (indifferently singular and plural) mangler her"—*some* (singular and plural) *word* (singular) or *words* (plural) wanting here". Cf. also the expression "a verdict of wilful murder against *some* person or persons *unknown*," where *some* and *unknown* belong to the singular as well as the plural forms; and Fielding's phrase (*Tom Jones*, iii., 65): "*Some particular* chapter, or perhaps chapters, *may be obnoxious*".

27. (13) The languages we have here dealt with tend evidently in their historical development towards general instead of special forms; but inseparable from this tendency is another, to get rid of the rules of concord. It is a characteristic feature of the

---

[1] This manner of letting the same word be governed by two verbs of different construction is found as far back as the *Ancren Riwle* p. 128: þe weond hateð & hunteð efter hire. In the following quotation, the same noun is first object and then subject; but this is very rare, and would no doubt be generally condemned. Thackeray, *Pendennis*, ii., 221: "all these facts gentlemen's confidential gentlemen discuss confidentially, and are known and examined by every person". Dean Alford, in *The Queen's English*, p. 103, mentions and blames the Oxford Declaration of the Clergy describing the Canonical Scriptures as "not only containing but being the Word of God".

older Arian languages that the adjective is made to agree with its substantive in number, gender, and case, and that the verb of the predicate is governed in number and person by the subject. The latter form of concord has disappeared from spoken Danish, where, for instance, the present tense of the verb meaning "to travel" is uniformly *rejser* in all persons of both numbers; while the written language till quite recent times kept up artificially the plural *rejse*, although it had been dead in the spoken language for some three hundred years. The old inflexion is, to use Madvig's words, "an article of luxury, as a modification of the idea belonging properly to the subject is here transferred to the predicate, where it has no business; for when we say 'mændene rejse' (die männer reisen), we do not mean to imply that they undertake several journeys".[1]

28. (13) By getting rid of this superfluity, Danish has got the start of the more archaic of its Arian sister-tongues. Even English, which has in most respects gone farthest in simplifying its inflexional system, is here inferior to Danish, in that in the present tense of most verbs it separates the third person singular from the other persons by giving it the ending -(*e*)*s*, and preserves in the verb *to be* some other traces of the old concord system, not to speak of the forms in -*st* used with *thou* in the language of religion and poetry. Small and unimportant as these

[1] Madvig, *Kleine philol. Schriften*, 28; Madvig, Siesbye, *Nord. Tsk. f. Filol.*, n. r. viii, 134.

survivals may seem, still they are in some instances impediments to the free and easy expression of thought. In Danish, for instance, there is no difficulty in saying "enten du eller jeg har uret," as *har* is used both in the first and second persons singular and plural. But when an Englishman tries to render the same sentiment he is baffled; "either you or I *are* wrong" is felt to be incorrect, and so is "either you or I *am* wrong"; he might say "either you are wrong, or I," but then this manner of putting it, if grammatically admissible, is somewhat stiff and awkward; and there is no perfectly natural way out of the difficulty, for Dean Alford's proposal to say "either you or I *is* wrong" (see *The Queen's English*, 8th ed., p. 155) is not to be recommended. As he himself admits, "the sound is harsh, and usages would be violated". The advantage of having verbal forms that are no respecters of persons is seen directly in such perfectly natural expressions as "either you or I must be wrong," or "either you or I may be wrong," or "either you or I began it,"—and indirectly from the more or less artificial rules of Latin and Greek grammars on this point, and from the following passages where English authors have cut the Gordian knot in different ways:—

Shakespeare, *Love's Labour's Lost*, v., 2, 346.
"Nor God, nor I, *delights* in perjur'd men" | *ibid*, *As You Like It*, i., 3, 99, "Thou and I *am* one" | Tennyson, *Balin and Balan* (Works, ed. Tauchn., xii., 227), "For whatso-

ever knight against us came Or I or he *have* easily overthrown" | Conan Doyle, *Adventures of Sherlock Holmes*, i., 214, "The vessel in which the man or men *are*".

29. (13) The same difficulty often appears in relative clauses; Alford (*loc. cit.*, 152) calls attention to the fact of the Prayer Book reading "Thou art the God that *doeth* wonders", whereas the Bible version runs "Thou art the God that *doest* wonders". Compare also:—

Shakespeare, *As You Like It*, iii., 5, 55, "'Tis not her glasse, but you that *flatters* her" | *ibid.*, *Measure for Measure*, ii., 2, 80, "It is the law, not I, *condemne* your brother" | *ibid.*, *Richard III.*, iv., 4, 269, "That would I learn of you, As one that *are* best acquainted with her humour" [the first folio, instead of "*that are*," reads "*being*"] | Mrs. H. Ward, *David Grieve*, i., 290, "It's you that's been teaching Lucy these beautiful sentiments".

In all of these cases the construction in Danish is as easy and natural as it generally is in the English past tense: "It was not her glass, but you that *flattered* her".

30. (14) The "luxury," which Madvig spoke of is still more striking in the inflexion of nouns and adjectives. If we compare a group of Latin words such as *opera virorum omnium bonorum veterum* with a corresponding group in a few other languages of a

less inflexional type: Old English, *ealra godra ealdra manna weorc*; Danish, *alle gode gamle mænds værker*; Modern English, *all good old men's works*, we perceive by analysing the ideas expressed by the several words that the Romans said really: "work," plural, nominative or accusative + "man," plural, masculine, genitive + "all," plural, genitive + "good," plural, masculine, genitive + "old," plural, masculine, genitive. Leaving *opera* out of consideration, we find that "plural" number is expressed four times, "genitive" case also four times, and "masculine gender" twice;[1] in Old English the signs of number and case are found four times each, while there is no indication of gender; in Danish the plural number is marked four times, and the case once. And finally, in Modern English, we find each idea expressed only once; and as nothing is lost in clearness, this method, as being the easiest and shortest, must be considered the best. Mathematically the different manners of rendering the same thing might be represented by the formula: $anx + bnx + cnx = (an+bn+cn)x = (a+b+c)nx$.

[1] If instead of *omnium veterum* I had chosen for instance *multorum antiquorum*, the meaning of masculine gender would have been rendered four times; for languages as a rule, especially the older ones, are not distinguished by consistency. It is only for the sake of convenience that I have taken my examples from Latin and Danish, which may here fairly stand as representatives of pretty much the same stages of development as primitive Arian and middle English, the examples being thus practically typical of four successive periods of one and the same language.

31. (15) This unusual faculty of "parenthesising" causes Danish, and to a still greater degree English, to stand outside of Schleicher's definition of that family of languages to which they historically belong; for according to him "the Arian noun (and adjective) as a living word can never be without a sign indicating case"[1]. I shall here quote an interesting passage from one of his books: "The radical difference between Magyar and Indo-Germanic [Arian] words is brought out distinctly by the fact that the postpositions belonging to co-ordinated nouns can be dispensed with in all the nouns except the last of the series, *e.g.*, *a jó embernek* 'dem guten menschen' (*a* for *az*, demonstrative pronoun, article ; *jó*, good ; *ember*, man ; *-nek* -*nak*, postposition with pretty much the same meaning as the dative case), for *az-nak* (*annak*) *jó-nak ember-nek*, as if in Greek you should say τὸ ἀγαθῷ ἀνθρώπῳ. An attributive adjective preceding its noun always has the form of the pure stem, the sign of plurality and the postposition indicating case not being added to it. Magyars say, for instance, *Hunyady Mátyás magyar királ y-nak* (to the Hungarian king Mathew Hunyady), -*nak* belonging here to all the preceding words. Nearly the same thing takes place where several words are joined together by means of *and*."[2]

[1] In the light of recent investigation, this sentence cannot even be maintained with regard to primitive Arian. See Brugmann's *Grundriss*, ii., 521.

[2] *Nomen u. Verbum*, 526. Cf. also Vilhelm Thomsen: Det

32. (15) Now, this is an exact parallel to the English group genitive in cases like "all good old men's works," "the Queen of England's power," "Beaumont and Fletcher's plays," "somebody else's turn," etc.; and as this peculiarity of English has developed in comparatively recent times from a grammatical construction analogous to the Latin concord (as will be shown at some length in a subsequent chapter), we may perhaps be entitled to ask, may not the absence of concord in Magyar be a comparatively modern simplification? In other words, may not the phenomena of concord be survivals from a primitive stage of linguistic development? In undeveloped minds we often find a tendency to be more explicit than seems strictly necessary, as in the frequent emphasising of a negation by seemingly redundant repetitions. In Old English it was the regular idiom to say: *nan man nyste nan þing*, "no man not-knew nothing"; so it was in Middle English, witness Chaucer's (*C. T. A.*, 70) "He *n*euere yet *n*o vileynye *n*e sayde In al his lyf unto *n*o maner wight," and so it is in the vulgar speech of our own day: says Rob Jakin (in *The Mill on the Floss*, i., 327), "There was *n*iver *n*obody else gen (gave) me *n*othin'"; whereas standard Modern English is contented with one negation: *no* man knew anything, etc. Concord

magyariske sprog (*Tsk. f. Philologi og Pædag*., vii., 170): *a nagy városban* (in the large town), *Buda-, Mohács- és Nándornál* (at Buda, Mohacs, and Belgrad), *Vladimir orosz fejedelemtől* (from the Russian prince V.).

seems to be a case in point, and this manner of viewing it will gain in plausibility by the phenomena of South African grammar treated in the opening of the next chapter.

33. Here let us sum up the results of this chapter. The grammatical system of Modern English is preferable to that of our remote ancestors, in that—

its forms are generally shorter;

there are not so many of them to burden the memory;

their formation and use present fewer irregularities;

their more abstract character assists materially in facilitating expression, and makes it possible to do away with the repetitions of languages which demand "concord".

CHAPTER III.

PRIMITIVE GRAMMAR.

34. (16) Nowhere do the phenomena of concord seem to grow more luxuriantly than in the languages of those primitive South African tribes known under the name of BANTU. I shall give some examples, chiefly taken from the late W. H. I. BLEEK's excellent grammar;[1] when these interesting facts are explained, we shall be able to draw some inferences from them with regard to our own group of languages.

The Zulu word for "man" is *umuntu*; every word in the same or in a following sentence having any

---

[1] *Comparative Grammar of South African Languages* (London), i., 1862; ii., 1869; the work has unfortunately never been finished. I have also made use of H. P. S. SCHREUDER, *Grammatik for Zulu-sproget* (Kristiania, 1850), and of the account of these languages in FR. MÜLLER's *Grundriss der Sprachwissenschaft*, i., 2 (1877), pp. 238-262. The remarks on Bantu grammar in the text were written (and printed in the Danish edition) before the appearance of TORREND's *Compar. Grammar of the South African Bantu Languages* (London, 1891); a perusal of this important work has not caused me to make any change in my presentation of the matter, as his objections to Bleek's examples relate only to the syntax of the verb, with which we have nothing here to do.

reference to that word must begin with something to remind you of the beginning of *umuntu*. This will be, according to fixed rules, either *mu* or *u* or *w* or *m*. In the following sentence, the meaning of which is "our handsome man (or woman) appears, we love him (or her)," these *reminders* (as I shall term them) are printed in italics:—

u*mu*ntu *w*etu o*mu*chle *u*yabonakala, si*m*tanda. (1)
man ours handsome appears we love.

If, instead of the singular, we take the corresponding plural *abantu*, "men, people" (whence the generic name of Bantu), the sentence looks quite different:—

*ab*antu *b*etu *ab*achle *ba*yabonakala, si*b*atanda. (2)

35. (16) In the same way if we successively take as our starting-point *ilizwe* "country," the corresponding plural *amazwe* "countries," *isizwe* "nation," *izizwe* "nations," *intombi* "girl," *izintombi* "girls," we get:—

*ili*zwe *l*etu *el*ichle *li*yabonakala, si*l*itanda. (5)
*amaz*we etu *am*achle *a*yabonakala, si*wa*tanda. (6)
*isi*zwe *s*etu *es*ichle *si*yabonakala, si*si*tanda. (7)
*izi*zwe *z*etu *ez*ichle *zi*yabonakala, si*zi*tanda. (8)
*in*tombi *y*etu *en*chle *i*yabonakala, si*y*itanda. (9)
*izin*tombi *zetu ezin*chle *zi*yabonakala, si*zi*tanda. (10)
(girls) our handsome appear we love.[1]

In other words, every substantive belongs to one

[1] The change of the initial sound of the reminder belonging to the adjective is owing to an original composition with the "relative particle" *a*, *au* becoming *o*, and *ai*, *e*. The numbers within parentheses refer to the numbers of Bleek's classes.

of sixteen distinct classes (termed by different authors declensions, species, concords, genera, principationes), of which some have a singular and others a plural meaning; each of these classes has its own "derivative prefix," to use Bleek's expression,[1] and by means of this class-sign the concord of the parts of a sentence is indicated. In the following example the same verb will be seen to have two reminders, one from the subject of the same sentence, and another from that of the preceding sentence:—

u*ku*tanda kuetu okukulu *ku*yabonakala, AB*A*ntu
love our great appears men
B*aku*bona, si*ku*bonakalisa. (15)
(they) (it) see we it make appear.

This example serves also to show us the resources of the language in other respects (*tanda, ukutanda*; *bona* "see," *bonakala* "appear," *bonakalisa* "make appear").

36. (16) It will be noticed that adjectives such as "handsome" or "our" take different shapes according to the word to which they refer; in the Lord's Prayer given by Fr. Müller "thy" is found in the following forms: *l*ako (referring to *i*gama, "name," for *il*igama, 5), *b*ako (*ub*ukumkani, "kingdom," 14), *y*ako (*in*tando, "will," 9). So also, the genitive case of the same noun has a great many different forms, for the genitive relation is expressed by the reminder of the governing word + the "relative particle" *a* (which

[1] An inhabitant of the country of *U*ganda is called *mu*ganda, pl. *ba*ganda or *wa*ganda; the language spoken there is *lu*ganda.

is combined with the following sound); take, for instance, *inkosi* "chief, king".—
*umuntu w*enkosi, "the king's man" (1; *we* for $w + a + i$).
*abantu b*enkosi, "the king's men". (2)
*ilizwe l*enkosi, "the king's country". (5)
*amazwe e*nkosi, "the king's countries". (6)
*isizwe s*enkosi, "the king's nation". (7)
*ukutanda k*wenkosi, "the king's love".[1] (15)

37. (17) "There is an appearance of redundancy," says Bleek (p. 107), "in this frequent repetition of the representative elements of the noun, when they are thus used with all parts of speech, which have a reference to it. But this will not much astonish those who have studied the literature of primitive races, and know the construction of their compositions,

With their frequent repetitions,
And their wild reverberations."

And he goes on to quote an interesting remark of Dr. Livingstone's: "The chief use in the extraordinary repetition of the signs of nouns which occur in pure Setshuana may be generally stated to be to give precision to the sentence. They impart energy and perspicuity to each member of a proposition, and prevent the possibility of a mistake as to the antecedent. They are the means by which with a single syllable or letter a recurrent allusion to the subject

[1] I have had to construct some of these forms on the basis of the materials given by Müller, p. 253 *sq.*, and Schreuder, p. 17. Bleek does not treat of the genitive.

spoken of is made, which cannot be accomplished by our lawyers without the clumsy circumlocution of 'said defendant,' 'said subject matter,' etc., etc. . . . I cannot quite sympathise with you [Bleek] when you speak of that use as 'cumbersome repetition'. The absence of it, in the mouths of half-castes, speaking an impure form of Setshuana, used to sound in my ears excessively harsh. And the fact of the sign being the easily recognisable initial sound of the noun, prevented any of that doubt which always clings to those abominations of the English language, 'former' and 'latter'."

38. (17) By way of contrast I translate a passage from an article by the German missionary, H. Brincker: "Another characteristic feature is that with these people eloquence generally consists, as it seems, in the employment of a great number of particles of one or more syllables, most of them untranslatable and meaningless. What a torrent of such waste-words (*flickwörter*) issues from the mouth of a native orator! Any one who is not familiar with the language is astonished to think how many thoughts must have been developed, and yet, at least, one-third of all the words pronounced were nothing but those obscure particles, repeated over and over again, while most of them might very well have been left out without any loss to the purport of the speech. Nevertheless, the natives attach a great importance to the use of these particles."[1]

[1] *Zur Sprachen- und Völkerkunde der Bantuneger*, in Tech-

This last remark of Brincker's shows that Livingstone is right in saying that the prefixes are necessary to the Bantu languages, and that the structure of these languages is such that the omission of the prefixes would involve obscurity and ambiguity. But still Bleek is right in speaking of the repetitions as cumbersome, just as the endings in the Latin *multorum virorum antiquorum* are cumbersome, however necessary and seemingly indispensable they were to Cicero and his contemporaries.

39. (18) But what is the origin of this South African system? The problem has not yet been completely solved, though Bleek is very much inclined to consider all Bantu nouns as originally compound words. As long as each component part is felt as relatively independent, it is natural, he argues, that the first part of the compound, which according to the structure of Bantu languages corresponds to the last element of our compound words, should be used as a representative of the whole word. Bleek illustrates this by means of English examples: the last syllable of the compound word *steamship* might be used to represent the whole word; and thus, after once mentioning "the steam*ship*," we might continue "our *ship*, which *ship* is a great *ship*, the *ship* appears, we love the *ship*". But in words where the syllable *ship* is a derivative suffix, it is incapacitated from being used by itself for the purpose of representing the whole compound noun. Thus in reference to the word "friend*ship*," it would be absurd to continue "our *ship*, which *ship* is a great *ship*, the *ship* appears, we love the *ship*"; but that is just what the Zulus do, even extending the use to cases in which the Zulu "derivative prefix" is as little felt to be an independent element as, say, the -*er* of steamer. This is as if in reference to "the steam-*er*," we should continue "our *er*, which *er* is a great *er*, the *er* appears, we love the *er*" (p. 107). Bleek very carefully investigates the several classes of nouns in all the cognate languages, in order to determine from the meanings of the words belonging to each class the original signification of the corresponding prefix, but he himself acknowledges that great difficulties attend this task; the want of old literary documents makes the whole investigation uncertain, as "will be easily understood by any one who may have tried to ascertain the original meaning of such English suffixes as -*dom*, -*ness*, -*ship*, etc., from an analysis of the nouns formed with them. A comparison of such nouns as 'kingdom, martyrdom, freedom,' etc., may give us an idea of the present value of the suffix -*dom*, and of the meaning which it would give to such nouns as we can now form with it. But this is a very different thing from knowing what was the meaning of the syllable -*dom* when used independently; and we imagine that any guess at that meaning, without tracing it back historically, might

mer's *Intern. Zs.*, v., 30 (1889). Brincker's explanation of these grammatical phenomena is purely fanciful and scientifically worthless.

be far from the truth" (p. 125). I shall mention a few points of interest in his disquisition.

40. (19) The fifteenth class is characterised by *ku*; we saw above *ukutanda*, "love". This is identified by Bleek (126) with the preposition *ku*, which corresponds to English *to*, both in the local meaning, as in ngi-ya-*ku*-laba-bantu, "I go to these people," and before infinitives, as in ngi-ya-*ku*tanda, which is literally "I go to love," and is used as a kind of future (comp. *I am going to love*, or *je vais aimer*); in u-*ku*-tanda *ku*-mnandi, "to love is sweet," the first *ku* is used as a derivative prefix, to which the second *ku* refers as a pronoun. Here I may be allowed to insert an interesting parallel; if such a word as *ukutanda* has been named in a previous proposition, and you want to introduce it later on, say as the object of some verb, this is achieved by repeating *ku* instead of *ukutanda* (cf. the last sentence in § 35), exactly as in modern colloquial English, instead of repeating an infinitive, you may content yourself with using *to* as a substitute for it.[1]

[1] Dickens, *Martin Chuzzlewit*, 217, "Now you won't overreach me; you want *to*, but you won't" | Darwin, *Life*, i., 117, "The little beggars are doing just what I don't want them *to*." | Stevenson, *Jekyll Hyde*, 60, "Take a quick turn with us. I should like *to* very much" | *Robert Elsmere*, i., 25, "You had given up water-colour; and she told me to implore you not *to*," etc., etc. How is this *to* to be classified? I should like to call it a new sort of pronoun; it replaces the infinitive very much in the same way as "it" does a substantive. This extremely convenient use of *to* seems to have developed in this century;

41. (20) To the fifteenth Bantu class belong first the unmistakable infinitives and some words in which the verbal idea is still more or less easily discernible, such as *uku*chla, "food" (really "eating"), and *uku*sa, "morning" ("dawning"), and, secondly, a number of words which cannot have been originally infinitives; in many of these, meaning "desert," "field," "open place," "winter," "rainy season," or some other particularisation of place or time, Bleek says that "the common origin of the prefix *ku*- and the preposition *ku*- (to) is almost evident". But whether we take this "common origin" to mean a development of the prefix from an original preposition, as Bleek seems to think, or the development of the preposition and the noun prefix from some common source, in any case a good many nouns remain in the class in the case of which no connexion can be traced between the meaning of the noun and any of the different meanings of the preposition. And this difficulty in seeing reasons for a noun belonging to a particular class and to no other is still greater in all the other classes, where it is often nearly impossible to perceive anything common to all or to most of the nouns in the class. Nay, where we are able to find a connexion, it seems in many cases to be a derived and not an original one; thus a great many names for living beings are comprised under the first class;

it has suffered the same persecution from schoolmasters and would-be grammarians as most other innovations, no matter how acceptable.

but it is probable that they were originally adjectives referred to *umuntu* and therefore taking the *umu*- prefix, which they subsequently kept even in cases where they were not joined to any *umuntu* (Bleek, p. 123).

42. (21) In several of the classes the words have a definite numerical value, so that they go together in pairs as corresponding singular and plural nouns (see the examples above): but though in the more advanced languages this is carried out pretty regularly, the existence of a certain number of exceptions shows that these numerical values cannot originally have been associated with the class prefixes, but must be due to an extension by analogy (Bleek, p. 140 *sqq.*). The starting-point may have been substantives standing to each other in the relation of "person" to "people," "soldier" to "army," "tree" to "forest," "ship" to "fleet" (*ibid*., 144); the prefixes of such words as the latter of each of these pairs will easily acquire a certain sense of plurality, no matter what they may have meant originally, and then they will lend themselves to forming a kind of plural in other nouns, being either put instead of the prefix belonging properly to the noun (*amazwe*, "countries," 6; *ilizwe*, "country," 5), or placed before it (*ma-luto*, "spoons," 6; *luto*, "spoon," 11). Sometimes we find that instead of being regulated by the class to which the subject belongs grammatically, the verb, etc., takes the reminders of some other class by some *constructio ad sensum*, just as in German the "reminder" *sie* may be used in referring to such neuter nouns as *weib* or *mädchen*; instead of *erumbi rándye ekúru ráya*, "my eldest brother" (5th class) "has gone away," you may hear *erumbi nándye omukúru náya*, where the reminders are of the first class (Bleek, p. 156, note). As has been mentioned above, the first class comprises a great many words signifying living beings.

43. (22) Thus an impulse is given to further deviations and changes; and we are told (Bleek, p. 234) that in the north-western branch of the Bantu languages "the forms of some of the prefixes have been so strongly contracted as almost to defy identification. Thus prefixes may have been confounded with each other, and correspondences differing from the original ones may have arisen through the force of analogy. At the same time, the concord appears to be frequently employed in the north-western languages rather as an alliterative process, than in its original grammatical sense, or as a division of nouns into classes." In one of the languages we have a two-hundred-year-old grammar by Brusciotto à Vetralla (see Bleek, i., 9). A comparison of the language described there with that spoken now-a-days in the same district (Mpongwe) shows that the class signs have dwindled down considerably; instead of a whole syllable we have as a rule only a vowel left; the phonetic shrinkage has been stronger in these grammatical elements than elsewhere;[1] the number

[1] Cf. Bleek, i., 47: "The more frequent use to which, generally, the grammatical elements of a language are subject has

of the prefixes and consequently of the classes has been reduced from 16 to 10: for instance, classes 11, 14 and 15 have been phonetically amalgamated (Bleek, 223; cf. 132).

44. (23) Here I shall say good-bye to Bleek and shall try to obtain from these South African phenomena some results bearing on the development of languages in general, and in particular of languages nearer home than those of South Africa. The reader will then, I hope, understand that it was not out of mere caprice that I undertook my rambling excursion to those far-off regions.

From the historical fact pointed out in the last section we may safely infer that if we were able to make acquaintance with the South African languages at a still earlier epoch, we should meet with a still greater number of classes than sixteen; and moreover, that the reminders we should see prefixed to adjectives and verbs would be still fuller in form and more like whole words. And, maybe, we should then be still more inclined to doubt the correctness of Bleek's view, according to which every Zulu noun was originally a compound word, whose first element was repeated with the following words of the sentence. He seems not to have proved or even rendered it probable that there either is or has been so great a partiality to composition that all non-compound words should have disappeared from the language. It would be very strange indeed if it were so.

45. (23) It seems to me much more probable that the origin of the whole system of reminders is to be sought in some primitive state of language necessitating a perpetual repeating of complete words in order to be understood. To take as an example the first Zulu proposition given above, we cannot, of course, tell how it would look in a language spoken in Africa centuries ago; but nothing hinders us from fancying its being originally made up of some such series of unconnected clauses as the following. (Unfortunately, we are obliged to keep the modern Zulu forms, and to use such pronouns as "ours" and "we," which may possibly not have come into existence at the time we are trying to imagine.)

umuntu, "man" = "I speak about the man";
umuntu etu, "man ours" = "the man is ours, it is our man";
umuntu yabonakala, "man appear" = "the man appears";
si umuntu tanda, "we man love" = "we love the

the tendency to more rapidly wear them off, and by such modifications to bring them, as a general rule, into a more advanced stage of phonetical development. It is on this account that, in the grammatical elements of the Hottentot language, clicks and diphthongs have entirely disappeared ... though three-fourths of the words of this language may be said to contain clicks." This offers a welcome confirmation of the theory advanced by me that the signification of a word or word element and the frequency of its use are important factors in its phonetic development. Cf. my article "Zur Lautgesetzfrage" in Techmer's *Internat. Zeitschr*, iii, 201, and *Nord. Tskr. f. Filologi*, n. r. vii, 224.

It seems by no means unlikely that some such method of joining sentences (and I am here speaking only of the joining of sentences and not of the forms or meanings of the separate words) should have obtained in remote antiquity; neither does it seem improbable that in course of time such an unconnected or loosely connected sequence should have developed into one organic whole. This would be somewhat analogous to the "integration" found in several languages, of which the following may stand as a specimen. Starting with a sequence of three co-ordinate sentences like these:—

all be it (= let it be so in all respects);
I neither lend nor borrow;
yet I will break a custom,—

we get a gradual coalescence into one organic whole, *albeit* becoming a conjunction introducing the subordinate clause, as when we read in Shakespeare (*Merchant of Venice*, i., 3, 62, folio) : "Shylocke, albeit I neither lend nor borrow By taking, nor by giuing of excesse, Yet to supply the ripe wants of my friend, Ile breake a custome". Compare also the development of Latin *licet* into a conjunction, or of Latin *fors-sit-an, forsitan*; English, *may-be*; French, *peut-être*; Danish, *maaske*, into adverbs; or that of such conditional sentences as "Suppose he had died, what then?" or "Had he been there, she would have been saved".

46. (24) So far, then, we seem to be on sure ground. Neither does there seem to be anything rash in assuming that accentual law to hold good in man's first language which we find everywhere in our own times and which is formulated by Sweet as follows:[1] "All words that express new ideas are more or less emphatic; while words that express ideas already familiar or that can be taken for granted are unemphatic"; if we begin a story with the words "A German came to London", we give stronger stress to German and London, than when we go on " . . . the German left London, and went to Liverpool". And this feebler stress has as a consequence a less distinct pronunciation of each of the sounds making up the words.

47. (24) Add to this another tendency found in all languages, as far as I am aware, that of shortening frequently repeated words, especially compound words when they are no longer *felt* as compound words, the meaning being associated with the word as a whole rather than with the several parts: when this is the case, it is of no consequence to the speaker that etymologically the word is, *i.e.*, once was, a compound. This shortening takes place extremely often in proper names;[2] in Greek, we see a great many abbreviations used as pet-names, *e.g.*, *Zeuxis* for Zeuxippos, Zeuxidamos, Zeuxitheos, etc., so in Old High German *Wolfo* stands for Wolfbrand, Wolfgang, etc. Icelanders say *Sigga* for Sigriðr, *Siggi* for

---

[1] *A Primer of Spoken English*, p. 29.
[2] Cf. Brugmann, *Grundriss d. vgl. Gram*, ii., 33, and the works there quoted.

Sigurðr, and so on in most languages. Abbreviations of this character do not belong to any particular time or to any particular country; they grow luxuriantly everywhere, and are not at all confined to children's language or to those cases which are sanctioned by tradition, like *Rob, Jim, Dick,* etc. Thus, in the beginning of this century Napoleon Bonaparte was generally called *Nap* or *Boney;* and Thackeray constantly says *Pen* for Arthur Pendennis, *Cos* for Costigan, *Fo* for Foker, *Pop* for Popjoy, *old Col* for Colchicum, etc., etc. This is quite natural; wherever a person is often spoken of, the speaker is understood by everybody before he is half through the name, if it is a rather long one, and therefore he often does not take the trouble to pronounce the latter part of it. He thus exemplifies the principle we meet with everywhere: people do not pronounce distinctly unless they feel that distinctness is necessary if they are to be understood; whatever is easily understood from the context or from the situation is either slurred over or left out completely.[1] This principle will account alike for most of the gradual sound changes in languages, and for such violent curtailings as *cab* for cabriolet, *caps* for capital letters, the *Cri* for the Criterion, *phiz* for physiognomy, *sov* for sovereign, or French *aristo* for aristocrate, *Boule-Miche* for Boulevard St. Michel, and so on.[1]

48. (24) Now I fancy it must have been by the same process that the Bantus have arrived at the use of *umu* as a representative of *umuntu*; the tendency to use a half-word in this manner may have been strengthened by the fact that in some cases a word was felt as a compound, so that the first part of it could be used independently.

However this may be, so much is certain, that in these languages we see the ORIGINATION OF PRONOUNS by natural means; whether Bleek is right in regarding the beginnings of words as first parts

Any shorthand writer knows how to utilise this principle systematically. I found a curious illustration of the identical shortening process in yet another domain, in the following scrap of conversation (Maupassant, *Bel Ami*, p. 8): "Voilà six mois que je suis employé aux bureaux du chemin de fer du Nord". "Mais comment diable n'as-tu pas trouvé mieux qu'une place d'employé au Nord ?"

---

[1] I must once more beg permission to refer to my article on *Sound Laws,* see above, § 43, note. Compare also the shortenings of reduplicated syllables (Brugmann, *loc. cit.,* ii., 11 *sqq.*); Noreen, *Urgermanische Lautlehre,* p. 225 *sqq.*). In *writing,* too, the same processes may be observed, not only in the use of initial letters instead of Christian names and of such standard contractions as *Esq., Mr., M.A., etc.,* but also in other cases; thus in letters the same proper name or technical term will often be found to be written distinctly the first time it occurs, while later on it is either not written in full or else written carelessly and illegibly.

[1] Cf. Tegnér, *Elliptiska Ord,* Filologmödet i Kristiania, 1881, p. 58; Storm, *Engl. Philologie,* 1881, pp. 158, 436; Earle, *Philol. Engl. Tongue,* 1871, p. 309; Pierson, *Métrique naturelle du Langage,* 1883, p. 247 *sqq.*; Passy, *Changements Phonétiques,* § 320; Behaghel, *Deutsche Sprache,* 1886, p. 68; Stoffel, *Studies in English,* p. 249. See also Addison, *The Spectator,* No. 135. Aug. 4, 1711.

of compounds, or whether they stand for complete words, they are originally nouns, "full words" (not "demonstrative roots"); and in their function as what I have called reminders they correspond to pronouns in our languages; for what else are many pronouns (especially the personal pronoun of the third person, the relative, and some of the demonstrative pronouns) but signs to remind us of what has been mentioned before?

49. (25) Further, we witness the ORIGIN OF OTHER GRAMMATICAL FORMS, that are to be classed partly with the flexional forms of nouns and adjectives ("our" = *wetu* when referred to umuntu, but *letu* when referred to ilizwe, which is much like Arian gender; in § 36 we saw something corresponding to our genitive), partly with verbal endings. And it should be remembered that we see these forms come into existence quite naturally from a more primitive and thoroughly concrete state of language, without any intention on the part of speakers to create anything new. They only indulge in the universal inclination to save oneself trouble, that is, in this case, to pronounce as few sounds as is compatible with making oneself understood.

50. (25) Finally we see the development of something that may be compared to our article; for as *umu* was used with other words as a reminder of *umuntu*, people seem to have come to look upon it as a reminder in the word *umuntu* itself, which was accordingly understood as *umu* (a sort of class-sign

to indicate the grammatical construction of the word, like the German *der, die, das*) + *ntu*, which thus appropriated to itself the meaning "man". This shifting of the popular linguistic conception of the constituent elements of a word is analogous to the popular misdividing of *anatomy* in English into *anatomy*, *an* being taken for the article, as in *an* atom, *an* attic, etc., and being subsequently subtracted ("the *atomy*"); or that of *acute* into *a*+*cute*, the word *cute* then being deduced from it. In the ending of words we see very frequently the same process; a few centuries ago *pease* was both singular and plural, corresponding to Old English singular, *pise*, plural, *pisan* or *piosan*; then the *s* was regarded as the common plural ending and subtracted so as to form the new singular *a pea*, which is not found in Shakespeare, and which is mentioned by Butler (A.D. 1633) as a cockneyism; in the same manner *cherry* is for *cherris* (cf. French *cerise*), *riddle* for *riddles* (Old English *rædels*), and there are many other cases.[1] Now, the same process of subtraction seems to have obtained, or at any rate to be now in operation, in Bantu languages, as lexicographers enter the word which I have mentioned so often, not in the form *umuntu*, but as *ntu*; it is true that Bleek protests against this division of the word;[2] but if he is

[1] I have collected not a few of these "back-formations," in my paper "*Om subtraktionsdannelser, særligt på dansk og engelsk*" in *Festskrift til Vilh. Thomsen*, 1894.

[2] See *Grimm's Law in South Africa*, Transact. Philol. Soc., 1873-4. 190.

right from an etymological point of view, he is perhaps wrong from the point of view of the actual linguistic instinct of the natives.

51. (25) If I sum up by emphasising the fact that in the Bantu languages this development of grammatical signs and categories has gone on indirectly and through a shortening of longer word-forms, and not through an extension of shorter words by means of formal elements, the reader will see how this long—perhaps too long—disquisition has some bearing on the comparative grammar of Arian; for the results arrived at go dead against a great many of those explanations of the origin of Arian forms which have hitherto been given by philologists.

52. (26) MADVIG'S philosophy of language was on the whole rationalistic; but he certainly in many respects exaggerated the intellectual faculties of "the creators of language,"[1] as will be seen very strikingly in the following passage: "Gender in languages was created by those who first hit upon (and adopted the habit of) keeping some particular phonetic modification of the demonstrative pronoun to indicate the special shade of signification of the noun; in our family of languages by those who added to the pronominal stem the open and soft vowel sound [a] . . . the quality of feminine being expressed by the more soft, open and lingering close of the uttered

[1] These were, according to him, exclusively men; women had no share in framing the first language (*Om Kunnet i Sprogene*, p. 18).

sounds". Madvig himself had an impression that he had here resorted to the method of explanation by means of sound symbolism, of which he is usually a fierce (in my opinion, too fierce an) antagonist, for he says by way of apology: "Such an origin, in which the character of the sound had a meaning and imparted it, we must specially imagine for ourselves in this case rather than in dealing with the formation of other primitive utterances, because we have not here to do with the name of some definite conception, but with a general modification, with the influence of an incidental condition". Now, I must confess that I can more easily imagine to myself primitive man hitting on a new sound to picture to his ear an entire perception which impressed him, but which his language was too poor to express, than fancy him adding an *a* to an existing genderless pronoun, in order thereby to denote the delicacy of *das ewig-weibliche*. And even if such a conceit might once come into his head, it is somewhat doubtful if his contemporaries would be able to see the drift of his long *a* and make an appropriate use of it with their own pronouns.

53. (27) Equally unsatisfactory are many other explanations that have been put forward by comparative philologists in their fondness for constructing hypotheses concerning primitive ages. Indeed, the history of comparative philology shows how very short-lived many of these explanations are: here to-day and in the waste-paper basket to-morrow! To show what sort of hypotheses I am alluding to, I shall have to quote somebody, for fear people should say that I am tilting at windmills; and I take a paper by the clever Norwegian philologist A. Torp,[1] for no other reason than because it is the last paper of this description that has come into my hands; I shall add a few criticisms within brackets. He says: "The common Indo-Germanic [Arian] language possessed several declensions; but it is *a priori* improbable that this should be the original state of things. The plurality seems necessarily to have developed out of an earlier unity. [Experience in historical times, in our family of languages as well as in that of South Africa, speaks rather in favour of a development in the opposite direction, from multiplicity towards comparative uniformity.] . . Among the most primitive elements of language I reckon particularly those stems that are seemingly formed from the verbal root by means of the suffix -*o*, both on account of the simplicity of their formation [simple things are pretty often of quite recent growth], their indefinite signification, as *nomina agentis*, as denoting products, as abstract terms, etc. [this is no decisive proof, the word "abstract" must create suspicion, if nothing else], and their number. [If the old languages of our family were dead, it would be possible by means of the same arguments to prove that the weak

[1] "*Vokal- og konsonantstammer*," in *Akademiske afhandlinger til Sophus Bugge*, Kristiania, 1889; cf. *Den Græske Nominalflexion*, af A. Torp, *ibid*, 1890.

verbs in English were the most primitive.] . . Later on, certain endings were joined to these stem forms, the language intending thereby a more definite denoting of the case relations (case endings). [Language neither can nor does intend anything; those who speak it intend nothing but to be understood at the moment; therefore they do not add anything to denote more definitely something of which they can have no notion.] These case endings have long been justly looked upon as consisting of pronominal stems. [It is possible that this may turn out in the end to be the correct view; but hitherto there is not one single ending with regard to which it has been shown with any degree of probability how a pronoun could modify the meaning and function of a noun in that particular way.] . . Thus -*s* in the nominative singular is certainly the same pronominal stem as that which is used as a demonstrative pronoun in the form *so, se* [but what is the origin of *so, se* itself?]; the -*m* of the accusative is the same element as that found in *me*, the pronoun of the first person, which was in all probability originally a demonstrative pronoun also. [Would it not be safer to confess that one has not the slightest idea of the derivation of -*m* than to bring forward an explanation presupposing violent changes of sense, without making the least attempt to commend such an assumption by adducing hypothetical connecting links?] . . the *ā*-stems are, I fancy, formed by an element -*ā*, which was, I suppose, properly a pronoun used to denote the feminine gender, being added to the *o*-stems before these had yet adopted case endings."

54. (28) If theories about the origin of things are not to be worthless, they must on every point be substantiated by analogies from processes going on now-a-days, and capable of direct observation and control. We must, accordingly, ask ourselves: Do we ever witness the genesis of any new flexional endings or similar elements? If we do, we cannot be far wrong in thinking that those formal elements of language whose origin lies far back in pre-historic times, must have arisen in similar ways and through the same agencies.

Now, there is one method of accounting for the genesis of the elements we are here speaking of, which seems so natural and obvious that it is no wonder that very extensive use has been made of it ever since the first beginnings of comparative philology, namely, the agglutination theory. According to this theory two words, originally independent of each other, so often stand together that at length they are combined into one indissoluble unity; one of the two gradually loses its stress, and finally becomes nothing more than a suffix of the other. Thus, without the least doubt, the Scandinavian passive voice originates in an agglutination of the active verb and the pronoun *sik*; Old Norse, *þeir finna sik*, "they find themselves," or "each other," gradually becomes one word, *þeir finnask*; Swedish, *de finnas*; Danish, *de findes*, "they are found".

Similarly the future tense of the Romance languages: Italian, *finirò*; French, *je finirai*; "I shall end," from *finire habeo (finir ho, finir ai),* "I have to end". The Scandinavian suffixed article is a third case in point, if we are allowed to consider it as a kind of flexion: Old Norse, *marmenn (manninn)*, accusative; Danish, *manden*, "the man"; Old Norse, *landet (landit)*; Danish, *landet*, "the land," for original *mann, land* + the demonstrative pronoun *enn*, neuter *et*.[1]

55. On the strength of these formations it has been concluded that all derivative and flexional endings had a similar history, that is, they were all independent words before they became agglutinated to, and fused with, the main word. This is the theory prevalent among all the leading linguists, not only of the times of Bopp and those of Schleicher, but also of quite recent days. Thus WHITNEY says: "Suffixes of derivation and inflexion are made out of independent words, which, first entering into union with other words by the ordinary process of composition, then gradually lose their independent character, and finally come to be, in a more or less mutilated and disguised form, mere subordinate elements, or indicators of relation". And again: "The grand conclusion, however, at which historical study has surely and incontrovertibly arrived, is that all the grammatical apparatus of languages is of secondary growth; the endings of declension and conjugation,

[1] Cf. also Roumanian *domnul*, "the master," for Latin *dominu(m) illu(m)*.

the prefixes and suffixes of derivation, were originally independent elements, words, which were first collocated with other words, and then entered into combination and were more or less thoroughly fused with the latter, losing their primitive form and meaning, and becoming mere signs of modification and relation; hence, that the historically traceable beginnings of speech were simple roots; not parts of speech even, and still less forms".[1]

H. PAUL says: "The strictly normal origin of all formal elements in language is always composition;" and in criticising the particular manner in which this process has been supposed to work, he still assumes the truth of the general theory: "the first foundation of derivation and of flexion was created by the coalescence of originally independent elements; but then, as soon as these foundations had come into existence, they had to serve as patterns for formations by analogy".[2]

BRUGMANN says: "What is included under the names of stem-formation and flexion depends on a more or less close fusion of originally independent elements".[3]

G. V. D. GABELENTZ expresses himself to the same effect: "As far as authenticated facts of linguistic history go, all external expedients of derivation and accidence originate in agglutination, that is, in the adding of originally independent words".[1]

Similar expressions might be adduced from other eminent philologists, such as TEGNÉR (who holds that the transition from agglutination to flexion constitutes a retrogression), SWEET, and HERMAN MÖLLER.[2]

56. Now, of course it cannot be denied that similar processes may have been going on at any time, and that some flexional forms of old Arian may have arisen in this way. But when the inference is that they are *all* to be explained in this manner, and that here we have the key to flexion in general, great exception may be taken. First, the number of actual forms proved beyond a doubt to have originated through agglutination is very small; the three or four instances named above are everywhere appealed to, but are there so many more than these? And are they numerous enough to justify so general an assertion? Secondly, these three or four instances can, at any rate, prove nothing as to the genesis of flexion in general from agglutination preceded by isolation; for in all of them the elements were fully flexional before the fusion (cf. Ital. *amerò, amerà, amerà,* etc.; Old Norse, *fınnask, fannsk; maðrenn, mannenn, mansens*). What they show, then, is really nothing

---

[1] *Life and Growth of Language*, 1875, 124-5. *Oriental and Linguistic Studies*, i. 283.
[2] *Principien der Sprachgesch.*, 2nd edit., 1886, pp. 274. 297.
[3] *Grundriss d. vgl. Gramm.*, ii., 1889, § 1.

---

[1] *Die Sprachwissenschaft*, 1891, p. 189.
[2] Tegnér, *Språkets Makt*, 1880, esp. pp. 53-54; Sweet, *New English Grammar*, 1892, § 559; H. Möller, *Tsk. f. Filol.*, n. r. x, p. 299.

but the growth of new flexional formations on an old flexional soil. Thirdly, it may be objected to the theory that, assuming it to be true, we should expect much more regular forms than we actually find in the old Arian languages; for if one definite element was added to signify one definite modification of the idea, we see no reason why it should not have been added to all words in the same way; as a matter of fact, the Romance future, the Scandinavian passive voice and definite article present much greater regularity than is found in the inflexion of nouns and verbs in old Arian.

(28) And finally, the agglutination theory must cease to be thought the only possible way of accounting for the origin of flexional endings, as soon as we are able to point out certain endings which undoubtedly have originated in quite a different manner. Such endings, however, are -*en* in English *oxen*, German *ochsen*, and -*er* in German *rinder*, *lämmer*. Here originally -*en* and -*er* belonged to the word through all cases and all numbers; *ox* was an *n*-stem in the same way as, for instance, Latin homo(*n*), homi*n*em, homi*n*is, etc., or Greek kuō*n*, kuna, ku*n*os, etc., are *n*-stems; cf. Sanskr. ukšan-; and the other words were originally *es*- and *os*-stems, comparable to Latin genu*s*, gene*r*is from older gene*s*is, Greek geno*s*, gene(*s*)os, for original *s* develops regularly through *z* to *r* in the Germanic languages, whenever it is preceded by a weak vowel. No one, in considering the Latin forms *homines* or *genera*,

would dream of the possibility of the syllables *in* (*en*) and *er* becoming the sign of the plural, when the same syllables appeared in the singular as well. Yet, in Germanic, where the declension was originally strictly analogous to that of Latin, this has actually come to pass: the final syllables of the nominative and accusative singular were dropped by a regular phonetic change, while in the plural *n* and *r* were kept because they were protected by a following syllable, which had first to be worn away. The result is that now plurality is indicated by an ending which had formerly no such function (which indeed had no function at all); for if we look upon the actual language, *oxen* is = *ox* (singular) + the plural ending -*en*, and similarly *rinder* = *rind* (singular) + the plural ending -*er*; only we must not on any account imagine that the forms were originally thus welded together (agglutinated).[1] Compare also the history of the English possessive pronouns; Old English *min* and *þin* keep the *n* throughout as forming part and parcel of the words themselves; but in Middle English the *n* is dropped first before nouns beginning with a consonant (*my father—mine uncle*; it is *mine*), and then before a vowel as well,

---

[1] When -*en* and -*er* had become established as plural signs, they were added by analogy to words which were not originally *n*- or *s*-stems, *e.g.*, German, *hirten*, *soldaten*, *thaten*; *wörter*, *bücher*; Middle English, *caren*, *synnen* (Old English, *cara*, *synna*; Modern English, *cares*, *sins*). Here we might speak of agglutination—but not in the sense of the welding together of originally independent words!

but only when the pronouns are used attributively (*my* father, *my* uncle—it is *mine*). The distinction between *my* and *mine*, *thy* and *thine*, which was originally a purely phonetic one, like that between *a* and *an*, gradually acquires a functional value, and serves to distinguish a conjoint from an absolute form; and as the former was the more commonly used, it came to be looked upon as the proper form, while the *n* of *mine* was felt as an ending serving to indicate the absolute function. That this is really the instinctive feeling of the people is shown by the fact that in dialectal and vulgar speech the *n* is added to *his, her, your,* and *their*, to form the absolute pronouns *hisn, hern, yourn,* and *theirn*.

58. (29) If we apply such considerations to the forms of primitive Arian speech, we shall be led to a change of front similar to that made in historic phonology when, instead of the *i* of the Greek *eipon* being considered as the root vowel and the *ei* of *leipo* as a strengthening of *i*, *ei* began to be taken as the original and fuller form, of which *i* was a weakening. And where the old school could only imagine language taking the most direct course possible we must realise the fact that it often takes the most unexpected round-about ways to reach its goal. It cannot but be beneficial always to remember that the signification borne at one time by a word or a word-element is very often widely different from the original one, and that sometimes an element which

had primarily no signification at all may gradually acquire a signification of great importance. Many endings may have acquired their special modifying force in a way analogous to that seen in the French *pas*. In the oldest French, *ne* alone is sufficient to express the negation; then it became habitual to strengthen the negation by the addition of such superfluous words as *pas*, "a step," *goutte*, "a drop," *mie*, "a crumb," or the like, just as we say in English, "not a bit, not a scrap". *Pas* became the most common of these expletives; and little by little it grew to be as indispensable in most sentences as the *ne* itself. Nay, now it is even more so, for *pas* has so completely appropriated to itself the negative meaning as to be used for "not" wherever there is no verb in the sentence (Pas de ça!) and in the colloquial style even with a verb, the word which originally carried the negative meaning being entirely ousted (C'est pas vrai!). A similar indirect course has been taken by the French *jamais*, "never," which now means the exact opposite of its etymological value (Latin jam + magis, "now + more").

59. (29) Many signs of the times seem to presage a change of front in the modern science of language. Numerous cases of agglutination formerly accepted have been proved by modern criticism to be untenable; nobody now thinks that the Germanic weak preterite is a compound of *did* (loved=love did), or that the *r* of the Latin passive is a disguised *se*; and after

Prof. Sayce's attack[1] it seems no longer possible to derive the person-endings of the verbs from personal pronouns. There is decidedly a growing disinclination to bring forward the kind of explanations by agglutination which were formerly so rife: not a few philologists carry positivism to the length of rejecting as mere metaphysical speculation any attempt at explaining the old forms; and the fresh explanations which are now given by the masters of the science of language are most of them indirect ones. I shall illustrate this by referring briefly to a few important investigations of recent date.

60. (30) The first of these is by the chief of the Leipzig school of philology, KARL BRUGMANN. In his paper *Das Nominalgeschlecht in den indogermanischen Sprachen*,[2] he puts the question: How did it come about that the old Arians attached a definite gender (or sex, *geschlecht*) to words like foot, head, house, town, the Greek *pous*, for instance, being masculine, *kephalē* feminine, *oikos* masculine, and *polis* feminine? The generally accepted explanation, according to which the imagination of mankind looked upon lifeless things as living beings, is, Brugmann says, unsatisfactory; the masculine and feminine as grammatical genders are merely unmeaning forms and have nothing to do with the ideas of masculinity

[1] The person-endings of the Indo-European verb, in Techmer's *Internationale Zeitschr. f. Allgem. Sprachwissenschaft*, i., 222.
[2] In Techmer's *Internationale Zeitschr. f. Allgem. Sprachwissenschaft*, iv. (1888), p. 100 ff.

and femininity; for even where there exists a natural difference of sex, language often employs only one gender. So in German we have *der hase, die maus*, and "der weibliche hase" is not felt to be self-contradictory. Again, in the history of languages we often find words which change their gender exclusively on account of their form.[1] Nothing accordingly hinders us from supposing that grammatical gender originally meant something quite different from natural sex. The question, therefore, according to Brugmann, is essentially reduced to this: How did it come to pass that the suffix *-a* was used to designate female beings? At first it had nothing to do with femininity, witness the Latin *aqua*, "water," etc.; but among the old words with that ending there happened to be some words denoting females: *mama*, "mother" (also with the meaning of "mother's breast," Latin *mamma*, French *mamelle*, and "aunt," German *muhme*), and *gena*, "woman" (compare English *quean, queen*). Now, in the history of some suffixes we see that, without any regard to their original etymological signification, they may adopt something of the radical meaning of the words to which they are added, and transfer that meaning to new formations. In this way *mama* and *gena* became the starting-point for analogical formations, as if the

[1] Thus, in German, many words in *-e*, such as *traube, niere, wade*, which were formerly masculine, now have become feminine, because the great majority of nouns in *-e* were feminine (*erde, ehre, farbe*, etc.).

idea of female was denoted by the ending, and new words were formed, *e.g.*, Latin *dea*, "goddess," from *deus*, "god"; *equa*, "mare," from *equus*, "horse," etc. Other suffixes probably came to denote "feminine sex" by a similar process.

61. (30) On account of the nature of the subject, Brugmann's investigation is more convincing in its negative criticism than in its positive conclusions. It must decidedly be greeted as a wholesome change that he does away with such explanations as those above mentioned, according to which the *a* in *equa*, etc., was a pronoun or a phonetic modification signifying the feminine quality, and having signified this from the very beginning. The division of Arian nouns into three genders, and the concord which is a consequence of that division (adjectives, etc., being made to agree with their nouns in gender), is, in fact, nothing but a class division analogous to that of the Zulu language described above. The analogy will be still more striking if we compare Arian, not with Zulu, but with the neighbouring, but totally unconnected, Hottentot language, for there a class division has been employed to distinguish natural sex which had nothing to do with sex originally.[1]

62. (31) The second instance of the beginning tendency towards *indirect* explanations of grammatical phenomena which I shall quote, is the important and learned book by the Berlin Professor JOHANNES

[1] Bleek, *Comparative Grammar*, ii., 118-122, 292-299.

SCHMIDT: *Die Pluralbildungen der indogermanischen Neutra* (Weimar, 1889). In this work Schmidt conclusively proves what before him some scholars had suspected,[1] namely, that the common Arian plural in *-a* was originally neither neuter nor plural, but, on the contrary, feminine and singular. The forms in *-a* are properly collective formations like those found, for instance, in Latin, *opera, -a* "work," comp. *opus*, "(a piece of) work"; Latin, *terra*, "earth," comp. Oscan, *terum*, "plot of ground"; *pugna*, "boxing, fight," comp. *pugnus*, "fist". This explains among other things the peculiar syntactic phenomenon, which is found regularly in Greek and sporadically in the Asiatic branch of the Arian family, that a neuter plural subject takes the verb in the singular. The Greek *toxa* is often used in speaking of a single bow; and the Latin poetic use of *guttura, colla, ora*, where only one person's throat, neck, or face is meant, points similarly to a period of the past when these words did not denote the plural. We can now also see the reason of this *-a* being in some cases the plural sign of masculine nouns: Lat., *loca* from *locus, joca* from *jocus*, etc.; Gr., *sita* from *sitos*. Joh.

[1] See Brugmann, *Grundriss*, ii., 682, second footnote, where he might also have mentioned F. A. March, who says (*Anglo-Saxon Gram.*, 1877, p. 36): "We take inanimate things in the lump; hence neuters tend to use no plural sign, or to use an ending like the feminine singular, as an abstract or collective form: Greek, Latin, *-a*, Anglo-Saxon *-u*, etc. Latin neuters plural frequently become feminine singular in the Romance languages; Greek neuters plural take a singular verb."

Schmidt refers to similar plural formations in Arabic; and we may call to mind our friends the Bantus, whose plural prefixes were, as we have seen, originally no more signs of plurality than the Arian -*a*. And thus we are constantly reminded that language must often make the most curious *détours* to arrive at a grammatical expression for things which appear to us so self-evident as the difference between *he* and *she*, or that between *one* and *more*. Simplicity in linguistic structure—that is, expressive simplicity—is not a primitive, but a derived quality.

63. (32) Comparative philology did not attain a scientific character till RASK and BOPP established the principle that the relationship of two languages had to be determined by a thorough-going conformity in the most necessary parts of language, namely, besides suffixes and similar elements incapable of independent existence, pronouns and numerals, and the most indispensable of nouns and verbs. But if this domain of speech, by preserving religiously, as it were, the old tradition, affords infallible criteria of the near or remote relationship of different languages, may we not reasonably expect to find in the same domain some clue to the oldest grammatical system used by our ancestors? And what sort of system do we then find there? We see such a declension as *I, me, we, us*: the several forms of the "paradigm" do not at all resemble each other, as they do in more recently developed declensions;

we find masculines and feminines such as *father, mother; man, wife; bull, cow*; while such methods of derivation as are seen in *count, countess; he-bear, she-bear*, belong to a later time; we meet with verbal flexion such as appears in *am, is, was, been*, which forms a striking contrast to the more modern method of adding a mere ending while leaving the body of the word unchanged.

64. (33) The general impression left by these and many similar instances is, that the grammatical system of our remote ancestors was, to say the least of it, very unsystematic and far from simple. Things which belong, or to us would seem to belong, closely together, were widely sundered as regards their linguistic expression. And it is only by a slow and gradual development that conformity and regularity are brought about, especially in those words which are in most constant use. The rarer a word is, the more difficult it is to remember its several forms unless they resemble one another; accordingly, rare words are more exposed to being accommodated on the spur of the moment to the most regular patterns of inflexion. These regular patterns being more present to the speaker's mind, he pays no regard to the fact that the word in question "ought properly to be irregular". Nor is it the rarer words alone which are reduced to rule: even in the case of the more frequently recurring words the levelling influences are at work; a greater and greater number of cases will run together, and irregularities will gradually disappear. Those little words which are used every minute, pronouns and so on, are uttered and heard so very often that their forms acquire an extreme power of resistance. And yet, even in these words we observe the great work of simplification going on. Let us take one of the clearest instances of all. The flexion of the second personal pronoun, which was universal in English some four hundred years ago, namely, nominative singular *thou*, accusative singular *thee*, nominative plural *ye*, accusative plural *you*, has now in ordinary conversational and prose language given place to perfect simplicity and uniformity: nominative singular *you*, accusative singular *you*, nominative plural *you*, accusative plural *you*. But if we look closer into the history of this important change, which will form the subject of a subsequent chapter, we shall see that a great many most widely different circumstances (phonetic, syntactic, and social) have concurred to produce so complete a revolution.

65. (33) To turn to the case of nouns, we cannot imagine even in the most primitive grammar such violent flexional changes as that seen in *I, me*, where a totally different root is needed. Nevertheless, we find in the oldest Arian languages plenty of comparative violent changes taking place in the declensions, as when different cases of the same noun have different accentuation and different gradation (ablaut); or as when in some of the most frequently occurring words some cases are formed from one "stem" and

others from another. Thus in the common Arian word for "water," Greek has preserved both stems: nominative *hudōr*, genitive *hudat-os*, where *a* stands for an original *n* or (*ə*)*n* which appears in some of the other related languages. Whatever the origin of this change of stems,[1] it is a phenomenon belonging only to the earlier stages of our languages;[2] in the later stages we always find a simplification, one single form running through all cases; this is either the nominative stem, as in English *water*, German *wasser* (corresponding to Greek *hudōr*), or the oblique case-stem, as in the Scandinavian forms, Old Norse *vatn*, Swedish *vatten*, Danish *vand* (corresponding to Greek *hudat-*), or finally a contaminated form, as in the name of the Swedish lake *Vättern* (Noreen's explanation) or in Old Norse and Danish *skarn*, "dirt," which has its *r* from a form like the Greek genitive *skōr*, and its *n* from a form like the Greek genitive *skatos* (older *skəntos*). The simplification is carried furthest in English, where the identical form *water* is not only used unchanged where in the older languages different case-forms of the noun would have been used (the water is cold; he drinks water; the surface

[1] See now Holger Pedersen, r-n-stämme, in Kuhn's *Zeitschr*, xxxii, 240.

[2] In these we sometimes find an alternation between the *r* stem in the nominative and a blending of both stems in the other cases; thus in Latin *jecur*, "liver," *jecinoris*; *iter*, "voyage," *itineris*; instead of *jecur—jecinis*, *iter—itinis*; cf. *femur*, thigh, *feminis*.

of the water; he fell into the water; he swims in the water), but also where it serves as a verb (did you water the flowers?) or as a quasi-adjective (a water melon, water plants). We see here an approach to the Chinese type of speech which we shall glance at in the next chapter.

CHAPTER IV.

THE HISTORY OF CHINESE AND OF WORD-ORDER.

66. (34) In CHINESE each word consists of one syllable, neither more nor less. The parts of speech are not distinguished: *tá* means, according to circumstances, great, much, magnitude, enlarge. Grammatical relations such as number, person, tense, case, etc., are not expressed by endings and similar expedients; the word in itself is invariable. If a noun is to be taken as plural, this as a rule must be gathered from the context; and it is only when there is any danger of misunderstanding, or when the notion of plurality is to be emphasised, that separate words are added, *e.g.*, *ki*, "some," *šŭ*, "number".[1] The most important part of Chinese grammar is that dealing with word-order: *tá kuok* = "great state," or "great states"; but *kuok tá* means "the state is great," or, if placed before some other word which can serve as a verb, "the greatness (size) of the state"; *tsi⁻ⁿ niü⁻* "boys and girls," but *niü⁻ tsi⁻ⁿ* "girl" (female child), etc.[2] Besides *words* properly so called, or, as the Chinese grammarians term them, "full words," there

[1] Gabelentz, *Chinesische Grammatik*, 1881, § 1054 *sqq.*
[2] *Ibid.*, *Anfangsgründe d. Chin. Gr.*, 1883, § 29.

are several "empty words" serving for grammatical purposes, often in a wonderfully clever and ingenious way. Thus *čï*[1] has besides other functions that of indicating a genitive relation more distinctly than it would be indicated by the mere position of the words; *mín* (people) *lìk* (power) is of itself sufficient to signify "the power of the people," but the same notion is expressed more explicitly by *mín čï lìk*. The same expedient is used to indicate different sorts of connexion; if *čï* is placed after the subject of a sentence it makes it a genitive, thereby changing the sentence into a sort of subordinate clause: *wàng paò mín* = "the king protects the people"; but if you say *wàng čï paò mín yêù* (is like) *fù* (father) *čï paò tsï*, the whole may be rendered, by means of the English verbal noun, "the king's protecting the people is like the father's protecting his child". Further, it is possible to change a whole sentence into a genitive; for instance, *wàng paò mín čï taò* (manner) *k'ò* (can) *kièn* (see, be seen), "the manner in which the king protects (the manner of the king's protecting) his people is to be seen"; and in yet other positions *čï* can be used to join a word-group consisting of subject and verb, or of verb and object, as an attribute to a noun; we have particles to express the same modification of the idea: *wàng paò čï mín*, "the people protected by the king"; *paò mín čï wàng*, "a king protecting the people". Observe here the ingenious method of distinguishing the active and passive voices by

[1] Gabelentz in Techmer's *Internat. Zeitschrift*, i, 276-7.

strictly adhering to the natural order and placing the subject before and the object after the verb. If we put *ì* before, and *kü* after, a single word, it means "on account of, because of" (cf. English *for . . .'s sake*); if we place a whole sentence between these "brackets" as we might term them, they are a sort of conjunction, and must be translated "because".

67. (35) These few examples will give the reader some faint idea of the language of the Celestial Empire; and, if the older generations of scholars are to be trusted, we have to picture to ourselves the primeval structure of our own language (in the root-period) as something analogous. Thus SCHLEICHER[1] says: "The structure of all tongues indicates that their oldest form was essentially identical with that which has been kept unchanged in some languages of the very simplest structure (*e.g.,* Chinese)". Similar utterances might be adduced from the writings of Max Müller, Whitney, etc.; and the same view is also held by the renowned Chinese scholar J. EDKINS, in his book on *The Evolution of the Chinese Language* (1888), from the preface of which I quote the following: "Chinese remains possessed of a primitive order of words, and a monosyllabic structure. These peculiarities give it a claim to be a direct descendant of the mother-tongue of humanity, but it is not itself that mother-tongue . . . there is no other language, or family of languages, which can be more reasonably assumed to be the speech first used in the world's grey morning than can the Chinese."

[1] *Die Darwinsche Theorie*, p. 21.

68. (36) However, different considerations have tended to shake this faith in the primitiveness of the Chinese language. As early as 1861, R. LEPSIUS, from a comparison of Chinese and Tibetan, had derived the conviction that "the monosyllabic character of Chinese is not original, but is a lapse from an earlier polysyllabic structure". And Mr. EDKINS, whose identification of Chinese with "the speech first used in the world's grey morning" I just now quoted, has been among the foremost to examine the evidence offered by the language itself for the determination of its earlier pronunciation. This, of course, is a much more complicated problem in Chinese than in our alphabetically-written languages; for a Chinese character, standing for a complete word, may remain unchanged while the pronunciation is changed indefinitely. But by means of dialectal pronunciations in our own day, of remarks on pronunciation in old Chinese dictionaries, of transcriptions of Sanskrit words made by Chinese Buddhists, of rhymes in ancient poetry, of phonetic or partly phonetic elements in the word-characters, etc., etc.,[1] it has been possible to demonstrate—with comparative certainty on the whole, though undoubtedly with no small uncertainty in many particulars—that Chinese pronunciation has changed considerably, and that the direction of change has been, here as elsewhere, towards shorter and easier word-forms. Above all, consonant groups have been simplified.

[1] Gabelentz, *Grammatik*, pp. 90-111.

69. (36) It is not impossible, as I think, that certain peculiarities in the living pronunciation of Chinese might, if correctly interpreted, lead us to the same conclusion. I refer to the change sometimes wrought in the meaning of a word by the adoption of a different musical tone.[1] Thus *wang* with the "lower even" tone means "king," in the "departing" tone it means "to become king"; *lao*, according to the tone in which it is spoken, is either "work" or "pay the work"; *tsung* with the "lower even" tone means "follow," with the "departing" tone it means "follower," and with the "upper even" tone "footsteps"; *haò* is "good," and *haó* is "love". Nay, meanings so different as "acquire" and "give" (*sheu*) or "buy" and "sell" (*mai*) are only distinguished by the musical accents.[2]

EDKINS makes an attempt to account for such changes, which I must confess I am not entirely able to follow; pointing with the hand seems to play some part in it, and then, "the wordmaker wanted the words 'to love' and 'to sell', and he formed them out of 'good' and 'buy' by adding an intonation existing in his environment". Similarly, though with much greater clearness, V. HENRY says: "Is not the process transparent? In primitive language,

[1] For a clear account of the true nature of the Chinese tones by a competent phonetician, see J. Storm, *Englische Philologie*, 2te ausgabe, 1892, pp. 212-214, 479-481.
[2] The examples taken from Gabelentz, *Gramm.*, § 230, and from Edkins, *loc. cit*, pp. 7, 40, 53.

in order to say 'I love,' one would say *hao*, 'this is good (for me),' accompanying this syllable with a gesture to take the place of the words that were understood; this gesture influenced the accent or tone of the syllable. . . . Further, we have in Chinese *mái* (to sell) and *mài* (to buy). . . . This double form seems to relate the history of exchange between men, as we find it in all works treating of political economy: unaccented *mai* probably denoted the rudimentary bargain or truck; but as this term had in each particular case to be exactly defined, the party saying *mai* (I acquire) would accompany the syllable with a centripetal gesture to indicate that the object came to him, and the other party who said *mai* (I cede) would naturally make the opposite gesture. The effect of this mimicry has been a divergent modification of the sound of the root".[1] Even granting the possibility of the gesticulation affecting the tone of the voice in the two cases,—which does not, however, seem quite beyond question,—this explanation presents some serious difficulties; for what if the speaker wanted to say "you buy"? Then the theory would make us expect the same gesture (and therefore the same tone) as in " I sell," contrary to the actual fact. And one does not see which gesture and which tone would have to be chosen to express the notion, "he sells to her," if both the persons spoken of were absent at the time. Or are we to suppose that men

[1] *Le Muséon*, i., p. 435 (Louvain, 1882); cf. P. Passy, *Changements Phonétiques*, p. 107.

at some remote period spoke only in the first person singular? Besides, the theory only assists us in the case of a very few pairs of words, and leaves us entirely in the dark about some of the above examples and numerous others. We must, therefore, be excused for looking about for another explanation; and I think I am able to suggest one. In the Danish dialect spoken in Sundeved (in Prussian South Jutland) two purely musical tones are distinguished, one high and the other low. Now these tones often serve to keep words or forms of words apart that would be perfect homonyms but for the accent, exactly as in Chinese. Thus *na* with the low tone is "fool," but with the high tone it is either the plural "fools" or else a verb "to cheat, hoax", *ri*, "ride," is imperative or infinitive according to the tone in which it is spoken; *jem* in the low tone is "home," and in the high "at home"; and so on in a great many words.[1] Now, in this language we need not go to gestures to explain the origin of these tonic differences, for the explanation is obvious to anybody familiar with the history of Scandinavian languages. The low tone is found in words origin-

[1] One of the forthcoming numbers of *Dania, Tidsskrift for Folkemaal og Folkeminder*, will, I hope, contain a detailed account of these tonic accents which have hitherto escaped notice; I have heard them in the pronunciation of Mr. N. Andersen, a native of Sundeved, who had of his own accord made comprehensive lists of homonyms distinguished by tones, without knowing anything of the existence and nature of similar tones in Scandinavian or other languages.

ally monosyllabic (compare standard Danish *nar*, *rid*, *hjem*), and the high one in words originally disyllabic (compare Danish *narre, ride, hjemme*). The tones belonging formerly to two syllables are now condensed on one syllable (originally, I suppose, in the form of a circumflex or compound tone).[1]

Although, of course, the Chinese tonic differences cannot in every respect be paralleled with those found in the Scandinavian languages, I see no reason why we should not set forth the provisional hypothesis that the above-mentioned pairs of Chinese words were formerly distinguished by derivative syllables or flexional endings and the like, which have now disappeared, without leaving any traces behind them except in the tones. This hypothesis is perhaps rendered more probable by what seems to be an established fact—that one of the five tones, at least in the Nan-king pronunciation, has arisen through the dropping of final consonants (p, t, k).

70. (37) However this may be, the death-blow was given to the dogma of the primitiveness of Chinese speech by ERNST KUHN'S lecture *Ueber Herkunft und Sprache der Transgangetischen Völker* (Munich, 1883). He compares Chinese with the surrounding languages of Tibet, Burmah, and Siam, which are certainly related to Chinese, and have essentially the same structure; they are isolating, have no flexion, and word-order is their chief grammatical instrument. But the laws of word-position prove to be different in these several languages, and Kuhn draws the incontrovertible conclusion that it is impossible that any one of these laws of word-position should have been the original one; for that would imply that the other races have changed it without the least reason and at a risk of terrible confusion. The only likely explanation is that these differences are the outcome of a former state of greater freedom. But if the ancestral speech had a free word-order, to be at all intelligible it must have been possessed of other grammatical appliances than are now found in the derived tongues; in other words, it must have indicated the relations of words to each other by something like or corresponding to our derivatives or inflexions.

71. (38) To the result thus established by Kuhn, that Chinese cannot have had a fixed word-order from the beginning, we seem also to be led if we

---

[1] Compare Norwegian *bön*, "prayer," with the "simple" tone, *bönner*, Old Norse *bø'nir*, "prayers," with the "compound" tone, while *bönner* (*bönder*), "peasants," has the simple tone of original monosyllables; cf. Old Norse *bø'ndr*. The same difference is made in Norwegian between *bund-en*, "the bottom," and *bunden* (similarly in Swedish), "bound". In standard Danish, the corresponding distinction is made by means of the glottal stop; thus, in everyday pronunciation, the only difference between the singular "day" and the plural "days" consists in the former having and the latter not having the stop or "stød," both forms being now monosyllabic *da*, whereas the literary language and "refined" pronunciation keeps up the old distinction between monosyllabic *dag* and dissyllabic *dage*. For an account of Scandinavian musical tones, see Storm, *Engl. Philologie*, 2nd ed., pp. 230, 247, 309, 327, and the works quoted there.

fully and thoroughly consider the question, what is a fixed word-order? And is primitive man likely to have arranged his words according to such fixed order? A Chinese sentence is arranged with the same logical precision as the direction of an English letter, where the most specific word is placed first, and each subsequent word is like a box comprising all that precede: Miss-Emily-Brown-23-High-Street-Brighton-Sussex-England. The only difference is that a Chinaman would reverse the order, beginning with the most general word and then in due order specialising.[1] The logical consistency in both cases is the same.

Now, is it probable that primitive man, that unkempt, savage being, still half brute, who did not yet deserve the proud generic name of *homo sapiens*, but would be better termed, if not *homo insipiens*, at best *homo incipiens*, is it probable that this *urmensch*, who was little better than an *unmensch*, should have been able at once to arrange his words, or, what amounts here to the same thing, his thoughts, in such a perfect order? I should prefer to suppose that logical, methodical, orderly thinking and speaking have only been attained by mankind after a long and troublesome struggle. And above all an exact order of words as a grammatically significant element of speech is what we should, least of all, look for in the case of primitive man, whose thoughts and words are most likely to have come to him rushing helter-

[1] Gabelentz, *Die Sprachwissensch*, 426.

skelter in wild confusion. Nay, "a fixed word-order" is without doubt to be considered the highest, finest, and accordingly latest developed expedient of speech to which man has attained. The rules of word-position have too long been the Cinderella of linguistic science—how many even of the best grammars are wholly or almost wholly silent about them! Thus, with regard to the Bantu languages it was only from a short remark made incidentally by Bleek (ii, 108) that I got a little bit of information, which was, however, of the greatest importance to me, namely, that these languages do not make use of a fixed word-order to indicate changes of meaning. Not a word was to be found on this point in the rest of my authorities. And although in English a change of word-order will in many cases completely alter the meaning of the proposition, this subject is, in many grammars, treated very inadequately, if at all. Yet there is no denying that the theory of word-order, of its importance, and of the mutual relation between this and other grammatical expedients, offers a great many problems to the thoughtful student of language.

72. (39) To take one of these problems: What is the reason of the prevalence of the word-order—subject-verb-object—in English, Danish, French, Chinese, to mention only a very small number of languages? The fact of "that heathen Chinee" using the same order as ourselves precludes the supposition, often resorted to in such cases, that one of the European nations has borrowed the usage from one of the others, and shows the phenomenon to be founded in the very nature of human thought, though its non-prevalence in most of the older Arian languages goes far to show that this particular order is only natural to developed human thought.

Again, a question is commonly indicated by an inversion of the usual order of words, as when we say: "Has John got his hat?"—did ever any philological writer examine the rise of this interrogatory form in those languages where it is found, and the extension of its use? Originally, in all the old Germanic tongues as well as in Latin, etc., inversion was very often used without any interrogatory sense being denoted by it; and traces of this state of things are still to be found, especially when the verb is not the first word of the sentence ("About this time *died* the gentle Queen Elizabeth"), and in parenthetic sentences ("'Oh, yes,' *said* he"). In German, especially in the ballad style, it is still possible to begin a sentence with the verb: "*Kam* ein schlanker bursch gegangen". But it is well worth noticing that in German, as well as in the other modern languages of Western Europe, such an arrangement is generally avoided, so that in those cases where the speaker wants to give a prominent place to the verbal idea by putting it before the subject proper, he will, so to speak, satisfy his grammatical instincts by putting a kind of sham subject before the verb; English speakers will use *there* ; Danes, *der* ; in German *es* is used; in French, *il* ; in Swedish, *det* : "*there comes* a time when . . .", "*der kommer* en tid, da . . .", "*es kommt* eine zeit wo . . .", "*il arrive* un temps où . . .", "*det kommer* en tid daa".[1]

The inverted word-order, then, was not originally peculiar to interrogatory sentences; a question was expressed, no matter how the words were arranged, by pronouncing the whole sentence, or the most important part of it, in the peculiar interrogatory rising tone. This manner of indicating questions is, of course, still kept up in our modern speech, and it is often the only thing to show that the words are to be taken as a question ("John?" "John is here?"). But although there was thus a natural manner of expressing questions, and although the inverted word-order was used in other sorts of sentences as well, yet in course of time there came to be a connexion between these two things, so that putting the verb before the subject came to mean a question and to be felt as implying a question. The proof of this is that that rising of the tone which is natural to questions is far less marked in an inverted sentence like "Is John here?" than if you ask the question by means of the sentence "John is here?" the word-order leading you to expect a question in

[1] Note that in English *there* serves as an accusative in such sentences as "Let there be no discussion about that"; compare "Let us discuss," etc., Shakespeare, *Cymbeline*, ii, 4, 108, "Let there be no honour where there is beauty" | Trollope, *Duke's Ch*, i., 95, "I cannot let there be an end to it".

the former case and a statement in the latter. This obliteration of the interrogatory tone is especially easy to see in the pronunciation of indirect questions in the form of direct ones, such as (Dickens, *David Copperfield*, ii., 384) "Dora asked me *would I* let her give me all her money to keep" | (George Eliot, *Mill on the Floss*, i., 252) "he had meant to imply *would she* love as well in spite of his deformity".

73. (39) Now, after this method of indicating questions had become comparatively fixed, and after the habit of thinking first of the subject had become all but universal, these two principles entered into a conflict, the result of which, in three of the languages here specially dealt with, has been in many cases a compromise, the interrogatory word-order carrying the day formally, while really the verb, that is to say, the verb which means something, is placed after its subject. In English, this is attained by means of the auxiliary *do*: instead of Shakespeare's "Came he not home to-night?" (*Romeo*, 1045), we now say, "Did he not, or Didn't he, come home to-night?" and so in all cases where a similar arrangement is not already brought about by the presence of some other auxiliary, "Will he come?" "May he come?" etc.[1] In Danish, the verb *mon*, used in the old language to indicate a vague futurity, fulfils to a certain extent the office of the English *do*; up to some two hundred years ago *mon* was really an auxiliary verb, followed by the infinitive: "*Mon* nogle miles færd Vel *være* saadan larm og saadan fare værd?" (Holberg); but now the construction has changed, the indicative is used with *mon*, as in "*Mon* den gudinde er, der plages saa af galde?" (*ibid.*), and *mon* must be considered no longer a verb but an interrogatory adverb; "Mon han kommer?" differs from "Kommer han?" in being more indefinite and vague: "Will he come, do you think?"[1]

74. (39) French, finally, has developed no less than two forms of compromise between the conflicting principles, for in "Est-ce que Pierre bat Jean?" *est-ce* represents the interrogatory and *Pierre bat* the usual word-order, and in "Pierre bat-il Jean?" the real subject is placed before, and the sham subject *il* after the verb. Here also, as in Danish, the ultimate result is the development of "empty words"; *est-ce que* is in pronunciation, if not in spelling, one inseparable whole, a sentence prefix to introduce questions; and in popular speech we find another empty word, namely *ti*. The origin of this *ti* is very curious. While the *t* of Latin *amat*, etc., coming

---

[1] The same arrangement is often used where an adverb is placed in the beginning of a sentence, by no author, perhaps, so frequently as by Carlyle; I note from comparatively few pages of the *Sartor*: "Thus did the editor see himself" (where a writer of two hundred years ago would have written, "Thus saw an editor himself") | "So had it lasted for some months" | "Well do we recollect the last words" | "Thus does the good Homer not only nod, but snore" | "Thus is the Law of Progress secured" | "In such wise does Teufelsdreck deal hits," etc.

[1] On *mon* see my note in *Dania*, i., 1890, pp. 79-80.

after a vowel, disappeared at a very early period of the French language, and so produced *il aime*, etc., the same *t* was kept in Old French, wherever a consonant protected it, and so gave the forms *est, sont, fait* (from *fact*, for *facit*), *font, chantent, chantait*, etc. From *est-il, fait-il*, etc., the *t* was then by analogy re-introduced in *aime-t-il*, instead of the earlier *aime il*. Now, towards the end of the Middle Ages, French final consonants were as a rule dropped in speech, except when followed immediately by a word beginning with a vowel ("liaison"); in spelling, the old consonants were generally retained. Consequently, while *t* is mute in sentences like "Ton frère *dit*," "tes frères *disent*," it is sounded in the corresponding questions, "Ton frère *dit-il*?" "Tes frères *disent-ils*?" As the *l, ls*, of *il* and *ils* in these connexions is generally dropped, even by educated speakers, the difference between interrogatory and declarative sentences in the spoken language will be seen to depend solely on the addition of *ti* to the verb: written phonetically, the pairs will be :—

tõ frer di — tõ frer di ti
te frer diˑz — te frer diˑz ti.

Now, popular instinct seizes upon this *ti* as a convenient sign of interrogative sentences, and turns "Ta sœur di(t)" into "Ta sœur di ti?" plural, "Tes sœurs dise ti?" etc. Even in the first person it is used: "je di ti?" "nous dison ti?" etc. Where popular language is reproduced in writing, in the comic papers, novels, and the like, you will often find this interrogative particle spelt as if the adverb *y* formed part of it: "c'est-y pas vrai?" "je suis t'y bête!" etc. In Daudet's *L'Immortel*, p. 308, a child asks, "Dites, c'est-y vous le monsieur de l'Académie qui va avoir cent ans?"[1]

These remarks will, I hope, show the interest of many problems connected with the history of word-position, and also throw a little light on some of those strange ways by which languages must often travel to arrive at new grammatical categories and new forms of expression.

75. (40) I now pass to two questions of the greatest importance to the main subject of this book. First, What is the relation between freedom in word-position and a complicated system of inflexions? How is it that in historical times simplification of grammar always goes hand in hand with the development of a fixed word-order? Is this accidental, and is there no connexion between the two phenomena? Or, is there a relation of cause and effect between them?

I dare say most readers, after bestowing some little thought on the question, will agree in answering the last question in the affirmative, and in seeing that a fixed word-order is the *prius*, or cause, and

[1] Cf. my paper, *Træk af det parisiske vulgærsprogs grammatik*, in the Transactions of the Philol. Society of Copenhagen, June 4, 1885, and G. Paris (*Romania*, vi., 438), who thinks it probable that this *ti* will soon find its way into standard French.

grammatical simplification, the *posterius*, or effect. It is, however, by no means rare to find underlying, in a more or less latent way, people's notions of these things, the theory that the inflexional endings were first lost "by phonetic decay," or "by the blind operation of sound laws," and then a fixed word-order had to step in to make up for the loss of the previous forms of expression. But if this were true, we should have to imagine an intervening period in which the mutual relations of words were indicated in neither way; a period, in fact, in which speech would be unintelligible and consequently practically useless. The theory in question is therefore untenable. It follows that the fixed word-order must have come in first: it would come quite gradually as a natural consequence of greater mental development and general maturity: when the speaker's ideas no longer came into his mind helter-skelter but in orderly sequence. If before the establishment of some sort of fixed word-order any tendency to slur certain final consonants or vowels had manifested itself, it could not then have become universal, as it would have been constantly checked by the necessity that speech should be intelligible, and therefore those marks which showed where the several words belonged to, should not be obliterated. But when once each word was placed at the exact spot where it properly belonged, then there was no longer anything to forbid the endings being weakened by assimilation, etc., or their being finally dropped altogether.

76. (40) To bring out my view, I have been obliged in the preceding paragraph to use expressions that must not be taken too literally; I have spoken as if the changes referred to were made "in the lump," that is, as if the word-order was first settled in every respect, and after that the endings began to be dropped. The real facts are, of course, much more complicated, changes of the one kind being interwoven with changes of the other in such a way as to render it difficult, if not impossible, in any particular case to discover which was *prius* and which *posterius*. We are not able to lay a finger on one spot and say: Here final *m* or *n* was dropped, because it was now rendered superfluous as a case-sign on account of the accusative being invariably placed after the verb, or for some other such reason. But, nevertheless, the essential truth of my hypothesis seems to me unimpeachable. Look at Latin final *s*. Cicero (*Orat.* 48, 161) expressly tells us—and a good many inscriptions corroborate his words[1]—that there existed a strong tendency to drop final *s*; but the tendency did not prevail. The reason seems obvious; try the effect in a page of Latin prose of striking out all final *s*'es, and you will find that it will be extremely difficult to determine the meaning of many passages; a consonant playing so important a part in the endings of nouns and verbs could not be left out without loss in a language possessing so much freedom in

---

[1] See Corssen, *Aussprache, etc., des Lat.*, 2nd edit., i., p. 285; Schuchardt, *Vokalismus des Vulgärlat.*, ii., pp. 45, 169, 389.

regard to word-position as Latin. Consequently, it was kept; but in course of time word-position became more and more subject to laws; and when, centuries later, after the splitting up of Latin into the Romance languages, the tendency to slur over final *s* knocked once more at the door, it met no longer with the same resistance as before; final *s* disappeared, first in Italian and Roumanian, then in French. In French the disappearance took place towards the end of the Middle Ages, and some cases of survival are still found in actual pronunciation; in Spanish, final *s* is just now, at the end of the nineteenth century, beginning to sound a retreat.

77. (42) The answer to the second question hinted at in § 75 cannot now be doubtful. The question is this: Is it beneficial to a language to have a free word-position? Or, on the other hand, is the transition from freedom to greater strictness in this respect to be termed not loss but progress?

The importance of word-position to the master of style is known or felt by everybody; but what style is to the individual the general laws of language are to the nation. When Schiller says:—

Jeden anderen meister erkennt man an dem, was er ausspricht;
Was er weise verschweigt, zeigt mir den meister des stils,[1]

we for our part must award the palm to that language which makes it possible "to be wisely silent" about things which in other languages have to be expressed

[1] Every other master is known by what he says, but the master of style by what he is wisely silent on.

by clumsy and troublesome means, and which have often to be expressed over and over again (Mult*orum* vir*orum* antiqu*orum*). Could any linguistic expedient be more worthy of the genus *homo sapiens* than using for different purposes, with different significations, two sentences like "John beats Henry" and "Henry beats John," or the four Danish ones "Jens slaar Henrik—Henrik slaar Jens—slaar Jens Henrik?—slaar Henrik Jens?" (John beats Henry—Henry beats J.—does J. beat H.?—does H. beat J.?) or the Chinese use of 打 in different places? Cannot this be compared with the ingenious Arabic system of numeration, in which 234 means something entirely different from 324 or 423 or 432, and the ideas of "tens" and "hundreds" are elegantly suggested by the order of the characters, not ponderously expressed as in the Roman system?

78. (43) It will be objected that freedom to arrange your words as you please is a great advantage. To this I answer: We must beware of letting our judgment be run away with by a word. Because freedom is desirable elsewhere it does not follow that it should be the best thing in this domain; just as above we did not allow the phrase "wealth of forms" to impose upon us, we must here be on our guard against the word "free". It will be an easy matter to turn the tables, if instead of inquiring into the advantages of freedom we put the question in this way: Which is preferable, order or disorder? It is true that viewed exclusively from the standpoint of the speaker, freedom would seem to be a great advantage, as it is a restraint to him to be obliged to follow strict rules; but an orderly arrangement is decidedly in the interest of the hearer, as it facilitates very considerably his understanding of what is said to him; and therefore, though indirectly, it is in the interest of the speaker also, because he speaks for the purpose of being understood, for we may leave out of account those persons who speak solely for their own pleasure. Add to this that the want of a fixed order of words necessitates for the speaker the use of a more circumstantial and clumsy wording, including a great many reminders and so on, and you will see that even from the speaker's point of view a fixed word-order has not a few advantages.

79. (43) If it be urged in favour of a free word-order that we owe a certain regard to the interests of poets, it must be taken into consideration, first, that we cannot all of us be poets, and that a regard to all those of us who resemble Molière's M. Jourdain in speaking prose without being aware of it, is perhaps after all more important than a regard to those very few who are in the enviable position of writing readable verse; secondly, that a statistical investigation would, no doubt, give as its result that those poets who make the most extensive use of inversions and other antiquated word-positions are not among the greatest of their craft; and, finally, that in those languages which have turned word-order to profit as a grammatical expedient,—at least, in those that I am acquainted with—so many methods are found of neutralising this restraint, in the shape of particles, passive voice, constructions of sentences, etc., that no artist in language (and that is what every poet should be) need despair.

80. Observe, however, the nature of my arguments in favour of a strict word-order, and you will notice that they imply a reservation of no small significance. Most languages have some rules of word-position which are like certain rules of etiquette, in so far that you can see no reason for their existence, and yet you are obliged to bow to them. Historians may, in some cases, be able to account for their origin and show that they had a *raison d'être* at some remote period; but the circumstances that called them into existence then are now no more, and now the rules are felt to be restraints with no concurrent advantage to reconcile us to their observance. No praise is due to rules of position of this sort, and in estimating languages we should, as far as possible, take this point too into consideration: What is the proportion between useful and useless rules of word-position?

This distinction, although implied in the language used, was not explicitly stated in the Danish edition; and as some critics have on that account failed to see the full scope of my views, I shall avail myself of the opportunity afforded by their objections to try and make my position more clearly understood. Mr. ARWID JOHANNSON, in an interesting article on

"Correctness in Language,"[1] adduces a certain number of ambiguous sentences from German :—

Soweit die deutsche zunge klingt und *gott* im himmel lieder singt (is *gott* nominative or dative?) | Seinem landsmann, dem er in seiner ganzen bildung ebensoviel verdankte, wie *Goethe* (nominative or dative?) | Doch wurde die gesellschaft *der Indierin* (genitive or dative?) lästig gewesen sein | Darin hat Caballero wohl nur einen konkurrenten, die Eliot, *welche* freilich *die spanische dichterin* nicht ganz erreicht | Nur Diopeithes feindet insgeheim dich an und *die schwester* des Kimon und *dein weib* Telesippa. (In the last two sentences what is the subject, and what the object?)

According to Mr. Johannson, these passages show the disadvantages of doing away with formal distinctions, for the sentences would have been clear if each separate case had had its distinctive sign ; "the greater the wealth of forms, the more intelligible the speech". And they show, moreover, that such ambiguities will occur, even where the strictest rules of word-order are observed (bei der festgeregelsten stellung ... [beispiele] die eine ganz regelmässige wortfolge aufweisen). I shall not urge that this is not exactly the case in the last sentence, if *die schwester* and *dein weib* are to be taken as accusatives, for then *am* should have been placed at the very end of the sentence ; nor that, in the last sentence but one, the mention of George Eliot as the "konkurrent" of Fernan Caballero seems to show a partiality to the Spanish authoress on the part of the writer of the sentence, so that the reader is prepared to take *welche* as the nominative case ; *freilich* would seem to point in the same direction. But these, of course, are only trifling objections ; the essential point is that we must grant the truth of Mr. Johannson's contention that we have here a flaw in the German language ; the defects of its grammatical system may and do cause a certain number of ambiguities. Neither is it difficult to find out the reasons of these defects, by considering the structure of the language in its entirety, and by translating the sentences in question into a few other languages and comparing the results.

81. First, with regard to the formal distinctions between cases, the really weak point cannot be the fewness of these endings, for in that case we should expect the same sort of ambiguities to be very common in English and Danish, where the formal case-distinctions are considerably fewer than in German ; but as a matter of fact such ambiguities are more frequent in German than in the other two languages.

---

[1] In the *Indogermanische Forschungen*, i., 1891 ; see especially pp. 247 and 248, note. I leave out of account his Swedish examples, on p. 246, as they will be of little interest to English readers ; besides, Prof. Ad. Noreen in a letter confirms my surmise that they are not quite idiomatic, and consequently prove very little indeed.

And, however paradoxical it may seem at first sight, one of the causes of this is the greater wealth of grammatical forms in German. Let us substitute other words for the ambiguous ones, and we shall see that the amphibology will nearly always disappear because most other words will have different forms in the two cases; *e.g.*:—

Soweit die deutsche zunge klingt und *dem allmächtigen* (or, *der allmächtige*) lieder singt | Seinem landsmann, dem er ebensoviel verdankte wie *dem grossen dichter* (or, *der grosse dichter*). | Doch wurde die gesellschaft *des Indiers* (or, *dem Indier*) lästig gewesen sein | Darin hat Calderon wohl nur einen konkurrenten, William Shakespeare, *welcher* freilich *dem spanischen dichter* nicht erreicht (or, den . . . *der spanische d.*) | Nur D. feindet dich insgeheim an und *der bruder des Kimon und sein freund* T. (or, *den bruder . . . seinen freund*).

It is the fact that countless sentences of this sort are perfectly clear, which leads to the employment of similar constructions even where the resulting sentence is by no means clear; but if all, or most, words were identical in the nominative and the dative, like *gott*, or in the dative and genitive, like *der indierin*, constructions like those used would be impossible to imagine in a language meant to be an intelligible vehicle of thought. And the ultimate reason of the ambiguities will thus be seen to be the inconsistency in the formation of the several cases. But this inconsistency is found in all the old languages of the Arian family: cases which in one gender or in one declension are kept perfectly distinct, are in others identical.[1] While in Latin *patres filios amant* or *patres filii amant* are perfectly clear, *patres consules amant* allows of two interpretations; and in how many ways cannot such a proposition as *Horatius et Virgilius poetæ Varii amici erant* be construed? Such drawbacks seem to be inseparable from the structure of the highly flexional Arian languages; although they are not logical consequences of a wealth of forms, yet historically they cling to those languages which have the greatest number of grammatical endings. And as we are not here concerned with artificial Volapüks, but with natural languages, we cannot accept the above quoted verdict of Johannson's: "The greater the wealth of forms, the more intelligible the speech". In fact, the author himself seems to have a scruple about it, for he adds in a footnote: "I do not, of course, mean to lend my sanction to a luxuriant and clumsy wealth of forms

[1] *Domini* is genitive singular and nominative plural (corresponding to, *e.g.*, *verbi* and *verba*); *verba* is nominative and accusative plural (corresponding to *domini* and *dominos*); *domino* is dative and ablative; *dominæ* genitive and dative singular and nominative plural; *te* is accusative and ablative; *qui* is singular and plural; *quæ* singular feminine and plural, feminine and neuter; etc. Such inconsistent and arbitrary clashings are dangerous, but they may, in the long run, help to introduce systematic simplifications. Cf. § 146 *sqq.*

such as that found for instance in the Bantu languages, but I always have in my mind the wealth of forms (formenschatz) found in Arian languages;" unfortunately, he does not tell us which of the several Arian languages he will regard as the *beau idéal* in which he finds the golden mean; are eight, or seven, or six, or perhaps five, distinct cases the *ne plus ultra?*

82. Secondly, we consider the position of words in Mr. Johannson's sentences, and we discover that Modern High German still enforces some old rules of word-order which have been given up in the other cognate languages, where they were formerly in common use. The most important of these is that of placing the verb last in subordinate sentences; in two of the examples it is this rule which causes the ambiguity, which would accordingly have been avoided in a principal sentence: *Die deutsche zunge klingt und singt gott im himmel lieder;* or, *die d. z. klingt und gott im himmel singt lieder | sie erreicht freilich nicht die spanische dichterin;* or, *die sp. d. erreicht sie freilich nicht.* In one of the remaining sentences the ambiguity is caused by the rule that the verb must be placed immediately after an introductory adverb: if we omit the *doch* the sentence becomes clear: *Die gesellschaft der indierin würde;* or, *die gesellschaft würde der indierin lüstig gewesen sein.* All of which exemplifies the distinction between useless and useful rules of word-position. Word-position in German is comparatively strictly regulated, but generally by arbitrary rules; if, therefore, you change the order of words in a German sentence, you will often find that the meaning is not changed in the least, but the result will be an unidiomatic construction (bad grammar); while in English a transposition will often result in perfectly good grammar, only the meaning will be an entirely different one from that of the original sentence. I do not mean to say that the German rules of position are all useless, and the English all useful; but only that in English word-order is utilised to express difference of meaning to a far greater extent than in German, which stands in this, as in many other respects, on a lower plane of development than English.

83. Before leaving Mr. Johannson, I must remark that as word-order in those languages which make the proper use of it is used much more consistently than any endings ever are in actually existing languages, it is not only more convenient, but also clearer than flexions. The alternatives, accordingly, are not, as he puts it, the avoidance of misunderstandings on the one hand, and the sparing of flexional endings on the other; for in the evolution of languages the discarding of old flexions is perfectly consistent with the development of simpler and more regular expedients that are rather less liable to produce misunderstandings than were the old endings. When Mr. Johannson writes, "In contrast to Jespersen I do not consider that the masterly expression is the one which 'is wisely silent,' and consequently leaves the meaning to be partly guessed at, but the one which is able to impart the meaning of the speaker or writer clearly and perfectly"—he seems to me rather wide of the mark. For, just as in reading the arithmetical symbol 234 we are perfectly sure that two hundred and thirty-four is meant, and not three hundred and forty-two, so in reading or hearing "The boy hates the girl" we cannot have the least doubt who hates whom. If in any way the understanding of English (or Chinese, etc.) sentences depended on guesswork like a missing word competition (or a missing flexion competition), well, then the language could not be said to be "*wisely silent*".

84. I must here turn to another critic, Prof. D. K. DODGE, who, in reviewing my *Fremskridt i Sproget*,[1] says: "To cite one example, which figures in almost every English Rhetoric as a violation of clearness: 'And thus the son the fervid sire address'd'. The use of a separate form for nominative and accusative would clear up the ambiguity immediately." No doubt it would; but so would the use of a natural word-order. If the example is found in almost every English Rhetoric, I am happy to say that such ambiguous sentences are scarcely, if ever, found in other English books. No person in his sober senses would ever speak so; no prose writer would ever indulge in such a style; and in the whole range of my reading in English poetic literature I do not remember a single instance of so bold an inversion, except where the context would unmistakably show

[1] *Modern Language Notes*, Nov., 1892.

which word was to be taken as the nominative.[1] And even if such examples are here and there to be found, the only thing they can prove is this, that a violation of the rules of grammar entails want of clearness, and in present-day English such an arrangement of words is to be considered as a fault to be classed almost with the use of *dominum* as a nominative in Latin.

Those who regret the want of separate forms for nominative and accusative, etc., seem generally to be considering how a language might be constructed which would combine the greatest clearness with simplicity and freedom; they see some drawbacks in the language that is most familiar to them, and they cannot help exclaiming: Oh, how easy it would be to remedy the defects, if only we had separate forms, etc. This manner of regarding linguistic problems presents no very great difficulties, especially as nobody will take you to task and call upon you actually to construct a language such as you dream of, one that would be perfect in every detail. People are apt to forget that these are really nothing but barren speculations with not the slightest scientific significance, and that the really important questions are, firstly, What is the direction of change in languages, *as they actually exist*? And secondly, Is this or is it not a direction towards progress?

85. My answer is: Languages tend on the whole to become more analytical. I shall give some reasons for this view, and also some reasons why this

[1] See, for instance, Longfellow's translation from Logau:—
"A blind man is a poor man, and blind a poor man is;
For the former seeth no man, and the latter no man sees".

more and more to utilise word-position for grammatical purposes; and this is really a progressive tendency, directly progressive, because it is in itself the easiest and nicest linguistic expedient, rendering the task of speaking easier, and involving less effort on the part of the listener; indirectly, because it facilitates the great work of simplification in language by making the unwieldy forms used of old to indicate concord, etc., more and more superfluous. The substitution of word-order for flexions means a victory of spiritual over material agencies.

Word-position has acquired grammatical significance; and if we ask how this has come to pass, we get the same answer as before, when we were considering other grammatical instruments: it has come by a slow growth, without any intention on the part of the speakers. By little and little, people accustomed themselves to arrange their words after the same pattern, until those case-endings which had hitherto been the primary grammatical sign to indicate subject and object, or to show what noun an adjective belonged to, and those tones which had been the chief means of indicating a question, became gradually more subordinate and were finally made wholly or nearly superfluous. Grammatical meaning was first expressed by certain more material instruments, independent of word-position, then by the same instruments with the words arranged in a fixed order, and finally by order, independent of those original instruments.

CHAPTER V.

THE DEVELOPMENT OF LANGUAGE.

86. (44) We have seen in the preceding investigations that the downhill theory does not hold good for languages in historic times; on the contrary, languages seem to be on the whole constantly progressive, not only with regard to the development of their vocabulary, where nobody ever denied it, but also in grammar, where philologists of the old school were able to see only decay and retrogression. And besides establishing this progressive tendency, we have also incidentally seen some at least of the often unexpected ways which lead languages to develop new grammatical forms and expressions. We are thus prepared to enter into a criticism of that theory concerning the prehistoric development of Arian speech which has met with greatest favour among philologists, and which has been expounded with greatest precision and consistency by Schleicher. The theory, as will be remembered, was this: an originally isolating language, consisting of formless roots, passed through an agglutinating stage, in which formal elements had been developed, although these and the roots were

(112)

mutually independent, to the third and highest stage found in flexional languages, in which formal elements penetrated the roots and made inseparable unities with them.

87. (45) First, as regards the postulated root stage, we have seen how the support which Chinese was supposed to lend to the theory has broken down. But also from other quarters the belief in such a starting-point has been shaken. An investigation of Old Arian phonetic laws has led some philologists to doubt the supposition, which is essentially due to the old Indian grammarians, that roots were always monosyllabic; and now many prefer fancying the roots as dissyllabics. A more important reason for objecting to the theory seems to be this, that we cannot imagine people expressing themselves by means of a language consisting exclusively of roots such as those given by Sanskrit scholars; the highly abstract significations assigned to them ("breathe, move, be sharp or quick, blow, go," etc.) would in themselves be sufficient to preclude the idea of such a language existing as a practically useful means of communication—especially between savage or worse than savage beings. No; of a certainty, roots never were spoken words; and there is no doubt a great deal of truth in such expressions as these: "a root is only something imaginary, an abstraction" (Pott); "the root is an ideal object" (Lyngby[1]); "roots are not natural entities, but investigators' hypotheses.

[1] *Annaler for nordisk Oldkyndighed*, 1854. p. 229.

Speakers seem to me to have spoken, from the first, and to speak now, without any general consciousness of their existence" (Ellis[1]). It seems, then, that the correct view of the nature of roots is that they are abstractions of that which is common to a group of words which are felt as etymologically related. But, according to this, the root is not older than the words that are "derived" from it; and consequently, in spite of the opposition of most living comparative philologists, we can speak with perfect justice of Greek, French, or English roots. Why not speak of a French root *roul*, found in *rouler, roulement, roulage, roulier, rouleau, roulette, roulis?* This only becomes unjustifiable if, in putting down *roul* as the root, we fancy we have historically explained the origin of the words in question, or if we suppose that *roul* is a root which at some time existed independently of the derived words; for then the linguistic historian steps in and objects that the words have been formed, not from a root, but from a real word, and one which is not even itself a primary word, but a derivative, Latin, *rotula*, a diminutive of *rota*, "wheel"[2]. To the popular instinct *sorrow* and *sorry* are undoubtedly related to one another; and a student of Living English should respect this feeling, and say that the words now belong to the same root; but a thousand

[1] *Transactions of the Philological Society*, 1873-74, p. 455.
[2] This example is taken from the sober critical article *La Langue Indoeuropéenne*, by M. Bréal (*Journal des Savants*, Oct., 1876. p. 632 ff.).

years ago they had nothing to do with each other, and belonged to different roots (Old English, *sorg*, "care," and *sarig*, "wounded," "afflicted"). If all traces of Greek and Latin, etc, were lost, a linguist would have no more scruples about connecting *scene* with *see* than most illiterate Englishmen have now. But who will vouch that the Arian roots found in our dictionaries have not originated in similar ways to the roots *roul-*, *sorr-*, and *see-*?

88. (46) According to Schleicher and his disciples, the root stage was succeeded by the agglutinating stage, in which the main part of the word was unchanged, while formal elements might be added as prefixes or suffixes. Now, as only very few languages present the same kind of structure as Chinese (which represented the first class), and as, on the other hand, only two families of languages (the Arian and Semitic) are allowed a place in the third or flexional class, this intermediate class is made to include the great majority of human tongues. Consequently, languages of the most widely different types are brought together under the heading of "agglutination," and it becomes next to impossible to form any idea of what is properly the connecting link between these languages. The definitions generally given seem to have been taken from Ural-Altaic languages, and to have been thence transferred with more or less of constraint to all the rest. The consequence is that in reading, for instance, in Schleicher or Fr. Müller, their descriptions of languages which are termed agglutinating, one is perpetually startled and driven inwardly to confess that one is unable to see any difference between the grammatical forms of these languages and those which in Latin and Greek we call flexions. It is especially so in dealing with so complicated a language as *Basque*; here the verbal forms indicate not only the person of the subject, but also that of the object proper and the object of reference (dative); and, further, "the Basque language distinguishes in the verbal flexion when a man, a woman, or a person who commands respect is spoken to: the two first forms are familiar; the third is generally used. Thus, *dut*, 'I have' (generally speaking); *diat*, 'I have' (to a man); *dinat*, 'I have' (to a woman)."[1] On the whole, the forms are so manifold that we understand how Larramendi, in his legitimate pride at having been the first to reduce them to a system, called his grammar *El Imposible Vencido*, "The Impossible Overcome". To give some notion of this jumble of forms I copy a few from Prof. Sayce's *Introduction to the Science of Language* (ii, 212): *det*, I have it; *aut*, I have thee; *ditut*, I have them; *dizut*, I have it for thee; *dizutet*, I have it for you; *diszkizut*, I have them for you; *diut*, I have it for him. Can this be called an invariable root with endings added loosely, and easily separated?

89. Some philologists have maintained that in French in the coalescence of the pronoun with the verb we have really something corresponding to the Basque

[1] Eys, quoted in Techmer's *Internat. Zeitschr.*, i., p. 440.

verbal forms (or to the American incorporations). They will say that the spelling of *je* and the other pronouns as separate words in *j'aime, il te le disait* goes for nothing, and that the pronouns are really part and parcel of the verb as much as the corresponding elements in the exotic languages mentioned; if French had had no literary tradition, *jaime, jelaime,* etc., would probably have been written in one word. There seems, however, to be a difference; the French elements are much more felt as independent of one another than can be the case in Basque, etc. This is shown first by the possibility of varying the pronunciation: *il te le disait* may be pronounced either [itlədize] or [itəldize] (or, even in more elevated style, iltaladize); secondly, by the regularity of these joined pronominal forms, for they are always the same, whatever the verb may be; and, lastly, by their changing places in certain cases; *te le disait-il? dis-le-lui,* etc. And, at any rate, the verbal form is totally independent of the pronoun, as seen in "Jean disait à sa mère; *disons* ça à sa mère," etc. All of which is impossible in the Basque forms, in which you can no more separate the pronominal and verbal elements or make them change places than you could the *am* and *o* in the Latin *amo*.

90. (44) The term agglutinative is still less applicable to such languages as some of those spoken by North American Indians and Eskimos, where the incorporation of expressions for various subordinate ideas into the verb is carried to such an extent that the whole utterance forms one inextricable web, which can hardly be termed either a word or a sentence, and into which the several elements enter, often in hardly recognisable shape. We are here nearly as far removed as possible from the simplicity and lucidity which distinguish those languages to which the term agglutination seems first and with greatest propriety to have been applied, namely, Finnic and Magyar and their cognate tongues. And yet, even with regard to these latter, an eminent authority on all of these languages writes: "The difference between these and the so-called flexional languages, to which our tongue belongs, is in many points comparatively vague, and there are here found not a few formations which can with perfect justice be said to rest on flexion".[1]

91. (47) The third stage, according to Schleicher, was flexion, characterised by the highest union of content and form, the root itself being subject to change to express modifications of the meaning, especially for grammatical purposes. Here we must first notice what Schleicher himself admits—that in flexional languages we find a great many things which cannot be called flexion as he defined it. In his view they are survivals of the previous stages of isolation and agglutination through which these languages passed in prehistoric times. And next we must remember that originally no modification of

[1] Vilh. Thomsen, in *Tidskr. f. Philologi og Pædag.*, vii., 1867 162.

meaning was associated with those inner changes in the root. If in Greek we have the three forms of gradation (ablaut) *lip, leip,* and *loip,* they owe their origin to differences of accent; and if they are used in three different tenses of the verb (*e-lipon* I left, *leipō* I leave, *leloipa* I have left) the tense relation itself is expressed by means of endings (and beginnings), but not at all, or at least neither originally nor exclusively, by vowel gradation. So too in the more recent phenomenon, mutation (umlaut): where it is used as a means of indicating a plural, as in *goose—geese,* Danish *gaas—gæs,* this is a comparatively modern development: originally the plural was expressed by an ending (-*es,* -*iz*), which in course of time modified the root vowel, and then, some time afterwards, was itself dropped. Here, then, we have again an originally accidental change of the word, which has eventually been made to do duty as an expedient for signifying a change of sense. And, curiously enough, in no other language has this been done in a greater degree than in that language which, according to Schleicher, shows the deepest decline from the flexional golden age, *viz.,* English. In English more than anywhere else change of vowel alone, without any concurrent change of endings or the like, is used to distinguish different shades of meaning: as, for instance, *sing, sang, sung, song.* But if we should ask whether Schleicher is right in looking upon this as the highest and most perfect of formal means in language, we must, I am afraid, express

ourselves a little more reservedly, as this inner change cannot be used with complete equality and regularity in all roots.

92. (48) What is, after all, the essential characteristic of flexion? I can find no better answer than this: Flexion means inseparableness of the word itself (the "full word" of Chinese grammar) and the formal elements (the "empty words" of the Chinese). The Latin *amo* shows flexion, the English *I love* does not, because the idea is here dissolved into two independent parts.[1] But if flexion is thus interpreted

[1] On account of this inseparableness, flexional forms are often shorter than those combinations of several words which in more analytic languages are used to translate them; thus Latin *dixi* is more compact than the corresponding English "I have spoken," or "I have said". "One single added consonant such as -*s* or -*t* can express the same thing which [in non-flexional languages] requires one or more words," says Prof. H. Möller, who finds me here at variance with myself, shortness of word-forms being named in § 16 as an advantage belonging to the later stages of languages. The solution of the discrepancy lies hidden in his own statement: "Nothing can possibly be shorter than flexion in those cases where one inflected word with no sequence of words in agreement is concerned". For we do not generally speak in single disconnected words, and in connected speech the languages which exact concord will not appear to advantage (cf. also the examples in § 30). Besides, we should not compare single features of one language with single features of another, but look at the typical characteristics of the two. Prof. E. Tegnér (see *Språkets Makt,* pp. 51-52) has calculated that the Gospel of St. Matthew in Greek contains about 39,000 syllables, while the more analytic Swedish translation has about 35,000, and the

as inseparableness, as opposed to analysis, it will be easily seen from all the above investigations that there exist many different gradations of both; in no single language do we find either synthesis or analysis carried out with absolute purity and consistency. Everywhere we find a more or less. Latin is synthetic in comparison with French, French analytic in comparison with Latin; but if we were able to see the direct ancestor of Latin, say two thousand years before the earliest inscriptions, we should no doubt find a language so synthetic that in comparison with it Cicero's would have to be termed highly analytic.

93. (48) Our principal conclusion, then, is this: the old theory which imagined the prehistoric development of Arian speech from roots through agglutination to flexion is untenable. The only way of arriving at sound hypotheses with regard to prehistoric times is by examining the development which takes place in epochs historically accessible to us. If, in historic times, we find definite and comprehensive laws of evolution, we cannot help assuming the same laws as valid for prehistoric times as well; if history shows us certain lines of direction, followed by all languages which are in process of change, we cannot avoid the conclusion that languages have changed along the same lines as long as human beings have spoken; so that to imagine the state of

Chinese only 17,000. I may add that according to my own calculations the same Gospel contains in Danish about 32,500, and in English (the Authorised Version) about 29,000 syllables.

primeval language we have only to follow these lines backwards beyond the earliest period of which we have any tradition.

Now, Modern English as compared with Old English; Modern Danish, Swedish and Norwegian as compared with Old Norse; Modern Low German as compared with Old Saxon; Modern High German as compared with Old High German (all modern Germanic tongues as compared with the Gothic of Wulfila); Modern French, Italian, etc, as compared with Latin; Modern Greek as compared with Old Greek; Modern Persian as compared with the language of the Avesta ("Zend") and the cuneiform inscriptions; Modern Indian dialects as compared with Prakrit and Sanskrit—all of these show, though in different degrees, the same direction of change; the grammatical forms of the modern languages are all shorter, fewer, simpler, more abstract and more regular; those of the older languages in general longer, more complicated, more concrete and more irregular. Semitic languages present, as I understand, similar phenomena. And we find traces of an evolution in the same direction in those languages where the want of early documents, or the peculiar character of the early documents, hinders us from following the historic development with the same exactitude as in the languages just mentioned (see the sections above on Bantu and on Chinese). We seem therefore justified in believing that the pre-Arian languages spoken in a remote past by our ancestors were still more complicated than the oldest languages we are now acquainted with; they must certainly in many points have presented similar features to those found in Basque or in those entangled, polysynthetic Indian languages, where the sentences consist in intricate words or word-conglomerations, embodying in one inseparable whole such distinctions as subject, verb, direct and indirect objects, number, tense, mood, etc, and being therefore very clumsy and imperfect instruments for the expression of thought.

94. But here it will be—as in fact it has been—objected that this polysynthesis and incorporation cannot be primitive, as we see similar phenomena which have developed in quite recent times. The French incorporation of pronominal forms has been mentioned above; it cannot be called a case in point. Prof. Möller says: "In English 'entangling' (or amalgamation, *sammenfiltringen*) is growing luxuriantly: *'s* [-z]=*is, has*; *'d = had, would*; *'ll = will*; *don't, won't, can't,* etc." But these developments cannot be paralleled with ficxion or polysynthesis; for, however closely together *he's* or *John's* (= *John is*) is generally pronounced, it is, and is felt to be, two words, as is shown by the possibility of transposition (Is he ill?) and of intercalation of other words (John never is ill). As for *don't, won't, shan't,* and *can't,* they are more like amalgamations of the verbal with the negative idea. Still, it is important to notice that the amalgamation only takes place with a few verbs all of them belonging to the auxiliary or "empty-word." class. Therefore, in saying "I don't write," etc, the full word is not touched by the fusion, and is even allowed to be unchanged in cases where it would have been inflected had the auxiliary not been used; compare *I write, he writes, I wrote,* with the negative expressions *I don't write, he doesn't write, I didn't write.* It will be seen, especially if we take into account the colloquial or vulgar form for the third person *he don't write,* that the general movement here as elsewhere is really rather in the direction of "isolation" than fusion; for the verbal form *write* is cleared of all signs of person and tense, the person being indicated separately, and the tense sign being joined to the negation. So also in interrogative sentences; and if that tendency which can be observed in Elizabethan English had prevailed—as some day it will perhaps—of using the "emphatic" form, *I do write,* in positive statements even where no special emphasis is intended, English verbs (except a few auxiliaries) would have been entirely stripped of all those elements which to most grammarians constitute the very essence of a verb, namely, the marks of person, number, tense, and mood, *write* being the universal form, beside the quasi-nominal or adjectival forms *writing* and *written.*

95. Prof. Herm. Möller holds, in opposition to my views, that the history of language does not show a continual progressive tendency, but rather a sort of gyration. He admits that many regular forms have been substituted for irregular ones; but, on the other hand, he finds that some formations which were regular in earlier stages become irregular in modern languages, and he infers that regularity and irregularity and regularity once more go on continually alternating. Similarly he notices that the Latin flexional future *amabo* has been succeeded by the analytical expression *amare habeo*, which in its turn is fused into a new flexional form *amerò*, *aimerai*; and from this he evolves a similar law of rotation from flexion through analysis to flexion once more, or, as he puts it in another place: first flexionless analysis, then agglutination, then flexion, and then again absence of flexion. But these results are only arrived at by considering a comparatively small number of phenomena, and not by viewing the successive stages of the same language as wholes and deriving general inferences as to their typically distinctive characters.[1] For if we find that two regular forms have become irregular, but that in the same period ten regular forms have been succeeded by regular ones; or if for every two instances of new flexions springing up we see ten older ones discarded in favour of analysis or isolation, are we not entitled to the generalisation that anomaly and flexion tend to give way to regularity and analysis? Prof. Möller seems to be under the same delusion as a man who in walking over a mountainous country thinks that he goes down just as many and just as long hills as he goes up, while

[1] This is best done by such tabulations as those printed below, chapter vi.

96. (49) On every point our investigation has led us to scepticism with regard to the system of the old school of philology. But while we perceive that their inferences were drawn too hastily and from insufficient materials, and while we feel tempted totally to reverse their system, we must be on our guard and not establish too rigid and too absolute a system ourselves. It would not do simply to reverse the order of the three stages of evolution, and say that flexion is the oldest stage, from which language tends through an agglutinative stage towards complete isolation; for flexion, agglutination, and isolation do not include all possible structural types of speech, nor do these words with sufficient definiteness characterise the successive stages of those languages whose history is comparatively best known. The possibilities of development are so manifold, and there are such innumerable ways of arriving at more or less adequate expressions for human thought, that it is next to impossible to compare languages of different families. Even if it is, therefore, probable that English, Finnish, and Chinese are all simplifications of primitive flexional or even incorporating languages, we cannot say that Chinese, for instance, was at one time in structure like English, and at some other time like Finnish. English was once a flexional language, and is now in some respects agglutinating, in others isolating or nearly so. With the reservation made in this paragraph, we may say that on the whole languages tend always in the exactly opposite direction to that indicated by Schleicher, namely, from polysynthetic flexion through agglutination to flexionless isolation. But it will, perhaps, be preferable to state the same idea thus: THE EVOLUTION OF LANGUAGE SHOWS A PROGRESSIVE TENDENCY FROM INSEPARABLE IRREGULAR CONGLOMERATIONS TO FREELY AND REGULARLY COMBINABLE SHORT ELEMENTS.

Schleicher's system is to be likened to an enormous pyramid; only it is a pity that he should make its base the small, square, strong Chinese root-word, and suspend above it the inconvenient flexion-encumbered Indo-Germanic sentence-word. Structures of this sort may with some adroitness be made to stand; but their equilibrium is unstable, and sooner or later they will inevitably tumble over.

97. (50) Although it will be seen that in a great many particulars the views advanced in these chapters have been previously enunciated with more or less of clearness by other philologists, I do not think that my theory of the progressive tendency and direction of language has been expounded before by any one. It is true that I find the following passage in Prof. Sayce's *Introduction to the Science of Language* (i., pp. 85-87): "In pursuance of Bopp's method, but independently of the distinctive theories of his school, WAITZ, the anthropologist, has propounded a new theory of language . . . the incorporating languages of America, in which an individual action is represented by a single sentence pronounced as one word, are a survival of the primitive condition of language everywhere. It is only gradually that the different parts of speech are distinguished in the sentence, and words formed by breaking up its co-ordinated elements into separate and independent wholes. . . . The agglutinative tongues in which the subordinate parts of a sentence are brought into duly dependent relation to the principal concept are more highly advanced than the inflexional. . . . An isolating language like the Chinese stands on the highest level of development, since here the sentence has been thoroughly analysed and each member of it rendered clear and distinct, their relations to one another being determined by position alone. Chinese, therefore, has given concrete expression in language to the philosophic analysis of ideas. . . . Waitz's theory of speech is the theory of an anthropologist who, as the student of the master-science, is better able to decide upon the origin of language than the comparative philologist with whom the existence of language has to be assumed. No science can of itself discover the genesis of its subject-matter."

98. (50) It will be understood that after reading this exposition of a theory which harmonised so completely with the whole tenor of my own thoughts, I eagerly seized an opportunity of consulting the first volume of Theodor Waitz's *Anthropologie der Naturvölker* (1859). It would have been so very pleasant to refer to the authority of the eminent anthropologist and to cry out to comparative philologists: Here you see, that more than thirty years ago, an outsider propounded a clear, consistent, and undoubtedly correct theory, which you have kept disregarding for all these years! But, oh! how great was my disappointment when on reading, and reading repeatedly, the section in question, I was utterly unable to find this fundamental theory. Waitz as an anthropologist cherishes a profound respect for philologists, and speaks of the reliable results of their method in determining the races of mankind as opposed to those which can be gained by measurings of skulls and the like ; certainly, it never entered into his mind to overthrow the edifice of linguistic science, or to start new theories on the development of the different types of speech.

On the contrary, Waitz makes a cardinal point of the fixed character of linguistic structure, and consequently keeps at a respectful distance from Max Müller's (*i.e.*, Schleicher's) view, according to which the three types of speech have developed out of one another with the isolating languages as the starting-point. The reverse evolution with isolation as the topmost stage is evidently very far from his thoughts, for he does not set so very great store by Chinese. "The wholly asyndetic isolating languages (so we

read on p. 276) leave our thoughts almost entirely to themselves ; they give hardly any hints as to their organisation, and leave our single ideas, which correspond to separate words, to stand by the side of each other in unrelated independence (in beziehungsloser selbständigkeit); the speaker is not led to analyse them, and must rest contented with marking a few rough distinctions between principal and subordinate conceptions." It will be seen that this is not exactly the same thing as the view attributed to Waitz by Sayce. "In opposition to this (we further read) the polysynthetic languages force the speaker as much as possible to grasp each conceptual whole as a unity, to join subordinate ideas as closely as possible to the principal idea, to view as it were at a glance the whole situation, that has to be rendered in speech, and not to make the modifications be added piecemeal and little by little to what is the chief element of thought ; these languages hinder the decomposition of ˸ideas to a far greater degree than the first (or isolating) class."
As for flexional languages, Waitz seems to look upon them as standing higher than the others, but his expressions are somewhat vague and partly contradictory ; on pp. 275 and 277 he says it is characteristic of flexion that secondary subordinate elements of thought are expressed by sounds which have no meaning of their own, but are inserted as integral portions of the main word ; while on p. 276 we read : "The fundamental idea of flexion is that the principal and the subordinate elements of thought remain in-

dependent and separate, and never coalesce into a single word". Sayce quotes this passage, but I fail to understand how Waitz's expressions can be interpreted as implying the inferiority of flexional languages.

99. (51) But, if the theory I looked for was not to be found in Waitz's work, it is in SAYCE'S; although he does not give it as his own, and although he can hardly be said to accept it. I seize the opportunity of acknowledging the great influence Prof. Sayce's works on linguistics have had on me; his suggestive remarks have often made me take up lines of thought which perhaps I should not have been led to, if it were not for him. So much the more must I from my point of view regret that this bold opposer of the *idola* of the ordinary linguistic school is in some very important points as much warped by prejudices as most other philologists. Though he repeatedly hints at the difficulties of drawing a sharply-defined line of division between agglutinating and flexional languages, yet he holds that there is a great gulf fixed between them, and he says: "The Finnic idioms have become so nearly inflexional as to have led a recent scholar to suggest their relationship to our Arian group; nevertheless, they have never cleared the magical [!] frontier between flexion and agglutination, hard as it may be to define, since to pass from agglutination to inflexion is to revolutionise the whole system of thought and language and the basis on which it rests, and to break with the past psychological history and tendencies of a speech".[1] Revolutions do, however, take place in the world of languages, even if they take more time than it takes the French to change their constitutions: if a thousand years suffices to change a type of speech like that of King Alfred into the totally different one of Queen Victoria, then the much longer period which palæontologists and zoologists accord to mankind on this earth could work still greater wonders. In spite of such expressions as this, "Species passes gradually into species, class into class," Sayce stands, with regard to those three or four types of speech which are distinguished by linguists, in much the same attitude which naturalists kept with regard to the notion of "species" before Darwin came; he uses the same sort of expressions, *e.g.*: "With all this gradual approximation the several types of language still remain fixed and distinct".

100. (51) Neither is he right in his manner of viewing the value of phonetic attrition (see above, § 16); he speaks, for instance, of Chinese as a "decrepit" language (i., 372), that "has been affected by phonetic decay to an enormous extent" (*ibid.*), and "the whole speech has grown old and weather-beaten. It is the Mandarin dialect which chiefly shows these marks of ruin" (ii., 221). We are here reminded of Schleicher's words (above, § 6) that the languages which we speak now-a-days in North-western Europe are "senile

[1] *Introduction to St. of L.*, i., 131; cf. *ibid.*, i., 366, and ii., 186.

specimens of speech," and we search in vain for any real thought in connexion with such expressions. A language which is old, weather-beaten, and decrepit, which is perhaps—that is only one step further—falling into dotage and second childhood! what can this mean? Are the English no longer able to express their thoughts by means of their language? Is the speech of the Chinese like that of an old toothless crone, whose ideas and sounds are equally incoherent?

Similarly, Sayce does not see the value and significance of the simplification of the Arian noun-declension which has taken place in historic times; he says: "The history of the noun is one of continuous decay... Long before the age of Arian separation,... the creative epoch had passed, and the cases and numbers of the noun had entered on their period of decay" (ii, 149-150). And although the pages he devotes to the relative estimation of languages (i., 374 *sqq.*) contain many excellent and suggestive remarks, and begin by stating the true principle, "what we really mean when we say that one language is more advanced than another, is that it is better adapted to express thought"; yet the writer does not go the full length of his own opinion, for on the very next page he tells us that it is all a matter of taste: "Preferences of this kind can as little be referred to an absolute standard as preferences in the matter of personal beauty. The European, for instance, has a wholly different ideal of beauty from the Negro, and the Negro from the Mongol." On some of the most vital points, Sayce has not attained to a settled and consistent belief.

101. (52) In favour of the theory here expounded it may be said that it leads on every point to a monistic view; while Schleicher, though clearly perceiving that all science and philosophy tends in our days towards monism,[1] is yet by the very nature of his standpoint obliged to set up a dualism in some decisive points. Thus, he establishes an opposition between phonetic decay and simultaneous development of richer resources in syntax and style; while according to our view the evolution in both departments goes hand in hand, if we consider phonetic evolution rightly as an evolution towards shorter and easier forms.

Inseparable from this is another dualism of Schleicher's, according to which grammar falls into two sharply divided parts: on the one hand, phonology and morphology, "the nature side of language," which is to be treated as a natural science by the "glotticist", and, on the other, syntax and style, "the more spiritual side of language, which is to a greater ex-

[1] "Die richtung des denkens der neuzeit läuft unverkennbar auf monismus hinaus" (*Die Darwinsche Theorie*, p. 8).

tent subject to the free determination of the individual," and which is therefore to be treated by the literary student (*der philologe*) on the historical method.[1] In contrast to this view it must be asserted that there is only one method for the whole of the science of language, and that a separation of grammar into two divisions, treated independently of each other, has only been, and can only be, injurious to the right understanding of linguistic phenomena; for form and meaning always influence each other to a degree unsuspected by readers of philological periodicals. Fancy just for one moment a division of a dictionary into two parts, one of them containing the forms of words without the least regard to their significations, and the other marshalling up nothing but the meanings. But as syntax is nothing but the theory of the functions, *i.e.*, meanings, of the grammatical forms—this expression taken in its widest significaction, including also word-position and tones—it will be seen that many recent "grammars on a comparative basis" correspond only too closely to the first part of the supposed dictionary. And this one-sidedness cannot possibly be conducive to scientific progress.

102. (53) The most important of Schleicher's dualisms, however, is that of two periods of directly opposite tendencies, a prehistoric period of progress, evolution, or construction, and an historic period of retrogression, decay, or destruction. In opposition

[1] *Deutsche Sprache*, 119, 120.

to this view we must assert that the moment of a nation's entering into history is of no consequence at all for the direction of linguistic change, which goes on in an essentially identical manner now and in the days of old. If history has any influence at all on linguistic evolution, it seems to be only that of accelerating the movement along the same lines as before; the languages of those nations whose lives have been most agitated by historical events have gone farthest in evolution. Besides the more lively exchange of thoughts, mixture of races may count here for much (see below, §§ 140, 143); an interesting contrast is that between the slow development of Lithuanian, which is rendered so precious to the antiquarian philologist by the great number of old forms which it has kept, and the rapid evolution of English, which on account of its great number of directly observable changes is an inestimable mine to the philosopher of linguistic history.

On the other hand, literature, which Schleicher places side by side with history, certainly, though perhaps not so powerfully as generally supposed, has the effect of retarding the tendencies of change in language by keeping older forms alive for a longer time than if language was only transmitted orally. But these accelerating and retarding agencies have no influence on the *direction* of change.

If the theory arrived at in the preceding chapters is really and completely monistic, and requires us at no point to assume any breach of continuity, it must also throw some light on that vexed question, the origin of speech. I think it does, and it will be my task in the last section of this book to show that; but before venturing out into that chaos of grey theories, it will be well for some time still to continue studying the "golden tree of life" in the development of some special points of the English language.

CHAPTER VI.

ENGLISH CASE-SYSTEMS, OLD AND MODERN.

103. (54) The arrangement of inflexions current in grammars, according to which all cases of the same noun, all tenses, persons, etc., of the same verb, are grouped together as a paradigm, is not a truly grammatical one: what is common to Old English *dæg—dæges—dæges—dagas—dagum—daga*, for instance, is not the flexional element, but the word, or stem of the word; the tie between all these forms, accordingly, is not of a grammatical, but of a *lexical* character. That such an arrangement may offer some advantages from a practical point of view cannot, indeed, be denied; but, on the other hand, it causes many things to be wrested from one another which belong together grammatically, *e.g.*, the termination *-um*, which is common to the dative plural of all the flexional classes. Besides, it forces us to separate from one another the two parts of grammar which treat respectively of the forms of words and of their uses. In the latter, we must of needs deal with (say) all datives under one head, all genitives under another, and so forth, while in accidence these forms are distributed according to declension classes. Such a disjunction, however, of accidence and syntax, beyond what is strictly necessary, is doubtless injurious in every respect (cf. above, § 101). At any rate, this *paradigmatic* arrangement of grammatical phenomena will not answer the purposes of this chapter, where we seek to get as perspicuous a survey as possible of the grammatical forms of two distinct stages of one and the same language.

104. (55) Many works of comparative philology, however, employ another arrangement. In this each case is dealt with more by itself, so that either (as in Schleicher's *Compendium*) the accusative singular, for example, is treated separately in each language, or (as in Brugmann's *Grundriss*) the mode of formation of one definite case in one definite class of nouns (*i*-stems, etc.) is followed out through all the allied tongues. According to this arrangement all those facts are brought into a single class which are related to one another from the point of view of a student of comparative philology; but, as an inevitable consequence, the survey of the forms of any one language (or stage of language) is obscured; the unity of time and place is effaced; and, moreover, we get only a formal conception of the phenomena. The morphological element has been brought to the front at the expense of the syntactical, which has to be treated in another section, so that the constant reciprocal action of form and function is generally lost sight of.

105. (56) Lastly, we come to that I will term the *purely grammatical* arrangement. The grammar of a language is, as it were, an answer to the question, What general means of expression does such and such a language possess?[1] Now, by the purely grammatical arrangement the methods of expression existing in a particular language at a particular time are tabulated in such a manner that those forms come together which are grammatically analogous. By this arrangement, forms which belong together from a dictionary point of view, *e.g.*, *dæg*, *dæg*, *dæges*, are wrested from one another, and the same may be the case with forms which belong together historically, *e.g.*, Old English nominative plural neuter *hof-u* and *word*; it is true that they were once formed with the same ending, but an Englishman of King Alfred's time could not possibly be aware of this point of agreement. Clearly by this mode of treatment the individual element, by which I mean that which is peculiar to each language or to each successive stage of language, is brought more distinctly into view; we are, moreover, enabled to survey the potentialities of development of each particular language: we see plainly where the differences between the various cases are so well marked that they can easily be kept distinct, and where they bear such a close resemblance to each other in form or function, or in both alike, as to run the risk of being levelled and blended.

In an ideal language it would be an easy matter to

---

[1] Cf. Sweet, *Words, Logic and Grammar*, p. 31.

carry out such an arrangement: since each modification of meaning would have its own expression, which would be constant for all cases and quite unambiguous, a separation of accidence and syntax would be precluded, *ipso facto*; whether we should say, the genitival relation is expressed by -a, or -a denotes the genitive, would be quite immaterial.

106. (57) Not so in the idioms actually existing or recorded with their countless freaks of chance and capricious exceptions. In Latin, for example, -*i* sometimes denotes the genitive singular, sometimes the nominative plural, and if, conversely, we ask how the genitive singular is formed, the answer will be: now by -*i*, now by -*is*, etc. Consequently, we get two different modes of arrangement, according as we take as our base

I. Analogies of form (such and such a termination expresses such and such a meaning)—the *morphological* classification,—

or,

II. Resemblances of function (such and such a relation is signified by such and such terminations)—the *syntactical* classification.

The two arrangements stand to one another as the two parts of a dictionary, in one of which the form (say, some German or French vocable) is given, and the signification sought (in other words, the English equivalent is appended) : in the other, the meaning is the known quantity, and the appended part is the German or French term which was required to be known.

107. (58) Before attempting to give a synopsis, arranged upon these principles, of English case-systems at different epochs of the growth of the language, I have to premise with regard to *Old English* that, as a matter of course, I shall have to give, in the main, West-Saxon forms, though for a thorough understanding of the historical process of development of Standard English it would have been better if I had been in a position to avail myself of a Mercian, or, still better, a London grammar representing the language as spoken about the year 800. Again, in stating the function, I shall have to be very brief, and content myself with merely giving names, leaving it to the reader to understand by "dative" (for example)—not the notion of dative in itself, for such a notion has no existence, but—" Old English dative". For the particular use which English people of a thousand years ago made of their dative case, I must refer to the Old English syntax, which is, unfortunately, still to be written. In the present chapter I can give nothing but a skeleton-like scheme, which does not aim at completeness.

108. (59) It will not fail to meet with general approval that, in drawing up this scheme, I have followed Sievers's excellent *Angelsächsische Grammatik* (2 Aufl., 1886). In accordance with my general views, however, as stated above, I shall differ from Sievers in paying much more regard than he does to what would naturally appear to King Alfred and his contemporaries as the significant element in language: I shall have to separate word and case-ending, as far as this is feasible, in the same manner as the instinctive linguistic sense of that time would have done, regardless of the prehistoric condition of things. Old English *eage*, for instance, is historically, it is true, an *n*-stem; but for my present purposes I shall have to look upon it as consisting of *eag* + the nominative ending-*e*, the genitive being *eag* + *an*, and so on. We want a special term for this distinction; and I propose to call the substantial part of the word, felt as such by the instinct of each generation as something apart from the ending (*eag* is the example chosen), the *kernel* of the word, while *eagan* is the historic "stem". No doubt, in some cases it will depend on a more or less arbitrary choice, how much of the traditional form is to be treated as kernel and how much as ending. For instance, *eage* itself might be said to be the kernel, the genitive ending being -*n*, before which the *e* of the kernel is changed into *a*. This division would, however, seem to be unnatural for Old English; although so much must be granted, that in Middle English we must look upon *eie* (not *et*) as the kernel, to which the ending -*n* is affixed in the nominative plural.[1]

The fact is, that along with the perpetual wearing away of words there is often an alteration in the feeling as to the relations of kernel and ending.

[1] In Old English *here* the kernel is *here*, but in *wine* it is *win*; cf. dative plural *herj-um* (written *hereum, herigum*, etc.), but *win-um*.

Now a little more, now a little less may be included in one or the other, exactly as when one generation considers the sound-combination *anaddere* as consisting of *a* + *naddere*, whilst the next looks upon it as *an* + *addere* (Modern English, *an adder*), or when *mine uncle* is transmuted into *my nuncle*.

109. (60) It will be seen that if Old English *eage* is said to be an *n*-stem, what is meant is this, that at some former period the kernel of the word ended in -*n*, while, as far as the Old English language proper is concerned, all that is implied is that the word is inflected in a certain manner. If, therefore, in the following pages, I shall speak of *n*-stems, *i*-stems, etc., it is only as designations for classes of declension. It follows, however, from my view that we are not properly entitled to put down, *e.g.*, *wyrm* as an *i*-stem, for by doing so we should fail to give a true picture of the real condition of things in the Old English period. If a modern linguist is able to see by the vowel-mutation (umlaut) that *wyrm* was an *i*-stem, an Englishman of that time could not have suspected any such thing, as the endings of the several cases of *wyrm* are identical with those of (the *o*-stems, *e.g.*) *dom*. When Sievers reckons *wyrm* among *i*-stems, or gives *sige* as an *es*- *os*-stem, he is writing for the benefit of those who take only a secondary interest in Old English grammar, and care chiefly for the way in which it reflects prehistoric phenomena. He is thinking little of those other students who make the first object of their investigation the mutual relations of the facts of a language at a definite historical epoch, and who go to the study of Old English partly for the sake of seeing the mechanism of this particular idiom as an organically connected whole, partly with a view to seeking in it the explanation of later developments of the English language.

110. (61) In the succeeding tabulations the following abbreviations are used:—

n	= nominative
a	= accusative
d	= dative
i	= instrumental
g	= genitive
s	= singular
p	= plural
m	= masculine
f	= feminine
nt (or n)	= neuter
b	= words with original short (*brief*) syllable
l	= words with original long syllable (long vowel or short vowel followed by long consonant)
st	= strong adjectival (pronominal) declension
w	= weak adjectival declension[1]
r	= rare

[1] The declension of adjectives and pronouns is only mentioned when deviating from that of nouns.

E	= early (Alfred inclusive)
L	= late
WS	= special West Saxon
N	= North of England
S	= Sievers's *Grammatik*.

Italicised letters indicate the stem (class of declension):—*o* (words like *dom, hof, word*; by others termed *a*-stems), *i*, etc.; *c* =those consonantal stems which do not form part of some larger group, such as *n, r*. What is said about the *ā*-class applies likewise to the *wā*-stems with a long vowel or a diphthong preceding the *w* (S, § 259), so that, in mentioning *wā*, I only mean those in which the *w* is preceded by a consonant (S, § 260); the *jā*-stems are only referred to when they present deviations from the other *ā*-stems (g p); *abstr.*=words like *strengu* (S, § 279). n a p n *o*b must be read: nominative and accusative plural of neutral *o*-stems consisting of an originally short syllable.

I. MORPHOLOGICAL CLASSIFICATION.

111. (62) The Old English language used the following formal means to denote case-relations:—

A. THE KERNEL OF THE WORD UNCHANGED.

(1) n a s. *o, jo* (except lm), *wo, i* (l)f, *u* lmf, *r, nd, c* mn, *c* lf [dom hof word, here secg cyn(n) rice westen, bearu searu (beadu), ben, feld hond, fæder modor, freond, fot scrud, boc].—Also N *i* b [wlit, S, § 263, anm. 5].

(2) n s f. (not a s.) *d* l, *jð* (*wd*) [ar, sib(b) gierd (beadu)] ; L also *i* (l)f [ben], -*e* being used in a s.

(3) d s. some *o* [(æt) ham, (to) dæg and a few more, S, § 237, anm. 2], of *r* only fæder sweostor ; r. *u* lf [hond] and *s* [dogor S, § 289] ; L *c* lf [ac, etc, S, § 284, anm. 2].

(4) g s. *r*[1] [fæder broðor, etc.] ; r. L *u* lf [hond].

(5) n a p. *o* ln, *jo* bn, *ww*, *c* n [word, -cyn(n), searu, scrud] ; also, though not exclusively, some *r* [broðor dohtor[2] sweostor], *nd* [freond hettend], *c* m [haeleð monað], *s* n [lamb for lambru by a complete transition to the *o*-class].

B. VOCALIC ENDINGS.

112. (63) —*a*.

(1) n s m. *n* [guma ; N also f] ; L *u* b [suna].

(2) a s m. L *u* b [suna].

(3) d s. *u* [suna[3] felda[4] dura[3] honda[5], also often words in -*ung* [leornunga, S, § 255]; also mæda, S, § 260.

(4) g s. *u* bm, f [suna,[6] dura honda ; r. lm felda[6]].

(5) n a p. *u* bm [suna],[7] f [dura[3] honda]; r. *u* lm [only hearga[7] appla[7]]. — *i* lm r. [leoda]. — *ð* [giefa[4] dohtra.

[1] L also -*es*, which appears perhaps first in compounds (heahfæderes, Sweet, *A. S. Reader*, 14 b, 136).
[2] *Oros*, 126, 7, Laud MS, his II dohtor, Cott. MS, his twa dohtra.
[3] L superseded by -*n*.
[4] L superseded by -*e*.
[5] L superseded by—(the kernel without any addition).
[6] L superseded by—-*es*.
[7] L superseded by -*u* -*as* (-*an*).

---

(2) n s f. (not a s.) *d* l, *jð* (*wd*) [ar, sib(b) gierd (beadu)]; L also *i* (l)f [ben], -*e* being used in a s. ... ara[1]], also instead of -*e* in *i* lf and *abstr*. [bena, strenga].—And finally L *o* bn [hofa, S, § 237, anm. 5].

(6) g p. wherever the ending is not -ana, -ena, -ra, see below [doma[2] hofa[2] worda,[2] her(i)g(e)a secg(e)a enda cynna ric(e)a westenna, bearwa searwa, giefa[2] ara,[2] sibba gierda, beadwa mædwa, win(ige)a spera, bena, suna felda dura honda (strenga?), fota scruda hnuta boca fæd(e)ra freonda]; r. *n* [bæcistra, S, § 276, anm. 1]. -*a* is also found in g p. in neutral adjectives when used as substantives [goda], *Cosijn Altws. Gr*, ii, § 49.

113. (64) —*e*.

(On *i* for classical O. E. *e*, see S, §§ 132 f, 237 anm. 2, 246 anm. 1, 252 anm. 1, 263 anm. 1, 269 anm. 2.)

(1) n a s. *jo* lm [ende] ; *i* bmn [wine spere] bf [only dene[3]], *jð* r. [-nisse -nysse, generally -nes], *n* nt [eage].

(2) n s. *n* f [tunge[3]] ; N also r. m.

(3) a s. *ð* [giefe are]; *abstr*. [strenge]; L also *i* lf [bene[4]].

(4) d (i) s. (on the difference between the older instr. in -*i* (-*y*) and the dative in -*ae*, see Sievers, *P. B.*

[1] L superseded by -*e*.
[2] N and L also (-*ana*), -*ena*, sometimes also -*na* [larna].
[3] L superseded by -*n*.
[4] The same difference between E and L as in *i* lf seems to hold with *wd* l; cf. *Orosius*, the older MS. (Laud, Sweet's ed., 92, 15), gelice and mon *mæd* mawe, the younger (Cott, Bosworth's ed., 51, 23), gelice and mon mæde mawe. Platt, *Anglia*, vi, 177, knows only the acc. *mæde*.

Beitr., viii, 324 f.; in classical O.E. this distinction is no more found)—everywhere except *u* and *n* and the rest of consonantic stems, where, however, *-e* begins to crop up (S, §§ 273 anm. 2, 274 anm. 1, 280 anm. 2, 281, 286). Accordingly *-e* is found, *e.g.*, in [dome hofe worde, her(i)ge secge ende cynne rice westenne, bearwe searwe, giefe are, sibbe gierde, headwe mæd(w)e, wine spere, bene, strenge; felde for older felda, r. dure nose flore eage fote freonde].—Also neutr. adj. used as substantives [gode], *Cosijn*, ii, § 49.

(5) i s. distinct from d s. only in some pronouns and *st* adj. [micle]; it occurs comparatively seldom, see *Cosijn*, ii, §§ 38-48.

(6) g s. *ð* [giefe are], *i* l f [hnute] lf [burge boce, etc., used concurrently with mutated forms; ace muse and others without mutation, S, § 284, anm. 1]; r. *u* f [dure S, § 274, anm. 1].

(7) n a p. *i* bm [wine¹ -ware], lm a few words [Engle], lf [bene²]; thence also *ð* [giefe are]; *st* m(f) [gode], also *nd* polysyllabics [hettende, besides -nd, -ndas].

(8) Mutated d s. og n a p. *c* bf [hnyte].

114. (65) —*u*.

(On *-o* see S, §§ 134 f, 237 anm. 4 and 5, 249, 252, 269 anm. 2 and 5, 279.)

(1) n s. *u* b [sunu duru]; *ð* b [giefu], *abstr*. [strengu], *c* bf [hnutu].

¹ Superseded by *-as*. ² Also *-a*.

(2) a s. *u* b [sunu duru]; L *ð* b and *abstr*., S, §§ 253 anm. 2, 279.

(3) d s. *u* b [sunu duru; generally -a], *ð* b and *abstr*. as in (2).

(4) g s. L *ð* b and *abstr*. as in (2).

(5) n a p n. *o* b [hofu; L also l: wordu, see on polysyllabics, S, § 243], *je* l [ric(i)u] and polysyllab. [westen(n)u], (*wo*: *u* for *-un*, searu), *i* b [speru]; similarly *st* b which have however often *-e* from m [hwatu].

n a p m f *u* b L [sunu duru]; *r* [broðru dohtru, which form also other plurals].

(6) (i s. horu Elene 297 from horh.)

C. NASAL ENDINGS.

115. (66) —*un*.

(1) d s. *st*. [piosum, godum]. —? miolcum, heafdum, see Kluge, *Pauls Grundr*., i, 386.

(2) d p. everywhere [domum hofum wordum, her(i)gum secg(i)um endum cynnum ric(i)um westennium bearwum searwum, giefum arum, sibbum gierdum, nearwum, winum sperum Englum, benum, sunum feldum durum hondum, gumum¹ tungum eagum, strengum, fotum hnutum bocum, fæd(e)rum, freondum, lombrum L lambum].

On -an, -on for -um see § 116.

—*m*.

(1) d s. pron. [him ðæm hwæm].

(2) d p. in some words after a vowel, for -um

¹ R -num: oxnum, nefenum, S, § 277, anm. 1.

[cneom beside cneowum, S, § 250, nr. 2 ; fream, etc., S, § 277, anm. 2], numerals [twæm þrim].

116. (67) —*an* (—*on*).

(1) d g s. and n a p. *n* [guman tungan eagan].
(2) a s. *n* m. and f. [guman tungan].
(3) n s. L weak adj.
(4) for -*um* L.
(5) g p.r. L [eastran, S, § 276, anm. 1 ; weak adj. § 304, anm. 2].

—*n*

for -*an* in some words after a vowel [frean, etc., S, § 277, anm. 2 ; beon tan, S, § 278, anm. 2].

117. (68) —*ena* [N *ana*].

g p *n* [gumena tungena eagena] ; L also in *o* and *á*, especially b [carena, S, § 252, anm. 4], not *já*.

—*na*.

g p in a few words [sceona, etc., S, § 242, anm. 2, N treona, § 250, nr. 2 ; Seaxna, etc., § 264 ; *n* l after r and g : larna eagna, § 276, anm. l, oxna, § 277, anm. l, gefana Sweona, § 277, anm. 2].

118. (69) —*ne*.

a s m. pron. [hi(e)ne þone þi(o)sne hwone] and *st.* [godne].

D. ENDINGS CONTAINING S.

119. (70) —*as*.

n p m. *o* [domas], *jö* [her(i)g(e)as endas], *wo* [bearwas], *u* l [feldas], *r* only fæderas ; becomes moreover frequent in *i* [winas], *u* b [sunas], *nd* [also -ras : wealdendras, S, § 286, anm. 2].

(G s. in -as r. ; perhaps Beowulf, 63, 2453, 2921.) —*es*.

120. (71) —*es*.

(1) g s m n. *o* [domes hofes wordes], *jö* [her(i)ges secges endes rices westennes], *wo* [bearwes searwes], *u* l [feldes], *nd* [freondes hettendes], *c* m [fotes] ; -es becomes frequent in *u* b [sunes], *n* [eages eares], *r* [fæderes] ; N also in most other stems.
(2) n a p. for -as L, S, § 237, anm. 3.

—*s*.

g s. very rare : eas (*Oros.*, 17, 23 ; *Chron.*, 896, 918, 919, 922) cus, S, § 284, anm. 4, sæs, S, § 266, anm. 3 (also n a p).

E. OTHER ENDINGS.

121. (72) —*ra*.

g p. p r o n. [hiera (heora) þara], *st.* [godra], *nd* polysyll. [hettendra] ;[1] = r + a : *s* n [lombra cealfra, etc. ; cildra also in texts which in n þ have cild].

—*re*.

g d s f p r o n. [þære þisre], *st.* [godre].

—*or*, —*ru*.

n a p n *s* [lomber, see Schmidt, *Pluralb.*, 149, lombru[2]].

—*rum*.

d p n *s* in the same words as -ru.

—*ð*

might be considered a case-ending in hæleð, monað, ealoð, d g s, n a p; but the words are generally inflected regularly.

---

[1] Also the numerals tweg(r)a þreora.
[2] Superseded by —, (-as).

F. CHANGES IN THE KERNEL.

122. (73) *I-mutation* is the only one of these changes which becomes a case-sign, namely in

(1) d s. *c* [fet[1] teþ men(n), bec[1] byr(i)g, ie,[1] etc.], *r* [breðer meder dehter], *nd* [friend[1]].

(2) gs. *c* lf [bec,[2] etc., ie[2]], *r* r. f [meder dehter].

(3) n a p. *c* [fet teþ men(n), bec ges byr(i)g], *nd* [friend[3]].

G. A TOTALLY DIFFERENT KERNEL.

Frequent in *pron.* [ic—me—wit—unc—us, etc.; se—þone, etc.].

123. (74) Those were the means used in Old English to denote case-relations; but we have not in our lists mentioned all the changes undergone by Old English words, for alongside of these significative changes we find a great many others which do not play any part in distinguishing cases. I shall briefly indicate the most important of these incidental changes.

(1) I-mutation, in isolated cases of i s. *o* [hwene, æne, S, § 237, anm. 2], in d s. *c* bf [hnyte] and r. *u* [dyre]. Where the i-mutation is found through all cases as in *cynn*, it does not concern us here.

---
[1] Unmutated forms are also used : fote boc, etc.; as for ea, note, *e.g., Oros.,* L. 14.28, from þære ie = C. 18.21, from þære ea ; L. 174.3. neah anre ie = C. 84.32, neah anre ea.
[2] Also unmutated forms: boce etc.; cf *Oros.*, L. 16.6 ie = C. 18.36 ea.
[3] Also unmutated freond.

(2) U-mutation, *o* n a d p n [gebeodu from gebed; it disappears at an early period, leaving perhaps but one trace, in the differentiation of *cliff* and *cleeve*, see Murray's *Dict.* and my *Studier over Engelske Kasus,* § 198] ; other instances of u-mutation, see S, §§ 241, 253, anm. 1, *Cosijn*, ii., p. 3 (cneoht); comp. also cucu, cwices, Sievers, *P. B. Beitr*, ix, 259.

(3) Interchange of *æ* and *a*, found with greatest phonetic regularity in st. adj. [hwæt, hwates hwate], while in the nouns (of the *o*-class) *æ* is carried through in the singular and *a* in the plural [dæg, dæges—dagas]. After a palatal consonant we have the peculiar change seen in geat, gatu, which is by-and-by levelled out in different ways. Note also gærs, grasu. For the still more complicated change in magu mæcge(s), plural mæcga(s) magum, see Kluge, *Literaturblatt f. germ. u. rom. Philol.*, 1889, 134, and Paul's *Grundriss*, i., 368.

(4) Interchange of long *æ* and long *a* : mæg, magas ; in ǣn ænne, long *a* and short *æ* interchange.

(5) Interchange of single and double consonant : cyn, cynnes, S, § 231 ; in the nominative cynn is also found, and it is not easy to see if the difference is only a graphical one or indicates a real difference in pronunciation. There is a tendency to utilise the difference for sense-distinguishing purposes in *mann*, "man," and *man*, corresponding to French *homme—on*, or still more closely to Danish *mand, man*, see *Cosijn*, ii., p. 47.

(6) Interchange between final voiceless and medial-

voiced consonants: wulf, wulves (wulfes (written wulfes), hus, huze (written huse), baþ baðas; see my *Studier over Engelske Kasus*, § 193 ff.

(7) The related interchange between *h* and *g*: beah, beages; *h* also interchanges with *w*: horh, horwes, the adj. ruh, ruwes (old "grammatical change," determined by Verner's law), and finally there is often an interchange between *h*-forms and forms with no consonant, but with contractions and perhaps lengthening of the vowel: furh, furum (? furum), sc(e)oh, sc(e)os, feoh, dative, feo. Here we very often see levellings, the *h*-less form being as a rule generalised.

(8) Interchange between forms with and forms without *w*: treo, treowes, later on levelled both ways: treo, treos; treow, treowes; compare also sna(w), S, §§ 174. nr. 3, 250, anm. 1. The forms are differentiated in æ "law" and æw "marriage," S, § 269, anm. 3.

(9) Interchange between *e* or *i*, *u* or *o* and the corresponding vowel-like consonants *j* and *w*: here, herias, herigas, hergeas, herigeas; bearu, bearwas (L bearuw, bearuwas).

(10) Interchange between the advanced and palatalised open *g* in dæg and the back open *g* in dagas;[1] so also byrig, burgum. In the latter word

[1] The two consonants corresponded probably to the Danish sounds of *tiger* and *bage* respectively; see my description in *Articulations of Speech Sounds* (Marburg, 1889), § 106, and in *Dania* (Copenhagen, 1890), vol. i., p. 52, nr. 50, and p. 53, nr. 56.

we have four sound changes: (*a*) the vowel of the principal syllable; (*b*) the vowel of the svarabhakti-syllable, which is also often left out; (*c*) the voiceless and voiced consonants, see above sub 6 and 7; (*d*) the palatalised and unpalatalised consonants.

(11) Vowel change in unstressed syllables, due to an old gradation (ablaut): -ung, ingum (S, § 255, anm. 1; see however *Cosijn*, ii., pp. 21, 22); broðor, broðer; morgen, mergen; see, for instance, *Oros*., L. 194, 12, on mergen = C. 92, 40, on morgen.[1]

(12) Interchange between a full vowel in final syllables and a weakened one in the middle of the word: rodor, roderas, S, § 129.

(13) Interchange between preserved and omitted weak vowel: engel, engles; deofel, deofles; see especially S, § 144. At a later period this leads sometimes to a differentiation of consonants, pointed out for *engel* by Napier, see the *Academy*, March 15, 1890, p. 188.

(14) Interchanging vowel quantity is probable before many consonant groups; an indubitable case in point is cild, cildru.

124. (75) A comparison of Old English with Proto-Arian will show that a good many case-endings have been given up, and that similarly the change of accent and that of vowels (by gradation) have disappeared from the declension; nor does the Germanic interchange of consonants according to Verner's law play

[1] With regard to *mergen* see, however, Sievers, in *P. B. Beitr.*, viii., p. 331, against Paul, *ibid.*, vi., 242.

any part in the declension (compare, however, §§ 123, 7 and 11).[1] Wherever the Old English language shows traces of these phonetic changes, it is always so that one form has been carried through in all cases, so that the other is only shown by the corresponding word in other connected languages, or by other derivatives from the same root. See on these traces especially Joh. Schmidt in Kuhn's *Zeitschrift*, xxvi, p. 8 ff., and *Pluralbildungen der idg. Neutra*, *passim*; Kluge in Kuhn's *Zeitschr*, xxvi, p. 92 ff.; and in Paul's *Grundriss*, i., p. 387 f.

125. (76) It is of greater importance to our subject to examine the extent in which cases which were distinguished either at an earlier stage of the language or in other Old English words, have coalesced in one and the same word. Such *coalescence of cases* is found very frequently, though sometimes the form which is identical with that used in another case is not the only one in use for that particular case.

(1) a s. = n s. in all words except (*a*) *â* [giefu ar, accusative giefe are]; from this class the distinction is transferred to *i* l [ben, bene, instead of the older ben, ben], while on the other hand the late O. E. levelling, by which for instance *lufu* comes to be used through the whole of the singular, obliterates the distinction.

(*b*) *n* mf [guma tunge, accusative guman tungan].

(*c*) *pron.* and *st.* mf.

(2) d s. = n a s.: (*a*) in some *o*-stems in certain connexions [ham, etc., see § 111, 3], also treo and

[1] Compare also *studu*, *suŋu*; see Sievers, *P. B. Beitr*, ix, 249.

similar words. (*b*) *jo* l [ende rice]. (*c*) *i* mnb [wine spere]. (*d*) *u* b [suna and sunu; duru]. (*e*) fæder sweostor; also L r ac boc, etc.

(3) d s. = a s. besides the words mentioned under

(2): *n* mf [guman tungan]

(4) instr. = dative everywhere except in some *pron.* and *st.* mn., even there not strictly distinguished.

(5) g s. = n s.: *r* [fæder broðor, etc.], *r u* bm [suna].

(6) g s. = a s.: *â, jâ, wâ* [giefe are sibbe gierde beadwe mæd(w)e], *n* mf [guman tungan], *r* [fæder, etc.]; L *i* lf [bene], *u* bm [suna].

(7) g s. = d s.: *â, jâ, wâ*; *i* lf [bene], *u* [suna dura honda, r. felda], *n* mfn [guman tungan eagan], *c* lf [bec, etc.], *r* [only fæder sweostor], *pron*. f [hiere þære þisse þisre], *st*. [godre].

(8) n p. = n s.: *o* n [word], *jo* bn [cynn], *wo* n [searu], *i* bm [wine], *u* bm [suna and sunu], *u* bf [duru], *r*: broðor dohtor sweostor, *nd* [freond hettend].

(9) n p. = a s. besides those under (8): *n* mf [guman tungan], L also *â* [giefe, are], *jâ* [sibbe gierde], *wâ* [beadwe mæd(w)e], *i* lf [bene].

(10) n p. = d s.: *i* bm [wine], *i* lf [bene], *u* [suna and sunu, felda dura honda], *n* [guman tungan eagan], *c* [fet hnyte bec], *r*: sweostor, *nd* [friend hettende]; also L the f mentioned in the end of (9).

(11) n p. = instr. s.: *st*. m [gode].

(12) n p. = g s.: *u* [suna felda dura honda], *n* [guman tungan eagan], *c* lf [bec], *r*: broðor dohtor sweostor; L the same words as in (9) and (10); finally L m when -es came to be used for -as.

(13) a p. = n p., so that the numbers (8-12) apply also to a p; the only exceptions are: we—us(ic), ge—eow(ic).

(14) d p. = d s.: pron. [þæm þi(o)sum], *st.* [godum], also weak adj. [godan], S, § 304, anm. 3.

(15) g p. = n a s.: *u* bm L [suna].
(16) g p. = d s.: *u* [suna felda dura honda].
(17) g p. = g s.: *u* [suna felda dura honda].
(18) g p. = n a p. *ā* [giefa ara], *jā* [sibba gierda], *wā* [beadwa mæd(w)a], *i* If [bena], *u* [suna felda dura honda], *r*: dohtra.

126. (77) This list, which does not include indeclinabilia like *strengu*, shows that the chances of mistakes were pretty numerous in Old English declensions. Take the form *suna*; it may be any case, except only dative plural; *sunu* is everything except genitive (singular and plural) and dative plural; *dura* is everything except nominative, accusative singular and dative plural; *fæder* may be any case in the singular; so also *sweostor*, which may moreover be nominative or accusative plural; the only thing we can affirm on such forms as *guman* or *tungan* is that they are neither nominative singular, dative plural, nor genitive plural, and in a late text we cannot even be sure of that, and so on.

II. SYNTACTICAL CLASSIFICATION.

127. (78) In the following survey of the manners in which the syntactic categories are expressed in Old English, I have not found it necessary to indicate in each case which stems had each ending, as I should then have had to repeat much of what has been said above. A dash denotes the unchanged kernel; -a denotes the kernel with an *a* added to it; + means the mutated, or otherwise changed kernel; the most frequent forms or endings are printed in black type, the rare forms or endings are put in ().

Nom. sg. —; -a, -e, -u, (-an).
pl. **-as**, —, -an, -a, -e, -u, +, (-ru, -es), (-n, +e).
Acc. sg. —, -e, -u, -an, -ne, (-a, -n).
pl. **-as**, —, -an, -a, -e, -u, +, (-ru, -es), (-n, -n, -a), (+ e).
Dat. (instr.) sg. **-e**, -an, -re, +, —, -um, (-m, -a, -u, -n, -a), (+ e).
pl. **-um**, (-an, -m, -n, -rum).
Gen. sg. **-es**, -an, -e, -re, +, (-a, -n), (—, -s, -u).
pl. **-a**, -ena [-ana], -ra, (-na), (-an).

128. (79) The Old English language has no expressions for the following syntactic categories, which were found in the Arian parent speech: (1) the dual number; the only exceptions are *wit, unc(it), uncer* and *git, inc(it), incer*; the nouns *duru, nosu,* and *breost,* in which traces of the old dual have been found by comparative philologists, were no doubt during the whole of the Old English period, and perhaps even much earlier, felt as singulars, and *sculdru* as a plural; (2) the vocative case, unless one feels inclined to consider the use of the definite form of the adjective in *leofa freond,* etc., as a sort of vocative.[1]

[1] See Rask, *Det Gamle Nordiske Sprogs Oprindelse*, p. 215.

Finally, three or four cases have coalesced to form the Old English dative, the old instrumental being, however, in some words distinct from the dative.

129. (80) I now pass to a similar survey of the case-relations and their expression in MODERN ENGLISH, and must at once declare that I shall deal only with the really spoken language, taking no account of what belongs only to the written language, *e.g.*, the distinctions made between

gen. sg. *king's*   nom. pl. *kings*   gen. pl. *kings'*
lady's   *ladies*   *ladies'*.

The three forms sound alike, and the systematic difference now made between them is quite recent. Before the middle of the eighteenth century they were all of them written alike; thus we find for instance in the original editions of Shakespeare, *Kings, ladies,* for the three cases. The apostrophe was at that time used (without any regard to case-function) where a syllable was added in pronunciation (*Thomas's*), or where the spelling *-es* was still commonly used, the apostrophe being then used to indicate that no new syllable was to be pronounced (compare the modern spelling *stabb'd*); in Shakespeare you will find, *e.g.*, *earth's* as a genitive singular and *prey's* as a nominative plural. Sometimes the apostrophe is even in our days used before the plural ending; thus in Shake-

speare's *Twelfth Night* (ii, 5, 96) the spelling "her very *C's*, her *U's*, and her *T's*" is kept unchanged in modern editions; and the same manner of spelling may be found also in proper names, especially when they are not familiar to English readers (*Hrolf's*, in Carlyle, *Heroes*, 29); similarly in *fly's* (carriages) as opposed to the more familiar *flies*; compare also the *Spectator*, No. 80, where Steele speaks of the manner in which people use "their *who's* and their *whiches*"[1]. Conversely the apostrophe is not written before every *s* denoting the genitive: *whose, its, hers, yours* being the received spelling, while it is true that some people write *her's* and *your's*.

In dealing with the forms of the spoken language I shall, however, for convenience' sake give them in their usual spelling, though it would, of course, have been more consistent had I written all my examples phonetically. The abbreviations will be the same as in the Old English section, as far as they are needed; "a." means the modern accusative, dative, or common oblique case (*him*, etc.); "abs." stands for the absolute form of the possessive pronouns (*mine*, etc.).

I. MORPHOLOGICAL CLASSIFICATION.

130. (81) A. **The kernel of the word unchanged.**

(1) n a s. in all words; as exceptions might be mentioned those few pronouns which have separate forms for the accusative (*me, us, him, her, them*).

Rask's identification of the ending *-e* in Danish *gode gud* with the Latin and Greek vocative ending is, of course, wrong, but that does not make his syntactical observation less correct.

[1] Cf. also Alford, *The Queen's English*, p. 12.

(2) n a p. (a) *you*. (b) *sheep* and *deer*.[1] (c) the ordinary compounds of *-man, gentleman* and *gentlemen* being pronounced alike; so *postmen, policemen*, etc.

(d) some words ending in -s [z]: e.g., *means, species*.

(e) many words are unchanged in the plural in special connexions, especially after numerals and collectively: six *pair* of gloves; twenty-three *snipe*; *people, fowl, fish, cattle*, etc.

131. B. **The ordinary s ending.**

(that is: the sounds -iz added to a sibilant [s, z, sh, zh];

the sound -s after a voiceless non-sibilant;

the sound -z after a voiced non-sibilant).

(a) g s. in all nouns and some pronouns: *prince's, duke's, king's, whose, somebody's*.

(b) n a p. in the majority of nouns and some pronouns: *princes, dukes, kings, somebodies*.

(c) g p. in the same words as under (b), if the g p. can at all be used: *princes', dukes', kings'* (*somebodies'*).

(d) The same ending denotes the idea of genitive in all those plurals which are not formed by the addition of *-s*: *men's, gentlemen's, children's*.

(e) absolute: *ours, yours, hers, theirs*.

132. (83) C. **Other endings.**

-s.

n a p. in *dice*; comp. also *pence, halfpence*.

---

[1] Here the common plural in -s seems also to gain ground; at any rate, Dr. Murray once told me that he had often heard *deers*; *sheeps* is found once in Shakespeare, *Love's L. L.*, ii, 219 (pun with *ships*).

(a) n a p. in *oxen*.
(b) abs. in *mine*.

133. (84) D. **Change in the kernel.**

(1) without any ending.

n a p.: *men, women, geese, teeth, feet, mice, lice*. The plural forms *these* and *those* might be mentioned here or perhaps better under (3), as *-se* [z] is felt as a sort of plural ending.

(2) with the ending *-ren* (or *-n*).

n a p. *children* (*brethren*).

(3) with the *-s* ending.

n a (g) p. *wives* (and *wives'*) and others in *f*; *paths* and others in *th*, *houses*, the change in the kernel consisting here in the substitution of the voiced for the voiceless sound.[1]

As an ulterior case in point might be mentioned the frequent omission of the *þ*- sound in such plurals as *months, sixths, elevenths*, etc. In words ending in *-nd* the plural is frequently pronounced without the *d*: *soun(d)s*, etc. We are perhaps allowed to consider Shakespeare's rhyming *downs* and *hounds* together (*Venus and Ad.*, 677) as an early instance of this pronunciation.

(4) an entirely new kernel is finally used to distinguish cases in some pronouns: *I, me, we, us*, etc.

---

[1] In *staff—staves* we have the same consonantal change combined with a change of the vowel sound, but the modern language tends to make two regular words out of the one irregular: *staff—staffs*, and *stave—staves*.

134. (85) *Coalescence* of formerly distinct cases is found very extensively.

n a p. = n a s. in the words mentioned above, A 2.
g p. = g s. consequently in nearly all the same words.

The three cases: *gen. sg.*, *nom.* (and *acc.*) *pl.*, and *gen. pl.*, have become identical in nearly all words, so that you can very soon enumerate the very few words in which they differ from each other, namely:—

All the three cases are different: *child's, children, children's*; similarly with *man, woman*, and finally with a few words where the gen. pl. is, however, scarcely used at all: *tooth, goose, mouse, louse; dice, pence, oxen*; compounds on the model of *son-in-law* would belong here if genitive plurals, like *sons-in-law's*, were not universally avoided.

g s. different from n a p., which is identical with g p.: *wife's, wives, wives'* and the other word mentioned under D 3.

The two genitives are different from the two nominatives in the nouns mentioned under A 2.

135. (86) A comparison with Old English will show that all the vocalic and most of the nasal case-endings have been abandoned; the changes of the kernel have been considerably limited so that more particularly those which were not in themselves sufficient to distinguish cases have been given up; further we see that one difference, which was unknown to Old English, has been made subservient to case-distinguishing purposes (O. E. genitive *wulfes*, nominative plural *wulfas*, both of them pronounced with *v*; modern, *wolf's, wolves*), and finally the provinces of the unchanged kernel and of the *s* form have been very considerably extended.

II. SYNTACTICAL CLASSIFICATION.

136. (87)

N a. sg.: —
 p l.: -**s**, +, (-n, —).
G e n. sg: -**s**, poss. pron.
 p l.: -**s**, + s, (-ns); poss. pron.

Here, as in a few places above, I have silently omitted the exceptional forms of the personal pronouns.

137. (88) A comparison with Old English will here show that—apart from a few pronouns, which distinguish a nominative and an objective case—the old nominative, accusative, dative and instrumental cases have coalesced to form a common case, which shows moreover a few traces of the fact that the old genitive plural grew to be formally identical with the common case of the singular number (*e.g.*, a *twopenny* stamp, a five *pound* note).

138. (89) The question naturally arises, How has it come about that the Old English system of declensions has been so completely metamorphosed? Is it possible to point out any single cause as the effectual agent in bringing about this revolution?

An answer which has been given often enough, and which is offered by some scholars even now, was formulated by one of the foremost masters of the historical science of language as follows :—

"Any violent mixture of two languages is against nature, and results in a rapid destruction of the forms of both. When a great mass of *French* words rushed in upon the English language, few if any forms passed over to its grammar, but the Saxon forms suddenly collapsed, because they did not agree with the new roots, and because the genius of the language was led by the crude employment of the foreign material to neglect the native flexion. . . . This rapid sinking from the more perfect Anglo-Saxon forms . . . is easily explained by *influence from Danish and Norman-French*. According to a universal and natural law, where two different tongues come in collision, grammatical forms are lost. One of the most important consequences was the thorough introduction of *s* in all plurals, which agrees with French usage and is not entirely unknown to the Saxon grammar." [1]

139. (90) Such an influence from Norman-French, however, is contradicted by various considerations, partly of a general, partly of a special nature. It would, indeed, have been at least imaginable, supposing that the two constituent elements of the population, the French-speaking and the English-speaking, had been co-equal in numbers. But this was not the case. Moreover, it is admitted that the vast majority of the conquered people spoke English and never learned to speak French; they were not, therefore, exposed to having their sense of the grammatical structure of their native dialects impaired by commixture with foreign modes of speech. And, where influence from the foreign idiom could not be avoided, it must have taken place essentially in the same manner as French and English influence each other at the present day, by the adoption, that is, of single words, which are then incorporated, substantially, into the native system of grammar.[1] Just as a modern Frenchman inflects the loan-words *leader, sport,* in accordance with the laws of his own language, and turns the English verb *stop* into *stopper* (*stoppant,* etc.),—just as, when some composite expression passes into his language, he does not shrink from forming such a derivative as *strugg(le)-for-lifeur* (Daudet),—precisely in the same manner did the English peasant act when he caught up a word from the courtly speech of the Normans. Quite instinctively he affixed to it his own terminations without troubling himself for a moment whether they would or would not "agree with the new roots".

140. (91) But, whilst the Norman Conquest exerted no *direct* influence on English grammatical

[1] Grimm, *Deutsche Grammatik,* i. (1819), pp. xxxii. and 177-178. So also Madvig, *Kleine philol. Schriften,* 27; Earle, *Philology of the Engl. Tongue,* 1st ed., p. 41; Elze, *Englische Philologie,* p. 245.

[1] Cf. Murray, *The Engl. Language,* in the *Encycl. Brit.,* viii, 393.

structure, there can be no doubt that it went far to accelerate the development of change *indirectly*. This was principally due to the fact that England was for some centuries without that retarding and conservative influence which will always make itself felt wherever cultivated classes speaking a "refined" speech exist side by side with a proletariat whose linguistic peculiarities are branded as vulgarisms, or as downright solecisms. Any such control as comes from an upper class whose more old-fashioned language is looked upon as a model, and, partly at least, imitated by the lower classes, was precluded at the period we are speaking of, inasmuch as the upper classes did not speak English, or, at best, spoke only bad English. In consequence of this, not only was the literary tradition of the English language lost or reduced to a minimum, but even in its oral transmission, which is always the more important matter, and was especially so then, one element was wanting which generally assists in stemming the tide of revolutionary tendencies.

141. (92) If now we look at the only detail in English accidence for which a Norman descent is claimed (namely, the plural -*s*[1]), some remarks will have to be made which perhaps have not been all propounded before.

(1) The growth of the plural -*s* cannot be separated from that of -*s* in the genitive case. Now the latter gained ground even more rapidly and extensively than the plural -*s*, and French influence is here utterly unimaginable. Why, then, resort to it with regard to the other ending?

(2) The plural in -*s* was long before the Conquest extended to many nouns which had formerly had other endings, belonging to the *i*- and *u*- classes, as also to some of the consonant stems (*wyrmas, winas, sunas, hæleðas*, etc., see § 119). This shows that the tendency of the language would have been the same even if William the Conqueror had never crossed the Channel.

(3) -*S* became universal in the North at an earlier date than in the South, where we should expect to find French influence strongest, but where -*en* seems for a long time to have had better chances of prevailing in all nouns than -*s*.

(4) In Old French -*s* was not used to the same extent as now as a plural ending; indeed, it can hardly be called a plural sign proper, as it was in the. most numerous and important class of nouns the sign of the nom. sg. and of the acc. pl., but not of the nom. pl. If, therefore, an Englishman of (say) the thirteenth century used the -*s* in the nom. pl, he was in accord with the rules of his native tongue, but not with those of French.

---

[1] Even Sayce says, *Introd. to Sc. of L.*, i, 172: "The great extension of the English plural in -*s*, confined as it was in Anglo-Saxon to a comparatively few words, seems due to Norman-French influence". The same view is taken by Strong, *Academy*, Oct. 20, 1893; cf. also the correspondence in the following numbers of that paper between Napier, Earle and myself.

(5) If -s was due to the Normans, we should expect it in the plural of the adjectives as well as of nouns; but, as a matter of fact, adjectives take it extremely rarely,[1] and hardly except in those cases where a Romance adjective is placed after its noun. Everywhere else, Middle and Modern English adjectives have no -s in plural, agreeing therein with the old native tradition, but not with French grammar.

(6) And, finally, it is worth noting that the two endings, Norman -s without any vowel, and English -es (originally -as) with the vowel pronounced, were kept distinct for about four hundred years in English; they are not confounded till, in the fifteenth century, the weak *e* disappears in pronunciation.

142. (93) Thus, at the one definite point where the theory of French influence has been advanced with regard to accidence, it is utterly unable to stand the test of historical investigation. And it is the same case, I believe, with many of the assertions put forward of late years by E. EINENKEL with regard to a French influence exerted wholesale on English syntax.[2] Einenkel's method is simplicity itself. In dealing with any syntactical phenomenon of Middle English, he searches through Tobler's *Verm. Beiträge zur Frz. Grammatik* and the ever-increasing literature of German dissertations on Old French syntax, in quest of some other phenomenon of a similar kind. As soon as this is discovered, it is straightway made the prototype of its Middle English analogue, sometimes in spite of the French parallel being perhaps so rare a use that even Tobler himself can only point out a very few instances of it, whilst its English counterpart is of everyday occurrence. In several cases French influence is assumed, although Einenkel himself mentions that the phenomenon in question existed even in Old English, or, not unfrequently, though it must be considered so simple and natural a development as to be quite likely to spring up spontaneously in a variety of different languages. A little knowledge of Scandinavian languages would, for example, with regard to many points have convinced Einenkel that these present the very same phenomena which when occurring in English he explains from Old French.

143. (94) A far greater influence than that exercised upon English by the Gallicised Normans must be ascribed to the *Danish* Wikings, who for such a long space of time were acting a prominent part in Britain, and whose significance for the life of the

[1] According to Ten Brink only twice in the whole of the poetic parts of the *Canterbury Tales* (*Chaucers Sprache u. Verskunst*, § 243), to which add *Hous of Fame*, 460, the "goddes celestials". Where Chaucer gives a direct prose translation from French, this -s occurs more frequently, thus in the *Tale of Melibeus*, which Ten Brink does not mention.

[2] See his *Streifzüge durch die me. Syntax*, 1887, his articles in the *Anglia*, xiii., and in Paul's *Grundriss der germanischen Philologie*, i., 907 and foll. Einenkel's syntactical investigations will, of course, in some measure keep their value, even though his theories on the origin of the phenomena he discusses are exaggerated and erroneous.

English people cannot easily be over-estimated. As for the language, it should be borne in mind that the tongue spoken by the Danes was so nearly akin with the native dialects that the two peoples could understand one another without much difficulty. But it was just such circumstances which made it natural that many *nuances* of grammar should be sacrificed, the intelligibility of either tongue coming to depend mainly on its mere vocabulary. It is in harmony with this view that the wearing away and levelling of grammatical forms in the regions in which the Danes chiefly settled was a couple of centuries in advance of the same process in the more southern parts of the country.

A fully satisfactory solution of the question of the mutual relations of North English and Scandinavian at that time must be regarded as hopeless on account of the small number, and generally inadequate character, of linguistic records; and, unless some fresh sources become accessible to us, we shall probably never learn clearly and unequivocally which points of correspondence in the two languages are attributable to primitive affinities, which others to loans from one language to the other, or, finally, how much may be due to independent parallel development in two areas which offered such striking analogies in so many essential particulars. But, as I hold, any linguistic change should primarily be explained on the basis of the language itself, while analogues from other languages may serve as illustra-

tions and help to show what in the development of a language is due to psychological causes of a universal character, and what is, on the other hand, to be considered the effect of the idiosyncrasies of the particular idiom.

144. (95) I return to the question of the cause of the simplification of the English system of declensions, and I will quote another answer, which agrees better than Grimm's with the linguistic theories prevailing now-a-days. This explanation is formulated by one of the most competent English scholars of our time, Dr. J. A. H. MURRAY, as follows:—[1]

"The total loss of grammatical *gender* in English, and the almost complete disappearance of *cases*, are *purely phonetic phenomena*".

In other words: a phonetic law which operates "blindly," *i.e.*, without regard to the signification, causes the Old English unstressed vowels -*a*, -*e*, -*u*, to become merged in an obscure -*e* in Middle English; as these endings were very often distinctive of cases, the Old English cases were consequently lost. Another phonetic law was operating in a similar manner by causing the loss of the final -*n*, which was equally utilised, though in a different way, in the Old English declension. Upon this I have to remark, first, that beside the phonetic laws must at all events be mentioned analogy. It is this which, for example, has led to the levelling of the nominative plural and dative plural : if phonetic decay had been

[1] *Encycl. Brit*, viii, 400.

the only factor, Old English *stanas* and *stanum* would still have been distinguished from one another, namely as *stones* and *stone*; whereas, in fact, the former form has been extended to the dative. This, however, must by no means be interpreted as an objection to Dr. Murray and the scholars who hold his view, and who are as fully alive to this principle of explanation as anybody else.

145. (97) I have stated elsewhere my reasons for disbelieving in the axiom of the so-called young grammarian school of the blind working of sound laws, and in the theory of sound laws and analogy sufficing between them to explain everything in linguistic development.[1] Here I shall add, with regard to the special question concerning us in this chapter, that the young grammarians' view does not look deep enough in its search for explanations. If simplification of forms is to be attributed in the main to the phonetic law of unstressed terminations, what, then, is the *cause of the phonetic law*? And if, on the other hand, analogy has played an important part in this development, the question arises, if it is not possible to suggest causes why the principle of analogy should have thus asserted itself.

Let us for a moment suppose that each of the terminations -*a*, -*e*, -*u*, bore in Old English its own distinctive and sharply defined meaning, which was necessary to the right understanding of the sentences in which the terminations occurred. Would there in

[1] See the paper on "Sound Laws," quoted above, § 43 note.

that case be any probability that a phonetic law tending to their levelling could ever succeed in establishing itself? Most certainly not; the all-important regard for intelligibility would have been sure to counteract any inclination towards a slurred pronunciation of the terminations. Nor would there have been any occasion for new formations by analogy, as the endings were already sufficiently alike.

146. (98) The above comparative survey of the declensions of Old and Modern English furnishes an answer to the questions proposed, and makes the whole causality appear in a much clearer light than would be possible by any other arrangement of the grammatical facts: *the cause of the decay of the Old English apparatus of declensions lay in its manifold incongruities*. The same termination did not always denote the same thing; the same case was signified now by this, now by that means; many relations plainly distinguished from each other in one class of words were but imperfectly, if at all, distinguishable in another class. And yet there is a still further cause of mixture and confusion which our arrangement does not bring out—the one, namely, which is latent in terms like dative, accusative, etc. In fact, these terms have no clear and definite meaning in the case of Old English, any more than in the case of kindred tongues; in many cases it did not even matter which of two or more cases the speaker chose to employ. Thus, not a few verbs existed which were employed now with one, now with another case; and it was often impossible to perceive any accompanying difference of meaning.[1] And so also with other parts of speech: the preposition *on*, as applied to time, sometimes governed the dative (instrumental), sometimes the accusative: thus we find in close succession (*Chron.*, 979, C.), *on þys geare* . . . *on þone sunnandæg*; (*ibid.*, 992, E.) *on þere nihte* ðe hi *on* ðone *dæi* togædere cumon sceoldon;[2] similarly (*Oros.*, 136, 23 and foll.) on westeweardum *þisses middangeardes*, . . . on easteweardum *þeosan middangearde* (comp. same page, l. 7), and so on.

147. (99) This condition of things naturally gave rise to a good deal of uncertainty, which manifested itself partly in a rather inaccurate pronunciation of the endings, partly in the use of them in places where they did not belong.

This now and then happened in such a manner as to bring about coincidences of sound without assisting clearness, nay, even at its expense, as, for instance, is the case when we find in the *Cura Past.*, 166, 2 and 20: to *anra* ðara ðreora burga, instead of *anre* (see Sweet's note in his *A. S. Reader*, p. 191). Generally, however, such uses of endings on analogy

[1] See particularly the materials collected by M. Sohrauer, *Kleine Beitr. zur ae. Gramm.*, pp. 10-26.

[2] *On* with the dative case here corresponded to an older *in*, while with the accusative it was the old *an* (comp. Germ. *in*, *an*), but I doubt very much if the old West Saxon author was alive to any difference in his use of *on* in the two phrases.

are apt to crop up in such places particularly where the traditional terminations are not sufficiently distinct, or where cases have been levelled which it is important should be kept apart. For example, *griefa* stands alike for the nominative plural and the genitive plural, and misapprehensions are the consequence. These are obviated by the extension to the nominative and genitive respectively of the termination -*e* from the *i*-class and -*ena* from the *n*-class (nominative *grief*, genitive *giefena*).

But if the transmutations, phonetic as well as nonphonetic, of the old declensions took their rise from the numerous inconsistencies of the system and its want of fixed boundaries, formal or functional, then what is described above as the true grammatical arrangement exhibits the prospects of the various cases and endings in their struggle for existence. By its aid we are, in some measure, in a position to cast the horoscope of the whole system and predict the main features of its destinies.

148. (100) The vocalic terminations (B) were evidently the least distinct and least sharply defined; each of these had many values, nor were they uniformly distributed in the different classes of inflexion. Here accordingly every succeeding generation when it came to learning the language was offered only scanty points of support and a great many chances of going wrong. It is therefore not surprising that these endings were confounded and effaced and in a later period entirely dropped, as there was no well-defined barrier between the use of the bare kernel of the word, and the kernel *plus* the vocalic termination *-e*, in which the endings *-e, -a, -u,* had at that time been merged.

The nasal endings were possessed of greater power of resistance. But they, too, were doomed, chiefly owing to the exceedingly common use of the ending *-an* in the weak forms of adjectives, where it was of no consequence whatever for the signification, and could therefore be neglected without any loss. In the case of verbal forms, too, where endings in *-n* occurred also, they did not perform any function of sufficient importance to check the tendency to drop the sound in pronunciation; in fact, at an early period we meet with collocations like *binde we, binde ge, mote we,* etc, in which the *-n* had fallen away (Siev., § 360).

149. (101) Where, on the other hand, the *-n* was protected by a following vowel, it could withstand the levelling tendencies better. This would be especially the case in the genitive plural, because of the distinctive meaning of this genitive. The same thing is also particularly true of the two *-s* endings, each of which was confined to a sharply limited sphere of use. The *-s* is too important to be left out; if, on the other hand, the two endings *-as* and *-es* are levelled in the Middle English *-es*, this is mainly due to the influence exercised by the other endings. As *-a* and *-e* were not distinctive enough in point of meaning to oppose a strong resistance to the tendency prevailing in all

languages to obscure vowels in weak syllables, nay, even invited this tendency, *-as* and *-es* had to submit to the resulting "phonetic law". This they did without any very great detriment to intelligibility, the connexion in which they occur being nearly everywhere sufficient to show whether the genitive singular or nominative plural was meant, especially after the rule had been established by which the genitive is always placed before its governing word (see chapter viii.).

As regards the prospects which changes of kernel have of maintaining themselves, we can only be certain of this much, that those which have become attended with inherent change of signification are, by a natural consequence, more likely to be permanent than the others, which are more liable to be affected by levelling tendencies, inasmuch as a new regular form which agrees with the shape of the word in other cases is sure to be understood as well as, or even better than, the traditional one. But, on the other hand, forces tending to change pronunciation are continually at work, and these give rise to fresh changes of kernel; we may mention, for instance, the laws of quantity which have split up the Old English *sceadu* into the two Modern English words *shade* and *shadow*. To foretell the durability of such modifications is, of course, a matter of impossibility.

150. (102) To sum up, setting aside changes of kernel, the other modifications of the nouns in Old English declensions are of a character to enable us

CHAPTER VII.

CASE-SHIFTINGS IN THE PRONOUNS.

151. (103) In the Oldest English pronouns we find the nominative, accusative, and dative cases distinct both in point of accidence and syntax, although in a few pronouns there is no formal difference between the nominative and accusative (in the plurals of the third person (*hie*); in the neuter (*hit, hwæt*, etc.), in the feminine form *heo* or *hie*).

The first step in the simplification of this system is the abandonment of the separate forms *mec, þec, usic, eowic, uncit, incit*, which are used only in the very oldest texts as accusatives distinct from the datives *me, þe, us, eow, unc, inc*, and which are soon ousted by the latter forms. By parallel developments occurring somewhat later, the old dative forms *hire* (*hir, her*), *him* and *hwam* (*whom*) are made to fill the offices held hitherto by the old accusatives *heo, hine* and *hwone*. In some of the southern counties *hine* is, however, preserved up till our times in the form of [en], see Ellis, *Early Engl. Pronunciation*, v., p. 43; in the literary transcription of these dialects this is written '*un, e.g.,* in Fielding's *Tom Jones* (Squire

---

to form an opinion on the main features of their destinies by considering the reciprocal relations of phonetic expression and inward signification, the more so as it was just the least ambiguous endings (-*as*, -*es*) that were used to denote the syntactical relations which are the most distinctive and appear to be the most indispensable in language, *viz.*, plurality and connexion (genitive). Logically to define the other case-relations is a matter of much more difficulty: the dative and accusative cases often come in contact with each other, and both have also some points of agreement with the nominative. Hence arises the chance of endless confusions, even where the forms are sharply distinguished (see the next chapter).[1] In fact, there is every occasion, be it said incidentally, alike from a formal and syntactical point of view, to prefer the arrangement of the cases prevalent in Denmark since Rask — nominative, accusative, dative, genitive—to any other, and more especially to that still current in Germany, where the genitive is placed between the nominative and the accusative.

[1] Professor H. Möller objects to my manner of "predicting after the event" the destinies of Old English endings, urging that in Old Frisian the endings were nearly identical with those of Old English, but that they have nevertheless been treated in various Modern Frisian dialects in different ways. But the forms adduced seem to me to prove nothing beyond the fact that some Frisian dialects have been slower in their development than others, and that the development is not exactly rectilinear, even where the direction is the same. Of course we could not expect any two dialects to change their common basis in precisely the same way.

Western, etc.), and in Thackeray's *Pendennis* (i., 62, "Show Mr. Pendennis up to '*un*").[1] In the plural, also, the dative form has expelled the old acc.; *hem* (O. F. *him*, *heom*; preserved in familiar and vulgar speech: "I know 'em") and the later *them* are originally datives;[2] the neuter singular, on the other hand, has preserved the old accusative forms *hit* (*it*), *þæt* (*that*), *hwæt* (*what*), at the expense of the old datives.

The reason of this constant preferring of the dative forms in the person-indicating pronouns is no doubt the fact that these pronouns are used as indirect objects more often than either nouns or adjectives;[3] at any rate, it is a phenomenon very frequently found in various languages; compare Danish *ham, hende, dem, hvem*, originally datives, now also accusatives and partly even nominatives (while it is true that in *mig* and *dig* the acc. has outlived the dative); North

---

[1] *Pendennis*, p. 50, Thackeray uses '*n* as a plural ("Hand down these 'ere trunks." "Hand'n down yourself"); but this is hardly due to a direct and correct observation of the real spoken language.

[2] *Chron.*, 893, the Parker MS. has "hie asettan *him* . . . ofer," but the Laud MS.: "hi ásetton *hi* . . . ofer"; it is perhaps allowable here to suppose a blending of the transitive "asetton hie" and the intransitive "asaton him"; cf. § 188. But in *Chron.*, 828, we have an indubitable outcome of the tendency to replace the old acc. by the dat., for the Parker MS. reads: "he *hie* to ea∫>modre hersumnesse gedyde," but the Laud MS.: "the *heom* ealle [N.B. not eallum!] to eadmodere hyrsumnesse gedyde".

[3] A. Kock, in *Nord. Tidskrift for Philologi*, n. r. iii., 256.

German *wem* for *wen*,[1] French *lui* as an absolute pronoun (while the acc. has carried the day in *elle*, *eux*, *elles*; *moi* and *toi* may be either); Italian *lui*, *lei*, *loro*,[2] etc.

152. (104) In this chapter I propose to deal at some length with those tendencies to further modifications of the pronominal case-system which may be observed after the accusatives and datives have everywhere become identical. The forms concerning us are in their present spelling:—

```
       nom.          acc.—dat.
       I, we         me, us
       thou, ye      thee, you
       he, she, they him, her, them
       who           whom.
```

Simplification has gone further in the case of the pronouns of the second person than in that of the others; in fact, if we were to believe the ordinary grammars, the substitution of *you* for *ye* is the only point in which a deviation from the old system has taken place. But ordinary grammars are not always trustworthy; in laying down their rules they are too

---

[1] Franke, in *Phonetische Studien*, ii, 50.

[2] Storm, *Engl. Philologie*, 208; compare also the interesting remarks in Franceschi, *In Città e in Campagna*, 585: "*lui, lei, loro*, per egli, ella, eglino ed elleno, che nel parlar famigliare parrebbe affettazione. . . . Questi e altri idiotismi e certe sgrammaticature . . . io fo di quando in quando scappar fuori dai miei personaggi, perchè vivono nella bocca del popolo toscano, come sa chi vi nacque o vi stette lungamente in mezzo, e portò amore alla sua parlata."

apt to forget that the English language is one thing, common-sense or logic another thing, and Latin grammar a third, and that these three things have really in many cases very little to do with one another. Schoolmasters generally have an astonishing talent for not observing real linguistic facts, and an equally astonishing inclination to stamp everything as faulty that does not agree with their narrow rules; and the precepts inculcated in the school-room have no doubt had some influence in checking natural tendencies, though the following pages will suffice to show that the best authors have in many points deviated more from the rules laid down in grammars than is generally supposed.

153. (105) Many of the phenomena I shall treat of have, as a matter of course, been noticed and partly explained by modern grammarians of the historical school; I shall specially mention KOCH, *Hist. Gramm.*, ii. (especially p. 244[1]); MÄTZNER, *Engl. Gramm.*, ii. passim; ABBOTT, *A Shakespearian Grammar*, § 205 ff.; A. SCHMIDT, *Shakespeare-Lexikon*; STORM, *Englische Philologie*, 1881, p. 207 ff.; GUMMERE, *The English Dative-Nom. of the Person. Pron.*, in *American Journ. of Philol.*, iv.; W. FRANZ, *Die dialektspr. bei Dickens, Engl. St.*, xii, 223 f, and *Zur syntax des älteren Neuenglisch, ibid.*, xvii, 212 ff.; KELLNER, in the Introduction to *Caxton's Blanchardyn* (EETS, Extra Series 58).

On the whole these authors content themselves with a purely lexical treatment of the matter, giving for instance all the examples of *I* for *me* and *vice versa* under one head, and only occasionally offering an explanation of some phenomena; the fullest and most satisfactory explanations are found in Storm's excellent work. In the following sections I shall attempt a systematic arrangement according to the psychological or phonetic principles underlying the phenomena and causing speakers or writers to use another case than that exacted by the rules of ordinary grammar. I shall first take those classes of case-shiftings which are of a more general character and may occur more or less frequently in all languages of our type, giving last those which belong more specially to English or to one particular period of English.

It must be specially mentioned that in many of the sentences quoted two or even more causes of shifting have operated concurrently.

I. Relative Attraction.

154. (105) A pronoun in the principal proposition is often put in the case which the corresponding relative pronoun has or ought to have. This is particularly easy to explain where no relative pronoun is used; the so-called relative ellipsis originates

---

[1] In the second edition of Koch's work, Prof. Zupitza has already remarked that the earliest of Koch's examples must be explained differently or are untrustworthy; but even Koch's "altenglische" examples prove nothing; thus *þam* in "*þer restid þam doun*" must certainly be the common reflexive dative (see below, § 188), and not the subject of the sentence.

in a construction *apo koinou*, the personal pronoun belonging equally well to both propositions. Examples abound, both where the relative pronoun is expressed and where it is understood.

Chaucer, *M.P.*, 5, 623, "*Him* that she cheest, *he* shal her have as swythe" | Caxton (see Kellner, xiv.), "*him* that he rought with full stroke was all in to brused" | Shak., *Cor.*, v., 6, 5 "*Him* I accuse (:) the city port by this hath enter'd" | *Ant.*, iii, 1, 15, "*him* we serues [serve's] away" | *Rom.*, 1032 (ii, 3, 85), "*her* I loue now Doth grace for grace, and loue for loue allow" (the oldest quarto *she whom*) | *Haml.*, ii, 1, 42, "*him* you would sound . . . be assured *he* closes . . ." | *Temp.*, v., 1, 15; *As*, i., 1, 46; 1 *H. VI.*, iv., 7, 75 | Tennyson, 370 "*Our noble Arthur, him* Ye scarce can over-praise, will hear and know" | Troll, *Duke's Ch.*, i., 161 (a lady writes), "I have come to be known as *her* whom your uncle trusted and loved, as *her* whom your wife trusted . . ."

Very often after *it is* :—

Marlowe, *Jew*, 1034, "Tis not thy wealth, but *her* that I esteeme" (= I esteeme her) | Sh., 2 *H. VI.*, iv., 1, 117, "it is *thee* I feare" | *Sonn.* 62, "Tis *thee* (my self) that for my self I praise" | Thack., *Pend.*, i., 269, "it's not *me* I'm anxious about" | *ibid*, iii, 301, "it is not *him* I want" | Troll., *Old Man*, 121, "It is *her* you should consult on such a matter".

Nom. for acc. is rarer in case of relative attraction.[1] Sh., *V. A.*, 109, "thus *he* that overrul'd I overswayed" | *Troil*, ii, 3, 252, "praise him that got thee, *she* that gaue thee sucke"; comp. *Hml.*, i., 2, 105; 2 *H. VI.*, iii., 2, 89; *R. III.*, iv., 4, 101 f. | Bunyan (see Storm, 211), "the encouraging words of *he* that led in the front".

II. Blendings.

155. (106) Contaminations or blendings of two constructions between which the speaker is wavering occur in all languages. The first class of contaminations concerning us here is caused by vacillation between *an accusative with infinitive and a finite verb*, exemplified in the Bible phrase: O. E., "*Hwæne* secgad men þæt sy mannes sunu?" Auth. V., "*Whom* do men say that I the son of man am?" (Matt., xvi., 13), as compared with the more "grammatically correct" construction in Wyclif: "*Whom* seien men to be mannus sone?" In the parallel passage, Luke, ix., 18 and 20, Wyclif writes: "*Whom* seien the puple that Y am? . . . But *who* seien ȝe that Y am?" From secular authors I shall quote :—

Chauc., *Morr.*, iii. 26, 803, "as ye han herd *me* sayd" [rhyme: apayd; for *me saye* or *I said*] | *B.*, 665, "yet wole we vs auyse *whom said*".

[1] Relative attraction is the reason of the three abnormal *he's* in Caxton which Kellner quotes on p. xv., but does not explain.

that we wole that [v. r. om. that] shal ben our Justyse" | Sh, *Cor.*, iv, 2, 2, "the nobility . . . *whom* we see haue sided in his behalfe" | *Temp.*, iii, 3, 92, "Ferdinand (*whom* they suppose is droun'd)" | *Meas.*, ii, 1, 72, "[my wife] *whom* I thanke heauen is an honest woman" | *Tim.*, iv, 3, 120, "a bastard, *whom* the oracle Hath doubtfully pronounced thy [fol. the] throat shall cut" | Fielding, *T. J.*, iv, 130, "I would have both *you* and *she* know that it is not for her fortune he follows her" | Darwin, *Life and L.*, i., 60, "to assist those *whom* he thought deserved assistance" | Muloch, *Halifax*, ii, 11, "one *whom* all the world knew was so wronged and so unhappy".[1]

Note also Sh, *Cor.*, i., 1, 236, "And were I anything but what I am, I would wish me only *he*," where *he* is the only natural form, as *him* would only obscure the meaning of the phrase.[2] In R. Haggard, *Cleopatra*, ii,

[1] The phenomenon is nearly akin to the well-known insertion of what should be the subject of the subordinate clause as the object of the principal proposition; see, for instance, Chaucer, *B.*, 4392, "Herkneth *thise blisful briddes* how they singe, And see *the fressche floures* how they springe" | Sh., *Wint. T.*, i., 2, 181, "*you perceive me* not how I give lyne". A good many examples have been collected by Kellner, *Blanch*, xvi. ("And God saw the light that it was good"); cf. also Wright's note, Sh., *Tw. N*, p. 100.

[2] Compare also Stevenson, *Treas. Isl.*, 171, "Some one was close behind, I knew not *whom*".

121, "rather than I would see her thy wedded wife and *thou* her loving lord," we have an approach to the phenomenon mentioned below, § 164.

When we find in the middle of the sixteenth century such sentences as these:—

Roister D., 38, "And let me see *you* play me such a part againe" | *ibid*, 76, "I woulde see *you* aske pardon,"

we may be pretty sure that the author meant *you* as the acc. case and the verbs *play* and *aske* as infinitives; but to a later generation neither the form of the pronoun nor that of the verb would exclude the possibility of *you* being the nominative before finite verbs (= let me see (that) you . . .).

158. (110) In these cases the blending was due to the fact that what was grammatically the object of one verb was logically the subject of another verb. This is particularly frequent in the combination *let us* (go, etc.), supplanting the older construction *go we*, etc.[1] The logical subject is here often put in the nominative, especially if separated from the word *let* :—

Genesis, xxi. 44, "Let *us* make a covenant, *I and thou*"[2] | Udall, *Roister*, 21, "Let all these matters passe, and *we* three sing a song"

[1] Still found in Sh, *e.g.*, *Macb.*, ii., 2, 65, "Retyre we" | v., 2, 25, "March we on".

[2] Compare the O. E. translation, "þæt freondscipe sig betwux unc, *me* and *þe*," which is a regular appositional construction; cf. § 163.

| Sh., *Merch.*, iii, 2, 21, "let fortune goe to hell for it, not *I*" | *Cæs.*, iii, 1, 95, "let no man abide this deede, but *we* the doers" | Byron, iv., 240, "Let *He* who made thee answer that" | Hughes, *Tom Brown's Sch.*, 3, "let *you and I* cry quits".

Storm (*E. Philol.*, 211) has some modern quotations (from Dickens, who writes also: "*Leave* Nell and *I* to toil and work"), and quotes the Norwegian [and Danish] colloquial *lad vi det* for *lad os det*. In the corresponding Dutch construction both the nom. and acc. are allowed: "laat *mij* nu toonen" as well as "laat *ik* nu toonen" (let me now show); similarly "laat *hem* [*hij*] nu toonen, laat *ons* [laten *wij*] nu toonen, lat *hem* [laten *ze*] nu toonen".[1] In a passage from Guy of Warwick, 3531, "*Let hym* fynde a sarasyn And *y* to fynde a knyght of myn," we have a transition case between this phenomenon and that dealt with in § 164.

A similar confusion after the verb *make* is found in Sh., *Temp.*, iv., 1, 217, "mischeefe which may make this island Thine owne for ever, and *I* thy Caliban for aye thy foote-licker"; here Caliban forgets the first part of his sentences and goes on as if the beginning had been "this island shall become". So also in *Rich. II.*, iv., 1, 216, "[God] *make me*, that nothing haue, with nothing grieu'd, And *thou* with all pleas'd, that hast all atchieu'd".

In these cases the nominative is used in spite of grammatical rules requiring the acc., because the word is thought of as the subject; this is even, though rarely, the case after a preposition; in *Roister Doister*, p. 72, I find: "Nay *as for they*, shall euery mother's childe die;" and a phrase in a letter that is read aloud twice in the same play runs the first time "*as for all them* that woulde do you wrong" (p. 51), but the second time "as for all they" (p. 57). In § 170 ff. we shall see some more instances of the nominative, as the case proper to the subject, getting the better of the acc., required by earlier grammatical rules.

157. (107) Other contaminations leading to confusions of two cases are found here and there. In Sh., *Temp.*, ii, 1, 28, we read: "Which, of *he*, or Adrian . . . First begins to crow?" This is a blending of "Which, he or A.," and "Which of [the two] him and A.," or else *of* may be a printer's error for *or*, as conjectured by Collier. In Sir Andrew's interruption, *Tw. N.*, ii., 5, 87, "[you waste the treasure of your time with a foolish knight.—] That's *mee* I warrant you," *me* is due to the use of the accus. in the preceding sentence (= with me); immediately afterwards he says: "I knew 'twas *I*;" in Malvolio's speech, "If this should be *thee*," *thee* is similarly the

---

[1] See *Taalstudie*, 1887, 376. Mr. C. Stoffel informs me that the two constructions are not exact equivalents, a difference being made, for instance, between *laat hij gaan*, "qu'il aille," and *laat hem gaan*, "allow him to go".

[1] Compare *Hamlet*, i., 4, 54, and H. Fritsche's note in his edition of that play, Berlin, 1880.

object of the preceding *I loue*. Comp. Thack., *Pend.*, iii., 87, "If ever I *saw* a man in love, that man is *him*". The opposite result of the contamination is found in Sh., *Troil.*, ii., 3, 102, "Achillis hath inveigled his foole from him.—*Who*, Thersites?—*He*" (= who is it? it is he); parallel cases occur at every moment in colloquial language.

158. (112) A good deal of confusion arises from *some words being both prepositions and conjunctions*. With regard to *but*, Dr. Murray says in *N. E. D.*:—

"In some of these uses, the conjunction is, even in Modern English, not distinctly separated from the preposition: the want of inflexions in substantives, and the colloquial use of *me*, *us*, for *I*, *we*, etc., as complemental nominatives in the pronouns, making it uncertain whether *but* is to be taken as governing a case. In other words 'nobody else went but me (or I)' is variously analysed as = 'nobody else went except me' and 'nobody else went except (that) I (went)', and as these mean precisely the same thing, both are pronounced grammatically correct." (Comp. also Murray's examples, especially under the heads C. 3 and 4.) It should, however, be remarked that the confusion in the use of *but* is not a consequence of the want of distinct case-endings in the nouns and the use of *me* instead of *I* in other connexions; in my view it is on the contrary the existence of such two-sided words as *but*, etc., that is one of the primary causes of mistakes of *me* for *I* or *vice versâ* and careless uses of the cases generally. Even in such a

language as German, where the cases are generally kept neatly apart, we find such combinations as "niemand kommt mir entgegen *ausser ein unverschämter*" (Lessing); "wo ist ein gott *ohne der herr*" (Luther); "kein gott ist ohne *ich*," etc.[1]

Sometimes both the preposition and the conjunction would require the same case as in these quotations from Murray's Dict.: "Se is æthwam freond butan dracan anum | bot þe haf i na frend". In the following examples there is a conflict between the two constructions; and in some of them (which I have starred) the nominative is used, although both the preposition and conjunction would require the accusative, or *vice versâ*.

Ancr. R., 408, "no þing ne con luuien ariht bute *he* one" | Chauc., *C.*, 282, "no man woot of it but god and *he*" (rhymes with *be*) | *Min. P.*, 2, 30, "no wight woot [it] but *I*" | Malory, 42, "neuer man shall haue that office but *he*" | Marlowe, *Jew*, 1576, "I neuer heard of any man but *he Malign'd the order of the Iacobines*"[2] | Sh., *Cymb.*, i., 1, 24, "I do not thinke, so faire an outward, and such stuffe within endowes a man, but *hee*" | *ibid.*, ii., 3, 153, "That I kisse aught but *he*" | *As*, i., 2, 18, "my father had no childe, but *I*" | *Macb.*, iii, 1, 54, (854).

---

[1] See Paul, *Principien der Sprachgesch.*, 1st ed. 225, 2nd ed. 318; in Danish similar examples abound ("ingen *uden jeg*," etc.).

[2] Relative attraction concurring.

"There is none but *he* whose being I doe feare" | *Romeo*, 250, (i., 2, 14), "Earth hath swallowed all my hopes but *she" | *R. III.*, ii., 2, 76, "What stayes had I but *they?" | 2 *H. VI.*, i., 2, 69, "here's none but *thee* and *I*" | *Temp.*, iii., 2, 109, "I neuer saw a woman But onely Sycorax my dam, and *she" | Thackeray, *Van. F.*, 521, "how pretty she looked. So do you! Everybody but *me* who am wretched" | R. L. Stevenson, *Child's Garden*, 17, "So there was no one left but *me*".[1]

159. (113) *Save* (*sauf*) presents similar phenomena of confusion, although it is comparatively seldom found as a preposition, as in Matth. Arnold, *Poëms*, i., 159, "For of the race of Gods is no one there, save *me* alone"; and in Tennyson, p. 319, "Who should be king save *him* who makes us free?"[2] In Chaucer *sauf* (*save*) is very common with nom. (*B.*, 474, 627; *G.*, 1355; *I.*, 25; *L. G. W.*, 1633; *Morris*, ii., 221, 493; 342, 801), so also in Shakespeare (*Tw. N.*, iii., 1, 172; *Cæs.*, iii., 2, 66, etc.), and in modern poets (*e.g.*, Byron, iv., 332, "Who shall weep above your universal grave, save *I*?"). Where the word is not meant as the subject, the accusative is used (*e.g.*, Chaucer, *B.*, 4491,

---

[1] *Instead of* is sometimes used in such a way as to approach a conjunction; see Mrs. Grand, *The Heavenly Twins*, p. 42, "Now they rule him instead of *him them*".

[2] Mätzner (ii., 501) has two examples of *save* with acc., from Rogers and Skelton.

"Save *you* I herde neuere man so singe;" where, however, one MS. (H) has *ye*). An example of an abnormal use of the nom. is Shak., *Sonn.* 109, 14, "For nothing in this wide universe I call, save *thou*, my rose".

For *except*, compare the following examples:—

Meredith, *Trag. Com.*, 28, "And everybody is to know him except *I*?" | Muloch, *Halifax*, ii., 22, "No one ever knew of this night's episode, except *us* three" | Mrs. Browning (a letter in Mrs. Orr, *Life and Letters of Rob. Br.*, 232), "Nobody exactly understands him except *me* who am in the inside of him and hears him breathe" | Hardy, *Tess*, 101, "Perhaps any woman would, except *me*".

160. (114) The conjunctions *as* and *than*, used in comparisons, give rise to similar phenomena. As it is possible to say both "I never saw anybody stronger *than he*" [scil. *is*], and "*than him*" (acc. agreeing with *anybody*), and "I never saw anybody so strong *as he*," and "*as him*," the feeling for the correct use of the cases is here easily obscured, and *he* is used where the rules of grammar would lead us to expect *him*, and conversely. The examples of complete displacement are here, as above, starred:—

Chauc., *B.*, 1025, "So vertuous a lyver in my lyf Ne saugh I never, such as *sche*" | *ibid*, *M. P.*, 3, 984, "Ne swich as *she* ne knew I noon" | Udall, *Roister*, 33, "for such as *thou*" (compare *ibid*, 44) | Marl., *Tamb*, 1814, "depend on such weake helps as *we*" | *ibid.*, 1877, "for these, and such as *we* our selues, For vs" | Greene, *Friar B*, 12, 66, "I do love the lord, As *he* that's second to thyself in love" (relat. attr.) | Sh., *Rom.*, 239, "For men so old as *we*" | *Shrew*, i., 2, 65, "'twixt such friends as *wee*" | *As*, ii., 5, 58, "Heere shall he see grosse fooles as *he*" | *Wint. T.*, ii., 1, 191 | *Ant.*, iii., 3, 14, "is shee as tall as *me*?" | Field, *T. J.*, ii., 115, "you are not as good as *me*" | Trollope, *Duke's Ch.*, iii., 31 (a young lord writes), "the Carbottle people were quite as badly off as *us*" | Orig. Engl., 42 (vulg.), "some people wot lives [= who live] on the same floor as *us*, only they are poorer than *us*" | Thomson, *Rule Britannia*, "The nations not so blest as *thee*, Must in their turn to tyrants fall" | Meredith, *Egoist*, 192, "What was the right of so miserable a creature as *she* to excite disturbances?"

After *such as* the nom. is now the rule :—Tennyson, *In Mem.*, xxxiv., p. 256, "What then were God to such as *I*?" | *ibid.*, p. 419, "Gawain, was this quest for thee?" "Nay, lord," said Gawain, "not for such as *I*" | Rob. Browning, iii., 78, "The land has none left such as *he* on the bier" | Mrs. Browning, *Sonnets f. t. Port.*, viii., "who hast . . . laid them on the outside of the wall, for such as

I to take" | Ward, *Dav. Grieve*, i., 193, "religion was not for such as *he*" | Buchanan, *Wand. Jew*, 74, "The Roman wars not with such foes as *he*" | Co. Doyle, *Sherl. H.*, i., 181, "God keep you out of the clutches of such a man as *he*".

Even after *as well as* the confusion is found, though in the mouths of vulgar persons :—

Sh., *Meas.*, ii., 1, 75, "I will detest my selfe also, as well as *she*" | Field, *T. J.*, iii., 121, "Dost fancy I don't know that as well as *thee*?"

The word *like* is normally used with the dative, but on account of its signification being often identical with that of *as*, the nominative is sometimes found :—

Sh., *Rom.*, 1992 (iii., 5, 83), "And yet no man like *he* doth greeue my heart," evidently on account of the following verb, whose subject in a way *he* is ; compare, on the other hand, *ibid.*, 1754-6, "wert thou as young as I . . . doting like *me*, and like *me* banished" | R. Wintle, *A Regular Scandal*, 35, "Yes, if it was a sweet young girl . . . and not one like *I*".

161. (115) Examples with *than* :—

Chaucer, *L. G. W.* (B), 476, "To me ne fond **I** better noon than *ye*" | Sh., *Cor.*, iv., 5, 170, "but a greater soldier then *he*, you wot one" | *As*, i., 1, 172, "my soule . . . hates nothing more then *he*" (compare *Troil.*, ii., 3, 199; *Cymb.*, v., 3, 72, "then *we*" (obj.) (relat. attr.) |

Field, *T. J.*, i., 49, "My sister, though many years younger than **me*, is at least old enough to be at the age of discretion" | *ibid.*, iii., 129, "you are younger than **me*" | *ibid.*, i., 221 (vulg.), "gentle folks are but flesh and blood no more than *us* servants" | Byron, ii., 351, "none Can less have said or more have done Than **thee*, Mazeppa" | *ibid.*, iv., 213, "Yet he seems mightier far than **them*" | iv., 223, "Higher things than ye are slaves; and higher Than **them* or ye would be so" | v., 226, "than **him*" | Shelley, 237, "I am . . . mightier than **thee*" | Thackeray, *Van. F.*, 412, "she fancies herself better than you and *me*" | Trollope, *Duke's Ch.*, i., 221 (a lady says), "[She should be] two inches shorter than *me*".

This use of the acc. after *than*, of which Bishop Lowth in his grammar (1762, p. 145) is already able to quote many examples from the writings of Swift, Lord Bolingbroke, Prior, etc., is now so universal as to be considered the normal construction; that is, to the general feeling *than* is a preposition as well as a conjunction. Even grammarians acknowledge the use of the accusative in this connexion,[1] though their reasons are not always of the best; thus W. Smith and D. Hall[2] mention: "A stone is heavy, and the sand weighty; but a fool's wrath is heavier than them both" (Prov. xxvii, 3), as "a construction founded on the Latin," namely, the ablative (without *quam*), to express the second member of a comparison (major Scipione), with which the English idiom of course nothing whatever to do. Nevertheless, many grammarians, and consequently many authors, reject this natural use of the accusative, and I think I am justified in considering the nominatives in some, at least, of the following examples as called forth by a more or less artificial reaction against the natural tendencies of the language:—

Carlyle, *Heroes*, 93, "the care of Another than *he*" | Troll, *Duke's Ch.*, i., 136, "he had known none more vile or more false than *I*" | G. Eliot, *Mill*, i., 186, "I have known much more highly-instructed persons than *he* make inferences quite as wide" | Tennyson, *Becket*, 1, "But we must have a mightier man than *he* for his successor" | Meredith, *Egoist*, 141, "if I could see you with a worthier than *I*" | Buchanan, *Jew*, 87, "Naming the names of lesser Gods than *I*" | Co. Doyle, *Sherl. H.*, i., 53, "I love and am loved by a better man than *he*".

The accusative is always used in *than whom* (found in Shakespeare, *Love's L.*, iii, 180, in Milton, etc.); Alford is right in observing that *than who* is here excluded because the expression does not admit of an elliptical construction. I only once remember

[1] Hyde Clarke, p. 132; Alford, *Queen's Engl.*, 111 ff.; see also Storm, *E. Philol.*, p. 233.
[2] *A School Manual of Engl. Grammar*, 1873, p. 119.

having found *than who*, namely in the sentence, "Mr. Geo. Withers, than who no one has written more sensibly on this subject," and then it occurs in the book on *The King's English* (p. 338) by Mr. Washington Moon, who is constantly regulating his own and others' language by what in his view *ought* to be, rather than what really *is* the usage of the English nation.

III. Anacoluthia.

162. (108) Of the different forms of anacoluthia we have here first to do with that which results when a speaker begins a sentence with some word which takes a prominent place in his thought, but has not yet made up his mind with regard to its syntactical connexion; if it is a word inflected in the cases he provisionally puts it in the nominative, but is then often obliged by an after-correction[1] to insert a pronoun indicating the case the word should have been in. This phenomenon is extremely frequent in the colloquial forms of all languages, but grammarians blame it and in literary language it is generally avoided. I shall first give some examples where the case employed is correct or the fault is at any rate not visible :—

[1] I translate thus Wegener's expression, "nachträgliche correctur" (see his *Grundfragen des Sprachlebens*, Halle, 1885, p. 72, where he deals with such German sentences as "das haus, da bin ich rein gegangen," etc.). The opposite process of placing the pronoun first is also common; see, for instance, Carlyle, *Heroes*, 19, "*it* is strange enough this old Norse view of nature".

Ancren Riwle, 333, "þe beste mon of al þisse worlde ȝif ure Louerd demde him al efter rihtwisnesse 7 nout efter merci, wo schulde *him* iwurden" | Chauc., *B.*, 4268, "oon of hem, in sleping as he lay, *Him* mette a wonder dreem" | Sh., *As*, iv, 1, 77, "verie good orators when they are out, *they* will spit" | *ibid.*, iv, 1, 177, "that woman that cannot make her fault her husbands occasion, let *her* neuer nurse her childe".

Next I quote some instances in which the nominative (or, in the first sentence, acc.) might be also caused by relative attraction (§ 154) :—

Oros., 78, 31, "þæt gewinn þæt his fæder astealde he . . . for þæm V gear scipa worhte" | *Cura P.*, 29, 2, "Se ðe god ne ongit, ne ongit god *hine*"[1] | *ibid.*, 31, 16, "Se ðe ænigne ðissa ierminga besuicð, him wære betere," etc. | Chaucer, *B.*, 4621, "For *he* that winketh, whan he sholde see, Al wilfully, God lat *him* never thee!" | Chaucer, *Morris*, iii, 165, "for certes *he* that . . . hath to gret presumpcioun, *him* schal evyl bitide" | *ibid.*, iii, 196, "*He* that most curteysly comaundeth, to *him* men most obeyen" | Malory, 150, "*ye* that be soo wel borne a man . . ., there is no lady in the world to good for *yow*" |

[1] This is the regular O. E. construction in relative clauses; compare the modern translation, "*He* who knows not God, God knows not *him*".

Matt., xii., 36, "*Every idle word* that men speak, they shall give account *thereof* in the day of judgment" | Sh., *Cor.*, i., 4, 28, "*He* that retires, Ile take *him* for a Voice" (compare *Haml.*, iii, 2, 252) | Sh., *R. III.*, iii., 2, 58, "that *they* which brought me in my masters hate, I liue to looke vpon *their* tragedie"[1] | Sh., *H. V.*, iv., 3, 35, "*he* which hath no stomacke to this fight, let *him* depart, his passport shall be made" | Carlyle, *Heroes*, 9, "*He* that can discern the loveliness of things, we call *him* Poet".

There is no relative attraction in the following sentences:—

Oros., 24, 7, "Seo ús fyrre *Ispania*, *hyre* is be westan garsecg" | *ibid.*, 188, 26, "Athium *þæt folc him* gebuhte" | Sh., *Meas.*, v., 134, "But yesternight my lord, *she* and that fryer I saw *them* at the prison" | Sh., *Wint. T.*, iii., 2, 98, "My second ioy, And first fruits of my body, from *his* presence I am bar'd".[1]

Sometimes no corrective pronoun follows:—

Sh., *Meas.*, v., 531, "*She* Claudio that you wrong'd, looke you restore" | Sh., *Wives*, iv., 4, 87, "and *he* my husband best of all affects" | Sh., *Tim.*, iv., 3, 39, "*Shee*, whom the spittlehouse and vlcerous sores Would cast the gorge at, this embalmes" [her; in the first folio a different punctuation is used] | R. Browning, *Tauchn.*, i., 235, "*She*, men would have to call your mother once, Old Gandolf envied me, so fair she was!"

163. (111) When two or more words are in *apposition* to each other it often happens that the appositum does not follow the case of the first word; the speaker forgets the case he has just employed and places the appositum loosely without any connexion with the preceding. M. Sohrauer[1] gives some O. E. examples (to *Nichodeme*, an ðæra Judeiscra ealdra), to which may be added:—

Chron., 984 A, "seo halgung *þæs æfterfylgendan bisceopes* Ælfheages, se ðe oðran naman wæs geciged Godwine" (rel. attraction!) | Sweet, *A. S. Reader*, 15, 7, "fram Brytta *cyninge*, *Ceadwalla geciged*" | *ibid.*, 1. 45, "*sumne arwurðne bisceop, Aidan gehaten*" | *ibid.*, l. 101, "to Westseaxan *kyninge, Cynegyls gehaten*" | *ibid.*, l. 144, "on *scrine*, of seolfre *asmiþod*".

This is extremely common in O. E. with participles; in more recent periods it is found in many other cases as well:—

Chauc., *B*, 1877, "prey eek for *us, we* sinful folk unstable" | Chauc., *M. P.*, 5, 421, "Beseching *her* of mercy and of grace, As *she*

---

[1] In the appendix to the next chapter I shall have occasion to mention these and similar ways of expressing the genitive of word-groups; see especially § 249.

[1] *Kleine Beiträge zur Altengl. Grammatik*, p. 29; see also Mätzner, *Gramm.*, iii., 343 ff.

that is my lady sovereyne" | Chauc, *Morris*, iii, 12, 325, "to folwe *hire*, as *she* that is goddesse" | Sh., 1 *H. IV*, i., 2, 16, "by *Phoebus*, *hee*, that wand'ring knight" | Sh., *Love's L.*, iv., 3, 7, "this loue . . . kils sheep; it kils *mee*, *I* a sheep" | Sh., *Wint. T.*, v., 1, 86, "Prince Florizell . . with his princesse (*she* The fairest I haue yet beheld)" | Sh, 1 *H. IV*., ii., 4, 114, "I am not yet of *Percies* mind, the *Hotspurre* of the North, *he* that killes me some sixe or seauen dozen of Scots"[1] | Shelley, *Poet. W.*, 250, "Know ye not *me*, The Titan? *he* who made his agony the barrier to your else all-conquering foe?"

Relative attraction may, of course, have also been at work in some of these sentences; and the following example (which I quote from A. Gil, *Logonomia*, 1619, p. 77) might be accounted for in no less than three of my paragraphs (154, 156, 163). This illustrates the complexity of the mutual relations of grammatical categories:—

"Sic etiam casus inter duo verba, nunc cum hoc, nunc cu*m* illo construitur: vt, Let Tomas cum in, J mēn hɩ̄ ðat kām yisterdai: aut I mēn him".

What is the reason of the accusative in Sh., *Cymb*, v., 4, 70, "we came, our parents and *vs* twaine"?

164. (109) There is a peculiar form of anacoluthia,

which for want of a better name I shall term *unconnected subject*. In English this phenomenon is not confined to those exclamations of surprise or remonstrance in which it is common in many languages (Dan., "Du göre det! Han. i Paris?" French, "Toi faire ça! Lui avare?" Italian, "Io far questo!" Latin, "Mene incepto desistere victam?" etc.), but is found in other cases as well, especially after *and*, by which the subject is more or less loosely connected with a preceding sentence.[1] I shall here in the first place give some quotations in which the case employed is the same as would have been used had the thought been expressed fully and in more regular forms:—

Sh, *Love's L.*, iii, 191, "What? *I* loue! *I* sue! *I* seeke a wife!" | *ibid*, 202, "And *I* to sigh for her, to watch for her," etc. | *Meas.*, ii., 2, 5, "all ages smack of this vice, and *he* To die for't" | *As*, iii., 2, 161, "Heauen would that shee these gifts should haue, and *I* to liue and die her slaue" (= I should) | *Tim*., iii., 1, 50, "Is't possible the world should so much differ, And *we* aliue that liued?" | *Macb*, i., 7, 58 (455), "If we should faile?— We faile!" (Here, however, the best reading seems to be "We faile." with a full stop, the verb being taken as an indicative) | *R. II*., iv., 1, 129, "And shall the figure of God's Maiestie . . . Be iudg'd by subject, and in-

---

[1] The phenomenon was more frequent from the fifteenth to the seventeenth century than it is now.

---

[1] Compare, for a fuller treatment of nominatives in apposition to genitives, § 222 ff. below.

ferior breathe, And *he* himself not present?" | Milton, S. A., 1480, "Much rather I [Manoa] shall choose To live the poorest in my tribe, than richest, And *he* in that calamitous prison left" [= if Samson is left . . .] | Field, T. J., ii, 85, "*A young woman* of your age, and unmarried, to talk of inclinations!" | G. Eliot, *Mill*, ii., 149, "*I* say anything disrespectful of Dr. Kenn? Heaven forbid!" | *ibid*, ii, 307, "Could anything be more detestable? A girl so much indebted to her friends . . . to lay designs of winning a young man's affections away from her own cousin?"

But in the following instances the nom. is used, although the construction, if regularly completed, would have led to the use of an accusative:—

Chaucer, E., 105, "I dar the better aske of yow a space Of audience to shewen our requeste, And *ye*, my lord, to doon ryght as yow leste" | Malory, 71, "hym thought no worship to have a knyght at suche auaille, *he* to be on horsback and *he* on foot" | Sh., As, i., 2, 279, "What he is indeede, More suites you to conceiue, then *I* to speake of" (Kellner [1] quotes from Sh. also *Err.*, i., I, 33; *All's*, ii., I, 186; *Timon*, iv., 3, 266) | *Cor.*, iii., 2, 83, "the soft way which . . . Were fit for thee to vse, as *they* to clayme" (compare also *Cor.*, iii., 2, 124, and ii., 2, 54).

165. (109) Similarly where no infinitive is used, but a participle or some other word:—

[Chaucer, *F.*, 700, "What coude a sturdy husbond more deuyse To preue hir wyfhood and hir stedfastnesse, And *he* continuing euer in sturdinesse?"] | Mal., 95, "whan Balen sawe her lye so with the fowlest knyghte that euer he sawe and *she* a fair lady, thenne Balyn wente thurgh alle the chambers" | Marlowe, *Tamb*, 244, "Me thinks I see kings kneeling at his feet, And *he* with frowning browes and fiery lookes Spurning their crownes" | Sh., *Romeo*, 537, "good manners shall lie all in one or two men's hands and *they* vnwasht too" | *Lear*, iii., 6, 117, "that which makes me bend makes the king bow, *He* childed as *I* fathered!" | Field, *T. J.*, ii, 249, "I thought it hard that there should be so many of them, all upon one poore man, and *he* too in chains" | Meredith, *Trag. Com.*, 165, "let her be hunted and I not by [and let me not be by; when I am not by], beast it is with her" | Ward, *David Grieve*, iii., 133, "It made her mad to see their money chuckled away to other people, and *they* getting no good of it".

In some of these sentences the construction might be called a kind of apposition; in others we have

---

[1] Introd. to *Blanchardyn*, p. lxvii. ff.; Kellner's explanation does not seem very clear.

something closely resembling the absolute participle, of which more will be said below, § 183; the use of an "unconnected subject" may have favoured the substitution of the modern "absolute nominative" for the old "absolute dative".

166. (109) Sometimes the phenomenon mentioned in § 164, of an unconnected subject with an infinitive, corresponds very nearly to the Latin accusative with the infinitive, only the nominative is used:—[1]

Malory, 40, "this is my counceill . . . that we lete purueyx knyȝtes men of good fame, & *they to kepe* this swerd" | *ibid.*, 60, "for it is better that we slee a coward than thorow a coward alle *we* to be slayne" | *ibid.*, 453 (quoted by Kellner), "*Thow* to lye by our moder is to muche shame for vs to suffre" | *ibid.*, 133, "And thenne hadde she me deuysed to be kyng in this land, and soo to regne, and *she* to be my quene".

But this use of a nominative with the infinitive does not occur often enough to be a permanent feature of the English language.

[1] Where the subject is a noun it is impossible to see which case is used; comp. *Ancr. R.*, 364, "is hit nu wisdom mon to don so wo him suluen?" | Malory, 67, "it is gods wyll youre body to be punysshed" | *ibid.*, 94, "it is the custome of my countrey a knyghte alweyes to kepe his wepen wih hym" | Sh, *Wint. T.*, v, 142, "Which . . . Is all as monstrous . . . As my Antigonus to breake his graue". Modern Engl. here has *for*: "it is wisdom for a man to do . . ."; compare the full and able treatment of this use of *for*, in C. Stoffel's *Studies in English*, p. 49 ff.

IV. Influence from the Nouns.

167. (116) The absolute absence of any formal distinction between the nominative and the objective cases in the nouns and adjectives, as well as in the neuter pronouns *it*, *that*, and *what*, must of course do a great deal towards weakening the sense of case distinctions in general.

168. (117) This is especially seen to be the case where the pronouns are themselves taken substantively, for then the normal case-inflexion is naturally suspended. This happens in two ways: either a pronoun is plucked from its context and quoted by itself, as in these examples:—

Sh., *All's*, iii., 1, 81, "write to her a loue-line. What *her* is this?" | Tennyson, *Becket*, act i., sc. 1, "It much imports me I should know her name. What *her*? The woman that I followed hither" | *Frank Fairlegh*, ii., 19, "so he left her there. 'And who may *her* be?' inquired Freddy, setting grammar at defiance";

or else a pronoun is used exactly like a noun, *he* or *she* signifying a male or a female respectively. This is extremely common in Shakespeare (see Al. Schmidt's *Sh. Lex.*); a few examples will here suffice:—

Bale, *Three Lawes*, 1439, "I am non other, but even the very *he*" | Sh., *Tw. N.*, i., 5, 259, "Lady, you are the cruell'st *shee* alive" | *Wint. T.*, iv., 4, 360, "to load my *shee* with knackes" | *As*, iii., 2, 10, "carue on euery tree The faire, the chaste and vnexpressiue *shee*" | *Love's L.*, v., 2, 469, "we . . . woo'd but the signe of *she*" | *Cymb.*, i., 3, 29, "the *shees* of Italy".

So also as the first part of a compound : *a she angel, you she knight errant* (Sh, *Wint.*, iv., 4, 211; 2 *H. IV*, v. 4, 25); comp.:—

Byron, v., 230, "The pardon'd slave of she Sardanapalus" | *ibid.*, v., 245, "wearing Lydian Omphale's She-garb".

But in the nineteenth century it is often the objective case that is used thus substantively:—

Troll, *Duke's Ch.*, i., 94, "that other *him* is the person she loves" | *ibid.*, 94, "reference to some *him*" | Gilbert, *Orig. Plays*, 1884, 129 (vulgar), "Mr. Fitz Partington shall introduce him.—It ain't a *him*, it's a *her*."

In philosophical language, the *me* and the *thee* are often used corresponding to the German *das ich, das du*:—

Carlyle, *Sartor*, 35, "Who am I; what is this ME?" | *ibid.*, 37, "our ME the only reality" | *ibid.*, 39, "that strange THEE of thine" | *ibid.*, 92, "a certain orthodox Anthropomorphism connects my *Me* with all *Thees* in bond of Love" | Ruskin, *Selections*, i., 503, "But this poor miserable *Me !* " | Meredith, *Egoist*, 489, "the miserable little *me* to be taken up and loved after tearing myself to pieces !"

Yet the nom. is sometimes found:—

Carlyle, *Sartor*, 132, "the THOU" | Mrs. Ward, *Dav. Grieve*, iii., 86, "was there any law— any knowledge—any *I ?*" | L. Morris, *Poet. Works*, 121, "And the *I* is the giver of light, and without it the master must die".

An English friend of mine once told me about a clergyman who in one of his sermons spoke constantly of *your immortal I*, but was sadly misunderstood by the congregation, who did not see why the *eye* should be more immortal than any other part of the body. It is perhaps to avoid such misinterpretations that the Latin form is sometimes used, as in Thack, *Pend.*, iii., 363, "every man here has his secret *ego* likely".

169. (118) When the pronoun is preceded by an adjective, it is sometimes inflected in the usual way ("poor *I* had sent a hundred thousand pounds to America; would you kill poor *me ?*" and similar examples are quoted by Storm, *E. Philol.*, 208, note); but in other places we find it treated like a substantive:—

Sh., *Sonn.* 72, "upon deceased *I*" | *ibid, Cor.*, v., 3, 103, "to poore *we*, Thine enmities most capitall".

In exclamations *me* is always used:—

Sh., *Sonn.* 37, "then ten times happy *me !* " | Thack., *Van. F.*, 120, "Poor little *me !* "

Compare the use of *me* in other exclamations : *O(h) me ! Woe me ! Ah me ! Ay me ! * (Milt., *P. L.*, iv.,

86, etc.), *Aye me detested!* (Sh, *Tw. N.,* v, 142) *Alas me!* (Keats, *Eve of St. Agnes,* xii.), *Me miserable!* (Milt., *P. L.,* iv., 73), etc. The use of *me in dear me! gracious me!* and other apologies for oaths is probably due to the analogy of the corresponding use of the pronoun as an object after a verb, as in *bless me!* etc. So perhaps also in Shak., 1 *H. IV.;* ii., 3, 97, "*Gods me,* my horse".

V. Position.

170. (119) Word-order is to no small extent instrumental in bringing about shiftings of the original relation between two cases. In Old English prose the subject is already placed before the verb in nearly every sentence; the exceptions are almost the same as in Modern German or Danish; thus inversion is the rule after adverbs such as *þa* (while, curiously enough, the subject precedes the verb where the clause is introduced by *hwæt þa* or *efne þa*). By-and-by these exceptions disappear or are reduced to a minimum, so that in Modern English the order, subject, verb, object, is practically invariable.[1] Cooper defines the difference between the nom. and the acc. in the pronouns in the following manner:[2] "*I, thou, he, she, we, ye, they,* verbis anteponuntur, *me, thee, him, her, us, you, them,* postponuntur verbis & præpositionibus". However naïve the grammarian may find this definition, it contains a

[1] See above, especially § 73 on *to* in interrogative propositions.
[2] See his *Gramm. Lingua Anglicana,* 1685, p. 121.

good deal of truth; this is the perception of the distinction between the two forms which in the popular instinct often overrides the older perception according to which the use of *I* and *me* was independent of position.

171. (120) *Before the verb* the nom. comes to be used in many cases where the acc. was required by the rules of the old language. Besides a few isolated instances, that may be more or less doubtful,[1] this is the case with *who,* as the natural position of this pronoun is always at the beginning of the sentence, the verb, as a rule, following immediately after it. For Middle English examples of *who* and *whom* see below, § 178; it would be an easy matter to find hundreds of examples from the Modern English period; I shall here print only a few selected from my own collections to supplement the numerous examples adduced by Storm (*Engl. Philol.,* 211 ff.):—

Marl., *Tamb.,* 4190, "*UUho* haue ye there, my Lordes?" | Greene, *Friar B.,* 1, 143, "Espy her loues, and *who* she liketh best" | Sh., *Tw. N.,* ii., 5, 108, "Ioue knowes I loue, but *who,* Lips do not mooue, no man must know" | *ibid., Wint.,* v., 1, 109, "[she might] make proselytes of *who* she but bid follow" | *ibid.,* i., 2, 331, "my sonne (*who* I doe thinke is mine, and loue as mine)" | *Spectator,* No.

[1] See, for instance, Sh, *Meas.,* 1, 221, "*Shee* should this Angelo haue married: was affianced to her [by] oath, and the nuptiall appointed," where most editors emend *she* to *her.*

266, "*who* should I see there but the most artful procuress?" | *ibid.*, 59, "*who* should I see in the lid of it [a snuff-box] but the Doctor?" | Dryden, "Tell who loves *who*" | Sheridan, *Dram. W.*, 39, "*who* can he take after?" | *ibid.*, 48, "*who* can he mean by that?" (cf. *ibid.*, 69) | Thack., *Van. F.*, 74, "*Who*, I exclaimed, can we consult but Miss P.?" | Mrs. H. Ward, *Rob. Elsm.*, ii., 141 (Lady Helen says), "*Who* does this dreadful place belong to?"

172. (120) As regards Shakespeare's use of *who* in the objective case, it must suffice to refer to Al. Schmidt's *Lexicon*; under the interrogative pronoun he gives fifteen quotations for the use in question, and then adds an *etc.*, which, to any one familiar with the incomparable accuracy and completeness of Schmidt's work, is certain proof that examples abound; finally he names nineteen places where the old editions do not agree. Under the relative pronoun he adduces twelve quotations for *who* as an acc., followed again by an *etc*, and by eleven references to passages in which the oldest editions give different readings. It is well worth noting that where such variations of reading are found it is nearly always the earliest edition that has *who* and the later editions that find fault with this and replace it by *whom*; most modern editors and reprinters add the *-m* everywhere in accordance with the rules of grammars, showing thereby that they hold in greater awe the schoolmasters of their own childhood than the poet of all the ages.[1]

Shakespeare also uses *whoever* as an accusative; *whomever* does not occur in his works; he also sometimes uses *who* after a preposition (see Abbott, § 274, and add to his examples, *R. III.*, i., 3, 54), but this seems now obsolete, because the natural word-order is to place the preposition at the end of the sentence, as Shakespeare does himself in numerous passages; for instance, *As*, iii., 2, 327, "Ile tell you who Time ambles withall, who Time trots withall, who Time gallops withal, and who he stands stil withall". It seems, then, as if the last refuge of the form *whom* is the combination *than whom*, where it had originally nothing to do; but as this combination belongs more to literary than to everyday language, *who* is now to be considered almost as a common case; compare what Sweet writes to Storm: "I think many educated people never use *whom* at all; always *who*".

173. (121) A great many verbs which in Old English were impersonal have become personal in Modern English, and one of the causes which most contributed to this change was certainly word-order. The dative, indicating the person concerned, was

[1] Schmidt has five instances from Shakespeare of *whom* (relative) for *who*: one is after *than*; three might be added to those I gave above in § 155; the fifth (*Temp*, v., 76) is an anacoluthia, which is corrected as early as in the second folio.

generally placed immediately before the impersonal verb; the reason of this position was undoubtedly the greater interest felt for the person, which caused the word indicating him to take a prominent place in the sentence as well as in the consciousness of the speaker. And so this "psychological subject," as it has been termed, eventually became the grammatical subject as well. But other circumstances favoured the same tendency. Some verbs in O. E. admitted of both a personal and impersonal construction, *e.g.*, *recan*, "to care"; compare from the thirteenth century the *Ancr. Riwle*, p. 104, where one MS. has "ȝif heo beoð feor, *me* ne recched," and another "þach ha beon feor, naut *I* ne recche". In one case, two originally distinct verbs grew to be identical in pronunciation by a purely phonetic development, namely O. E. *þyncan*, "seem" (German *dünken*), impersonal, and *þencan*, "think" (Germ. *denken*), personal. In the former the vowel *y* by the usual process lost its lip-rounding and so became *i*; in the latter *e* was raised to *i* before the back nasal consonant, as in O. E. *strenȝ*, Mod. *string*, O. E. *hlence*, mod. *link*, O. E. *Englaland*, Mod. *England*, pronounced with [i]; compare also the history of the words *mingle*, *wing*, *cringe*, *singe*, etc.

The number of verbs that have passed from the impersonal to the personal construction is too great for me here to name them all; I shall refer to the lists given by Koch, *Gram.*, ii, § 109; Mätzner, ii, p. 198 ff.; Einenkel, *Streifzüge*, p. 114 ff.; and Kellner, *Blanchardyn*, p. xlvii. ff. But I shall supple-

ment the remarks of these scholars by attempting to analyse the psychological agencies at work in the transition; I shall for this purpose print those examples from my own collection which seem to be the most illustrative, confining myself generally to only a few of the most usual verbs coming under this head.

174. (122) The original construction will be seen from the following quotations:—

Ancr. R., 238, "*me luste* slepen" | Chauc., *B.*, 1048, "*hir liste* nat to daunce" | Bale, *Three L.*, 1264, "And maye do what *him lust*" | *Ancr. R.*, 338, "hit mei lutel *liken God* [dative], and misliken ofte" | Chauc., *M. P.*, 22, 63, "al that *hir list and lyketh*" | *ibid*, *Morr.*, iii, 145, "whan *him liketh*" | Malory, 100, "I shold fynde yow & damoysel . . . that shold *lyke yow & plese yow*" [the two verbs are synonymous] | Greene, *Friar B.*, 4, 55, "this motion *likes me well*" | Sh., *Haml.*, ii, 2, 80, "It *likes vs well*" | *ibid*, *Troil.*, v, 2, 102, "I doe not like this fooling . . . But that that *likes not you pleases me best*" | Milton, *Reason of Church Governm.*, ii, "much better would it *like him* to be the messenger of gladness" | Thack., *Van. F.*, 89, "Some [women] are made to scheme, and some to love: and I wish any respected bachelor . . . may take the sort that best *likes him*"[1]

---

[1] *Like* is here used in the old sense of *please*; this is now-a-

Chauc, *M. P.*, 3, 276 (and very often), *"me mette* [I dreamt] so inly swete a sweven" | *Ancr. R.*, 136, "hit schal *þunche þe* swete" | Chauc., *B.*, 4578, "*hem thoughte* hir herte breke" | Malory, 65 (four times), "*hym thoughte*" | Latimer (*Skeat's Spec.*, xxi, 91), "*me thynketh* I heare" | "*methinks, methought(s)*".

175. (123) In many cases it is impossible to decide whether the verb is used personally or impersonally, as, for example, when it stands with a noun or with one of the pronouns that do not distinguish cases. It goes without saying that the frequency of such combinations has largely assisted in bringing about the change to modern usage. A few examples will suffice:—

Ancr. R., 286, "hwon *þe heorte likeð* wel, þeonne cumeð up a deuocioun" | Chauc., *Morr.*, iii, 147, "al that *hir housbonde likede* for to seye" | *ibid.*, *B.*, 477, "*God list* to shewe his wonderful miracle" | *ibid.*, *Morr.*, iii, 145, "hem *that liste* not to heere his wordes" | *ibid.*, *B.*, 4302, "how *Kenelm mette* a thing".

The construction is similarly not evident in the case of an accus. with the infinitive:—

days extremely rare. In Middle English *like* was often used with *to*: Chauc., *Morr.*, iii, 191, "what day that it like *yow* and *unto your* noblesse" | *ibid., E.*, 345, "It lyketh *to* your fader and *to* me". Compare Chauc., *Morr.*, iii, 172, "it displeseth *to* the jugges," but 183, "displese God".

Chauc., *M. P.*, 5, 108, "That *made me to mete*" | *ibid.*, 115, "[thou] *madest me* this sweven *for to mete*".

176. (124) The transition to the new construction is shown by the possibility of joining two synonyms, of which one has always been a personal verb:—

Prov. of Alfred (*Specimens*, i., p. 148), "þat ye alle a-drede vre dryhten crist, *luuyen* hine and *lykyen*" | Malory, 35, "the kynge *lyked and loued* this lady wel".

As early as Chaucer we find passages in which a nominative is understood from an impersonally constructed verb to a following verb of personal construction:—

B., 3731, "For drede of this, *him* thoughte that he deyde, And [he] ran into a gardin, him to hyde" | *M. P.*, 7, 200, "*her* liste him 'dere herte' calle And [she] was so meek" | *M. P.*, 5, 165, "Yit lyketh *him* at the wrastling for to be, And [he] demeth yit wher he do bet or he".

Sometimes both constructions are used almost in a breath:—[1]

Ch., *L. G. W.*, 1985, "*me* is as wo For him as ever *I* was for any man" | Malory, 74, "Arthur loked on the swerd, and *lyked*[2] it".

---

[1] See also below, § 193.
[2] This and the just mentioned are the only examples of personal (or rather half-personal) use of *lyke* I have noted in Malory, who generally uses the acc. (dat.) with it, *e.g.*, 61, "it lyketh you" | 157, "yf hit lyke yow".

passynge wel; whether *tyketh yow* better, said Merlyn, the suerd or the scaubard? *Me lyketh* better the swerd, sayd Arthur" | Greene, *Friar B*, 6, 138, " Peggy, how *like you* [nom.] this?—What *likes my lord* is pleasing unto me" | Sh., *Troil.*, above, § 174. In Ch, *M.P.*, 5, 114, "[thou] dauntest whom *thee* lest," some of the manuscripts read *thou*, probably in order to avoid the two accusatives after each other.

177. (125) Sometimes the impersonal expression is followed by a connexion of words that is strictly appropriate only after a personal verb:—

Ancr. R., 332, " Ase ofte ase ich am ischriuen, euer *me puncheð me* unschriuen (videor mihi non esse confessus) | *ibid.*, 196, "swetest *him puncheð ham* [the nuns : they appear to him [God] most lovely" | Chauc., *E.*, 106, " For certes, lord, so wel *vs lyketh yow* And all your werk and ever han doon ".

The last quotation is of especial interest as showing a sort of blending of no less than three constructions : the impersonal construction with *us lyketh* as a third personal sg. with no object, the old personal construction, where *like* means " to please," *us lyken ye*,[1] and finally the modern personal use, *we lyken yow* ; the continuation " and ever han doon" (= " and we have always liked you ") shows that the last construction was at least half present to Chaucer's mind.

[1] Not *us lyketh ye*, as Prof. Skeat would have it in his note to the passage.

Other blendings of a similar nature are found with *think; me thinks* and *I think* are confused in *me thinke*, found, for instance, in a sermon of Latimer's (Skeat's *Specimens*, xxi., 176);[1] *thinks thee?* and *thinkst thou?* give *thinkst thee?* in Shakespeare's *Hamlet*, v., 2, 63 (folio; the old quartos have *thinke thee*; some modern editors write *thinks't thee*, as if contracted for *thinks it thee*; but this is hardly correct, as this verb is very seldom used with *it*, at least when a personal pronoun is added).

178. (126) Note particularly *who* in the following sentences :—

Ancr. R., 38, "*hwo se puncheð* to longe lete þe psalmes" | Chauc., *B.*, 3509, " Hir batailes *who* so *list* hem for to rede . . . Let him vnto my maister Petrark go" | Sh., *Troilus*, i., 398, " and *who*-so *liste* it here".

These we may consider either the oldest examples of *who* as an accusative (centuries before any hitherto pointed out), or else the oldest examples of O. E. *byncan* and *lystan* used personally.[2] I suppose, however-

[1] Compare also *Roister Doister*, 71, " me thinke they make preparation . . . me think they dare not," where *thinke* seems to be in the plural on account of the following *they*.

[2] The Chaucer quotations given by Einenkel (*Streifzüge*, p. 115) are too dubious to prove the personal use of *listen* : iii, 1 (= F. 689), the Ellesm. MS. reads, " For he to vertu *listneth* not entende" [what is *entende* here? a noun? an adv.? (in the ende??). I understand it no more than did those scribes who placed *listeth* instead of *listneth*]; iv, 136, has *that*, which may as well be acc. as dat.; finally, iii, 268, proves nothing, as some

ever, that the correct way of viewing these sentences is to say that the two tendencies, neither of which was strong enough to operate by itself, here combined to bring about a visible result.

179. (127) Here I shall finally give a few examples of the prevailing personal use:—

Sh., *Rom.*, 37, "as *they list*" | Milton, *P. L.*, iv., 804, "as *he* list" | *Gesta Rom.* (ab. 1440, quoted by Kellner), "*þou* shalt *like* it" (in Elizabethan language also *like of*) | Greene, *Friar B*, 10, 45, "if *thou please*" | Sh., *Shrew*, iv., 3, 70, "as *I please*"[1] | Chauc., *B.*, 3930, "And eek a sweuen vpon a nyghte *he mette*".

In some cases the personal construction has not become universal, as in the case of *ail* (O. E. *eglan*). Though Dr. Murray is able to show the personal use of the word in a quotation as early as 1425, and though Shakespeare never uses it impersonally (comp. also Marlowe, *Jew*, 1193, "What ayl'st thou"), the old construction still survives. The reason is undoubtedly the fact that the verb is so very often used in the

MSS. read "if *the* list," not *thou*. Kellner, *Blanchard.*, xlix., quotes Einenkel's two examples, showing that he has found no more examples in Chaucer, while he has some from Caxton. Compare, however, *M. P.*, 7, 200, quoted above, § 176.

[1] Milton, *P. L.*, vi., 351, shows the personal use of *please* and the impersonal use of *like*: "As *they please*, They limb themselves, and colour, shape, and size, Assume, as *likes them* best, condense or rare". Compare *ibid.*, vi., 717.

common formula: *What ails him?* (her, etc.), where the personal pronoun is placed *after* the verb; see, *e.g.*, Sirith, 337; Chauc., *B.*, 1170, 1975, 4080; *H.*, 16; *M. P.*, 3, 449, etc., etc.; Tennyson, p. 132: "What ail'd *her* then?" G. Eliot, *Mill*, i., 80, "there's nothing ails *her*".

With *seem* the shifting observable in the case of *like*, etc., has not taken place, although there were formerly tendencies in this direction; Kellner[1] gives two instances from old wills of the personal use (with the person to whom it seems, in the nom.), and in Somersetshire[2] *I zim* now means "it seems to me" exactly as the Danish *jeg synes*.[3] The following examples of a corresponding use I give with some diffidence:—

Malory, 76, "So whan the kynge was come thyder with all his baronage and lodged as *they semed* best"; comp., on the other hand, *ibid.*, 77, "*me semeth*" | Spalding, *Eng. Lit.*, 358, "*we seem* often as if we were listening to an observant speaker".

180. (128) I must here mention the history of some peculiar phrases. When the universal tendency to use impersonal expressions personally seized upon the idiom *me were liever* (or *me were as lief*), the

[1] *L.c.*, p.1. Kellner does not seem to be right in asserting that the O. E. verb means "think, believe".

[2] Elworthy, *Word-book* (E.D.S), p. 851.

Danish offers a great many parallels to the English development of personal constructions out of impersonal.

resulting personal construction came in contact with the synonymous phrase *I had liever* (or *I had as lief*),¹ and a considerable amount of confusion arose in this as well as in the kindred combinations with *as good, better, best, rather*. I give some instances of the various constructions found, starring those in which the case employed seems to run counter to logic:—

Oros., 220, 26, "*him leofre was þæt* ..." | *Ancr. R.,* 230, "ham was leoure uorte adrenchen ham sulf þen uorte beren ham" | *ibid.,* 242, "asken þe hwat te vœre leouest" | Sirith, 382, "*Me were levere* then ani fe That he hevede enes leien bi me" | Chauc., *B,* 1027, "*she hadde* [var. l. *Hire hadde] lever a knyf Thurghout hir brest, than ben a wommman wikke" | *ibid., C,* 760, "if that yow be so leef To fynde deeth" [two MSS. **ye be,* others *to you be*] | *ibid., E,* 444, "al *had* *hir leuer haue born a knaue child" | Malory, 87, "*he had leuer* kyng Lotte had been slayne than kynge Arthur" | *ibid.,* 92, "*I had leuer* mete with that knyght" | Sh., *Cor.,* iv., 5, 186, "*I had as liue* be a condemn'd man".

Chauc., *M. P.,* 5, 511, "*him were as good* be stille" | *ibid.,* 5, 571, "*yet were it bet for the* Have hold thy pees" | Bale, *Three L.,* 889, "**Thu were moch better* to kepe thy pacience" | Udall, *Roister,* 26, "*ye were best sir for a while to reuiue againe" |

¹ He is dear to me = I have (hold) him dear.

PROGRESS IN LANGUAGE.

Marlowe, *Jew,* 1798, "*he were best to send it" (cf. *ibid.,* 869, 1851, 1908) | Sh., *Meas.,* iii., 2, 38, "*he were as good* go a mile" | *ibid., As,* iii., 3, 92, "*I were better to bee married" | *ibid., R. III,* iv., 4, 337, "What *were* *I best to say?" | *ibid., Shrew,* v., 1, 108, "Then *thou wert best saie that I am not Lucentio" | *ibid., Cymb.,* iii., 6, 19, "*I were best not call" | Milton, *S. A.,* 1061, "But *had we best* retire?" | Field, *T. Jones,* ii., 110, "Your La'ship *had almost as good* be alone" | Thack., *Pend.,* iii., 131, "*you had much best* not talk to him".

Marlowe, *Jew,* 147, "*Rather had I* a Jew be hated thus, Then pittied" | Sh., *R. II.,* iii., 3, 192, "**Me rather had,* my heart might feele your loue".¹

¹ Those who object to the form *had* in "I had rather speak than be silent," etc. (see for instance a letter from Robert Browning in Mrs. Orr's *Handbook,* 6th ed., p. 14), seem wrongly to take *rather* as an adverb instead of an adjective; it is incorrect to urge that the omission of the adverb would "alter into nonsense the verb it qualifies," for *had rather* is to be taken as a whole, governing the following infinitive. *Had rather* is used by the best authors, by Shakespeare at least some sixty times, while *would rather* is comparatively rare in his writings and generally confined to such cases as *Two Gent,* v., 4, 34, "I *would* haue beene a breakfast to the Beast, *rather* then have false Protheus reskue me," where, of course, *rather* belongs only indirectly to *would.* In an interesting paper, "Had Rather and Analogous Phrases," in the Dutch periodical *Taalstudie* (viii., 216), C. Stoffel shows that so far from

CASE-SHIFTINGS IN THE PRONOUNS.

181. (135) I must here also mention the peculiarity of the English language by which not only what would be the direct object of the active verb but other parts of the sentence may be made the *subject of a passive verb*. As I have not collected sufficient materials to give an exhaustive treatment of this interesting subject, I shall confine myself to a few remarks. There can be little doubt that nouns were employed in this way as "free subjects" of passive verbs at an earlier time than pronouns in which the nom. and the acc. had distinct forms. I shall arrange my examples under four heads.[1]

(1) The verb originally governs the dative case, but has no direct object in the accusative. Such an instance as (*Ancren Riwle*, 82) *God beo iðoncked* is not quite beyond question, as the form *God* is used in that text in the dative as well as in the nominative; but the following is indubitable, as *Louerd* is not used as a dative:—[2]

Ancr. R., 8, "vre Louerd beo iðoncked" | Chaucer, *L. G. W.*, 1984, "He shall be holpen" | *ibid*, *Morr.*, iii., 11 (compare Einenkel, 111), "I may be holpe" | Malory, 125, "he myght neuer be holpen" | *ibid.*, 36, "youre herte shalbe pleasyd" | *ibid.*, 463, "he was answerd".[3]

(2) The verb is combined with a preposition; then the word governed by the latter is considered as the object of the composite expression (verb and prep.), and can therefore be made the subject of a passive proposition.

Maundev., 22 (quoted by Koch), "Thei ben sent

---

had rather being an "incorrect graphic expansion" of *I'd rather* instead of *I would rather*, the *had* form historically is the better of the two. Stoffel is undoubtedly right in his conclusions; still it is interesting to notice how the feeling of the etymological connexion has been lost on account of the phonetic identity of the unstressed forms of *had* and *would* [əd]; the change in the popular instinct is already seen in Shakespeare's *Rich. III.* (iii, 7, 161), where the folio emends the *had rather* of the old quartos into *would rather*. A further step in the gradual forgetfulness of the old idiom is shown by the occasional introduction of *should*, as in Conan Doyle, *Adv. of Sherlock Holmes*, i. 228, "Or should you rather that I sent James off to bed?" Nor are signs wanting that in other cases as well as before *rather* the feeling of the difference between *had* and *would* has become obscured; I shall give two quotations, one from Tennyson's *Becket* (act iii., sc. 3), "You *had* safelier have slain an archbishop than a she-goat," and the other from a little Cockney, who writes, "If anybody else *had* have told me that, I wouldn't have beleeved it" (see *Original English, as Written by our Little Ones at School*, by H. J. Baker, Lond., 1889). A. Trollope writes (*Old Man's Love*, 263), "Had you remained here, and have taken me, I should certainly not have failed then," where, by a singular confusion, *had* seems first to have its proper meaning, and then to be taken as an equivalent of [əd] = *would*.

---

[1] Cf. Koch, *Gram.*, ii., § 147 ff.

[2] The dative is *louerde*; see pp. 160, 168, also p. 58, where the MS. has *lourde* according to Kölbing, and not *lourd* as Morton prints it.

[3] This is given by Kellner (*Blanchard*, lv.) as the only instance found in Malory.

fore" | Malory, 35, "we were sent for"; similarly, though with a noun as the subject *ibid.*, 47, twice, p. 67, p. 38, "lete hym be sent for" | Latimer, *Spec.*, iii., 21, 46, "they wyl not be *yl* spoken of" | *ibid.*, 251, "that whiche I can not leaue vnspoken of".

| Sh., 1 *H.IV.*, iii., 2, 141, "your vnthoughtof Harry" | *ibid.*, i., 2, 225, "Being wanted, he may be more wondred at" (see *ibid.*, i., 3, 154; iii., 2, 47; *R. II.*, i., 3, 155, etc.) | Meredith, *Trag. Com.*, 76, "The desire of her bosom was to be run away with in person".

Compare the somewhat analogous phenomenon in *Ancr. R.*, 6, "sum is old & atelich & is ðe leasse dred of" (*is dred of* is a sort of passive of *habben dred of*); here, however, we have rather a continuation of the old use of *of* as an adverb = "thereof".

(3) The verb governs both an accusative and a dative; in this case there is a growing tendency to make the dative the subject when the verb is made passive. The oldest examples are:—

Ancr. R., 112, "he was þus ileten blod" | *ibid.*, 260, "swinkinde men & blod-letene" | *ibid.*, 258, "heo beoð ileten blod"; similarly, 262 (he), 422 (ge, twice).

It should, however, be remarked that *let blood*, more than most of these combinations, is felt as *one* notion, as is seen also by the participle being used attributively (p. 260) and by the verbal noun *blod-*

lettunge (14, 114). Something approaching the indirect passive construction is found in the following passage:—

Ancr. R., 180, "ȝif *me*[1] *is* iluued more þen anoðer, & more ioluhned, more *idon god, oðer menske,*

from which it would perhaps be rash to conclude that the author would have said, for instance, "*he is idon god oðer menske,*" if these expressions had not been preceded by the direct passives *iluued* (loved) and *ioluhned* (caressed). At any rate these constructions do not become frequent till much later; in Chaucer I have found only one instance (*L. G. W.*, 292, "And some were brend, and *some wer cut the hals*"); Mätzner quotes one from the *Towneley Mysteries* ("alle my shepe are gone; *I am not left one*"); Kellner knows none in the whole of Caxton's[2] which may be explained by the fact that Caxton's translations closely follow the original French in most syntactical respects. For examples from Shakespeare and recent authors I may refer to Koch, ii., § 153, and Mätzner, ii., p. 229. The following passage shows the vacillation found to a great extent even in our own century:—

Sh., *Macb.*, i., 5, 14-17 (305-308), "ignorant

---

[1] *Me* is the indefinite pronoun (*men*, *man*), corresponding to French *on*.

[2] The dative is used for instance in Malory, 89, "there was told *hym* the adventure of the swerd" | "therefore was gyuen *hym* the pryse".

of what greatnesse *is promis'd thee* (in Macbeth's letter) . . . Glamys thou art, and Cawdor, and shalt be what *thou art promis'd*" (comp. *Wint. T.*, iv., 4, 237, "I was promis'd them").

To this category belongs also such a phrase as the following:—

Shak., *As*, i., 1, 128, "*I am giuen* sir secretly to vnderstand that your younger brother . . .".

(4) The verb beside a direct object has attached to it a preposition and a word governed properly by the preposition, but coming to be taken as the object of the composite expression, verb + object + preposition:—

"I was *taken no notice of*" | Carlyle, *Sartor*, 29, "new means must of necessity be *had recourse to*".

Here, too, I am able to point out a sentence in the *Ancren Riwle* containing, so to speak, a first germ of the construction:—

Ancr. R., 362, "Nes Seinte Peter & Seinte Andreu istreiht o rode . . . and loðlease meiðenes þe tittes ikoruen of, and to-hwiðered o hweoles, & hefdes bikoruen?"

182. This extension of the passive construction is no doubt in the first place due to the effacement of the formal distinction between the dative and the accusative; but a second reason seems to be the same fact which we met with before in the case of verbs originally impersonal: the greater interest felt for the person makes the speaker place the noun or pronoun by which the person is indicated before the direct object, as in the sentence: "He gave the girl a gold watch". This makes it natural that in the passive voice the dative should be placed at the very beginning of the sentence: "The girl was given a gold watch". But this position immediately before the verb is generally reserved for the subject; so *the girl*, though originally a dative, comes to be looked upon as a nominative, and instead of "*her* was given a gold watch," we say, "*she* was given a gold watch". On the other hand, the nature of these constructions reacts on the feeling for case-distinctions in general; for when "I was taught grammar at school" comes to mean the same thing as "me was taught grammar," or "she was told" as "her was told," etc., there is one inducement the more to use the two cases indiscriminately in other sentences as well, or at least to distinguish them in a different way from that which prevailed in the old language.

183. No doubt the position before the verb has also been instrumental in changing the old *absolute dative* (as seen, for instance, in *Chron*, 797, "*Gode fultomiendum*, God helping") into the modern nominative.

A few instances will show that the modern construction was fully established in Shakespeare's time:—[1]

[1] See also Mätzner, iii., 75 ff.; Koch, ii., 130 ff. I have not had access to Ross's dissertation, *The Absolute Participle in Middle and Modern English* (Johns Hopkins Univ., 1893).

Sh., *Venus*, 1010, "For *he* being dead, with him is beauty slain" | *ibid.*, *Cymb.*, ii, 4, 8, "*they* [the hopes] fayling, I must die" | *ibid.*, iii, 5, 64, "*Shee* being downe, I haue the placing of the British crowne" | *ibid.*, *Temp.*, v., 1, 28, "*they* being penitent, the sole drift of my purport doth extend Not a frowne further" | *ibid.*, *Cor.*, v., 4, 37, "and *he* returning to breake our necks, they respect not vs" | *ibid.*, *R. III*., iv., 2, 104, "How chance the prophet could not at that time Haue told me, *I* being by, that I should kill him" | *ibid.*, *Errors*, iii., 2, 87, "not that *I* being a beast she would haue me".

Gil, in his *Logonomia*, 1619, p. 69, mentions the modern construction only, showing thereby that the old one was completely forgotten at that time, even by learned men:—

"Nominatiuus absolutus apud Anglos ita vsurpatur, vti apud Latinos Ablatiuus: vt I bïing prezent, hî durst not have dun it . . . Hï bïing in trubl, hiz frîndz forsük him."

We are, therefore, astonished to find Milton using the old dative towards the end of that century:—

P. L., ix., 130, "and *him* destroyed . . all this will soon follow" | *ibid.*, vii., 142, "by whose aid This inaccessible high strength, the seat of Deity supreme, *us* dispossessed, He trusted to have seized" | *Sams.*, 463, "Dagon hath presum'd, *Me* overthrown, to enter lists with God".

But this peculiar use of Milton's is undoubtedly due rather to an imitation of Latin syntax than to a survival of the Old English construction, and Milton in other places employs the nominative:—

P. L., ix., 312, "while shame, *thou* looking on . . . Would utmost vigour raise" | *ibid.*, ix., 884, "Lest, *thou* not tasting, different degree Disjoin us".

I have already mentioned that the phenomenon I termed "unconnected subject" may have contributed something towards the growth of the absolute nominative, see § 165; I shall here call attention to another circumstance that may have favoured this construction, namely, that in such sentences as 'the following an apposition (in the nominative) is practically not to be distinguished from the absolute construction:—

Field, *Tom Jones*, ii., 42, "The lovers stood both silent and trembling, *Sophia being* unable to withdraw her hand from Jones, and *he* almost as unable to hold it" | C. Doyle, *Sherl. Holmes*, i., 36, "they separated, *he driving* back to the Temple, and *she* to own house".

It is true that these sentences are modern and penned long after the absolute nom. had been settled; but although I have no old quotations ready to hand, similar expressions may and must have occurred at any time.

184. (129) Having dealt (in §§ 170-183) with the substitution of the nominative for an original accusa-

CASE-SHIFTINGS IN THE PRONOUNS.

tive or dative before the verb, we shall now proceed to the corresponding tendency to use an objective case *after the verb* where a nominative would be used in the old language. This is, of course, due to the preponderance of the instances in which the word immediately following the verb is its object.[1] The most important outcome of this tendency is the use of *me* after *it is*. I have already had occasion to mention a few connexions in which the accusative will naturally come to be used after *it is* (see §§ 154 and 157); to these might be added accusatives with the infinitive, as in Greene, *Friar Bacon*, 10, 57, "*Let it be me*". But even where there is no inducement of that kind to use *me*, this form will occur after *it is* by the same linguistic process that has led in Danish to the exclusive use of *det er mig*, where some centuries ago the regular expression would have been *det er jeg*, and which is seen also in the French *c'est*, used in Old French with the oblique form of nouns and then also of pronouns, *c'est moi*, etc.[2]

With regard to the English development from O. E., *ic hit eom*, through the Chaucerian *it am I* (*Cant, B.*, 1109, *M. P.*, 3, 186, etc.) to *it is I*[3] and *it is me*, I shall refer to a letter from A. J. Ellis, printed in

[1] When Trollope writes (*Duke's Ch.*, ii, 227), "There might be somebody, though I think not *her*," *her* is viewed as a sort of object of "I think".
[2] On the French development see, for instance, Lidforss in *Öfversikt af Filologiska sällskapets i Lund Förhandlinger*, 1881-88, p. 15.
[3] Malory, 36, "I am he".

Alford's *The Queen's English*, p. 115, and to Storm, *Engl. Philol.*, 1881, pp. 209-10, 234 ff.; the latter author gives a great many modern examples of the accusative in familiar speech. Ellis goes so far as to say that "the phrase *it is I* is a modernism, or rather a grammaticism, that is, it was never in popular use, but was introduced solely on some grammatical hypothesis as to having the same case before and after the verb *is*. ... The conclusion seems to be that *it's me* is good English, and *it's I* is a mistaken purism." The eminent author of *Early English Pronunciation* is no doubt right in defending *it's me* as the natural form against the blames of quasi-grammarians: but I am not so sure that he is right when he thinks that *it is I* is due only to the theories of schoolmasters, and that "it does not appear to have been consonant with the feelings of Teutonic tribes to use the nominative of the personal pronouns as a predicate". He seems to have overlooked that it was formerly used so often with the nom. that we cannot ascribe the usage exclusively to the rules of theorists; see, for instance :—Chaucer, *B.*, 1054, "it was *she*" | Malory, 38, "it was *I* myself that cam" | *Roister Doister*, 21, "that shall not be *I*" | *ibid*, 58, "it was *I* that did offende" | *ibid.*, 26, "this is not *she*" | Marlowe, *Jew*, 656, "'tis *I*" | Shak., *Macb.*, 877, 1009, 1014 (and at other places), "it was *he*," or "'tis *hee*".

185. (129) The nom. accordingly seems to have been the natural idiom, just as *det er jeg* was in

Danish a few centuries ago, and as *det är jag* is still in Sweden; but now it is otherwise, and *it is me* must be reckoned good English, just as *det er mig* is good Danish. In Shakespeare (besides the passages accounted for above) we find the accusative used in three passages, and it is well worth noting that two of them are pronounced by vulgar people, *viz., Two Gent.,* ii., 3, 25, "the dogge is *me*" (the clown Launce), and *Lear,* i., 4, 204, "I would not be *thee*" (the fool; comp. *Pericl.,* ii., 1, 68, "here's *them* in our country of Greece gets more," spoken by the fisherman); the third time it is the angry Timon who says: "[I am proud] that I am not *thee*" (iv., 3, 277). The stamp of vulgarity would have disappeared completely by now from the expression had it not been for grammar schools and school grammars; even to the most refined speakers *it's me* is certainly more natural than *it's I*.[1] And Shelley has consecrated the construction as serviceable in the highest poetic style by writing in his *Ode to the West Wind*: "Be thou, spirit fierce, my spirit! *Be thou me,* impetuous one!"

Latham, Ellis, Sweet and Alford defend *it is me* as the only natural expression; the reason of their not extending this recognition of the objective case equally to the other persons will be found below

[1] Trollope makes a young lord say: "I wish it were *me*" (*Duke's Childr.,* iii., 118); comp. *ibid.,* ii., 64, "It is *you*. . . . '*Me!*' said Miss Boncassen, choosing to be ungrammatical in order that he might be more absurd." Many other examples in Storm.

(§ 194); yet in Thackeray's *Vanity Fair,* p. 163, a young lady says *It's her*; and in *Cambridge Trifles,* p. 96, an undergraduate says *It couldn't be them*—to mention only two examples.

186. (130) Not only the predicate but also the subject itself is liable to be put in the accusative after the verb. *Shall's* (= *shall us*) for *shall we* is found six times in Shakespeare. As four times it means exactly or nearly the same thing as *let us* (*Cor.,* iv., 6, 148, "Shal's to the Capitoll"; *Wint.,* i., 2, 178; *Cymb.,* v., 5, 228; *Pericl.,* iv., 5, 7), it is probable that this idiom is originally due to a blending of *let us* and *shall we* (compare the corresponding use of a nom. after let, § 156). But it has been extended to other cases as well: *Tim.,* iv., 3, 408, "How shal's get it?" | *Cymb.,* iv., 2, 233, "Where shall's lay him?" Towards the end of the last century *shall us* was common in vulgar speech according to Sam. Pegge,[1] who adds:

[1] See his *Anecdotes of the Engl. Language* (1803; re-edited 1814 and 1844, with additions by the editors; Pegge himself died in 1800). This is a very remarkable work, excellent alike for the power of observation it displays and for the author's explanations of linguistic phenomena, by which he is often many years ahead of his time, and often reminds one of that eminent philologist who was to take up the rational study of vulgar English about eighty years later: Johan Storm. Of course, it is no disparagement to Pegge to remark that many of the phenomena he deals with are now explained otherwise than was possible to h**i**m, before the birth of comparative philology. I shall here quote an interesting remark of his: "Before I undertook this investigation, I was not aware that *we all speak so incorrectly* in our daily colloquial language as we do". This

"The Londoner also will say—"Can us," "May us," and "Have us". Storm quotes (p. 209) from Dickens some instances of vulgar *shall us, can't us, do us, hadn't us*; is this phenomenon still living in the mouth of uneducated people? I do not call to mind a single instance from the Cockney literature of the last ten years or so.

187. (131) I find a further trace of the influence of position in Shakespeare, *Macb.*, 2044 (v., 8, 34), "And *damn'd be him*[1] that first cries hold, enough!" *Damn'd be* is here taken as one whole meaning the same thing as, and therefore governing the same case as, *damn* or *God damn*. The person that should properly be the subject of the verb is sometimes even governed by a *to*:—

Field., *T. Jones*, i., 297, "Are not you ashamed, and *be d—n'd to you*, to fall two of you upon one?" | *ibid.*, ii., 118, "*be d—ned to you*" | *ibid.*, iv., 87, "You my son-in-law, and *be d—n'd to you!*" | Thack., *Van. F.*, 158, "*be hanged to them*"; similarly, *ibid.*, 274, 450; *Pendennis*, ii., 146, 314, 317[2] | Darwin, *Life and Lett.*, iii., 76, "I went to Lubbock's, partly in hopes of seeing you, and, *be hanged to you*, you were not there" | Mrs. Ward, *D. Grieve*, i, 220, "*be d—d to your Christian brotherhood!*"

Here the phrase *be damned*, or its substitute *be hanged*, has become an exclamation, and *to you* is added as if "I say" was understood; compare also *Hail to thee* (Middle Engl. *heil be þow*); *farewell to you; welcome to you; good-bye to you*.[1]

An earlier form of the phrase *Would to God* is *Would God*, where *God* is the subject:—

Chaucer, *M. P.*, 3, 814, "God wolde I coude clepe her wers" | Malory, 66, "so wold god I had another" [hors] | *ibid.*, 81, "wolde god she had not comen in to thys courte" | Greene, *Friar B*, 6, 40, "would God the lovely earl had that".

But when people lost the habit of placing a subject after the verb, they came to take *would* as an equivalent of *I would* and *God* as a dative; and the analogy of the corresponding phrase *I wish to God* (or, I pray to God) would of course facilitate the change of *God* into *to God*.

188. (132) The position after the verb has probably had no small share in rendering the use of *thee* (and *you*) so frequent *after an imperative*, especially in the

[1] *Hamlet*, ii, 2, 575, qu.; this phrase properly contains two *yous*; compare also Stevenson, *Tr. Isl.*, 256, "I've got my piece o' news, and *thanky to him* for that" (*thanky* = thank ye, thank you).

[1] *And damn'd be him* that first cries hold, enough!

[2] *Pendennis*, ii, 321, "Field of honour be hanged!"

[1] Of course, Pope and most later editors "emend" *him* into *he*.

first Modern English period; the usage is still seen in the poetical phrase "*Fare thee well*". Here we have, however, a concurrent influence in the use of a reflexive pronoun (without the addition of *self*) which was extremely common in all the early periods of the language, and which did not perceptibly alter the meaning of the verb to which it was added.[1] This reflexive pronoun was sometimes originally added in the accusative case, *e.g.*, after *restan* (see Voges, p. 333), but generally in the dative; this distinction, however, had obviously no significance for any but the very earliest stages of the language. As now it was made no difference whatever whether the speaker said *I fear me* or *I fear me* (compare, for instance, Marlowe, *Jew*, 876, with 1110), the imperative would be indifferently *fear* or *fear thee (fear yow)*;[2] but it was equally possible with the same meaning to say *fear thou (fear ye)*, with the usual addition of the nominative of the pronoun to indicate the subject. Examples from Malory of the latter combination: 73, "doubt ye not," 74, "telle thow" | 75, "go ye not," etc.[3] In other words: *after an imperative a nominative and an accusative would*

[1] See Voges, *Der reflexive dativ im Englischen*, in *Anglia*, vi., 1883, p. 317, ff. To supplement my own collections, I take the liberty of using those of his numerous quotations which seem best suited to illustrate the process of case-shifting, a subject which Voges deals with only in a cursory manner.
[2] Chaucer, *L. G. W.*, 1742, "dreed thee noght" | Malory, 61 and 85, "drede yow not".
[3] Sometimes both cases are used in the same sentence: "Slep *thou the* anon" (Judas, quoted by Voges, 336).

very often be used indiscriminately. Thus, *Care ye not* (Malory, 72) means exactly the same thing as *care not yow* (*ibid.*, 135); *stay thou* (Sh., *Cæs.*, v., 5, 44) = *stay thee* (3 *H. VI*, iii., 2, 58); *get ye gon* (Marlowe, *Jew*, 1226) = *get you gone* (common, Sh.); *stand thou forth* (Sh., *All*, v., 3, 35) = *stand thee by* (*Ado*, iv., 1, 24); *turn ye* unto him (Isaiah, xxxvi, 6; Ezek., xxxiii, 11) = *turn you*, at my reproof (Prov., i., 23); *turn you* to the stronghold, *ye* prisoners of hope (Zech., ix., 12); *turn thee* unto me (Ps., xxv., 16) = *turn thou* unto me (*ibid.*, lxix., 16¹); *fare ye well* (Sh., *Merch.*, i., 1, 58 and 103) = *fare you well* (*ibid.*, ii., 7, 73); seldom as in *Tim.*, i., 1, 164, *Well fare you, fare thou well* (*Temp.*, v., 318) = *fartheewell* (*Tw. N.*, iii., 4, 183); *far-thee-well* (*ibid.*, iii., 4, 236); *far thee well* (*ibid.*, iv., 2, 61); *sit thou* by my bedde (Sh., 2 *H. IV.*, 5, 182) = *sit thee* downe vpon this flowry bed (*Mids. N.*, iv., 1, 1; also with the transitive verb *set thee down*, *Love's L.*, iv., 3, 4, in some editions emended into *sit¹*).

189. (132) It will now be easily understood that *thee* (or *you*) would be frequently added to imperatives where the thought of a reflexive pronoun would not be very appropriate; in *hear thee, hark thee, look thee* and similar cases, Voges finds a reflexive dative,

[1] The quotations from the Bible are taken from Washington Moon's *Ecclesiastical English*, p. 170; this author blames the translators for their inconsistency and for their bad grammar; he does not know that Shakespeare is guilty of the very same "faults," and he does not suspect the historical reason of the phenomenon.

whereas Al. Schmidt quotes them under the heading "*thee* for *thou*"; it is rather difficult to draw a line here. When Troilus says (act iv, 5, 115): "Hector, thou sleep'st, *awake thee*," no less than three grammatical explanations are applicable: *awake* may be intransitive, and *thee* the subject (Al. Schmidt), *awake* is intransitive, but *thee* is a reflexive dative (Voges, *l. c.*, p. 372), and finally, *awake* may be a transitive verb having *thee* as its object (comp. Murray's Dict.); but whichever way the grammatical construction is explained, the meaning remains the same.[1]

It is evident that all this must have contributed very much to impair the feeling of the case-distinction, and it should be remarked that we have here a *cause of confusion that is peculiar to the pronouns of the second person*.[2]

[1] We may perhaps be allowed to conclude from the following passage that *you* after an imperative was at the time of Shakespeare felt as an accusative: *As*, i., 3, 45. "Mistris, dispatch you with your safest haste, And get you from our court. *Me* Vncle?"

[2] When in Living English a pronoun is added to an imperative, it is generally placed before it: "*You* try! *You* take that chair!" | "Never *you* mind!" | C. Doyle, *Sherl. H.*, i., 63, "And now, Mr. Wilson, off *you* go at scratch" | Jerome, *Three Men in a Boat*, 30, "Now, *you* get a bit of paper and write down, J., and *you* get the grocery catalogue, George, and *somebody* give me a bit of pencil". When the auxiliary *do* is used, the pronoun comes before the principal verb: "*Don't you* stir!" | C. Doyle, *l. c.*, 94. "I shall stand behind the crate, and *do you* conceal yourselves behind those" | *ibid.*, ii, 71, "*Don't you* dare to meddle with my affairs". Compare from

---

190. (133) In connexion with the reflexive expressions mentioned just now I shall remind the reader that we have a still more radical change in the case of the *reflexive pronoun when joined to self*. *Him self* was originally added to the verb with the meaning of a dative, "to, or for, himself"; but it came to be regarded as an emphatic apposition to the subject (he has done it *himself*; he *himself* has done it), and finally it is sometimes used as a subject by itself (*himself* has done it). We see the first beginnings of this development in Old English phrases like these:—

Oros, 194, 21, "þa angeat Hannibal, & *him self* sæde"[1] | *ibid.*, 260, 33, "[Nero] gestod *him self* on þæm hiehstan torre" | *Ancr. R.*, 226, "ȝe beoð tures *ou sulf*, 'ye yourselves are towers'" | *ibid.*, 258, "*he him sulf* hit seið".

It would be a waste of paper and ink to give examples from more recent times, as they abound everywhere; I shall therefore only state the fact that in the modern use of *himself* and *themselves* (and last century Fielding, *T. Jones*, iv, 131, "Well then," said Jones, "*do you* leave me at present" | *ibid.*, 157. "*Do you* be a good girl" | *ibid.*, 302, "Harkee, sir, *do you* find out the letter which your mother sent me". It will be seen that in this deviation from the position rules of former times we have an application of the rule laid down in § 72 ff.

[1] For this can hardly mean at this place: "he said to himself"; the Latin original has: "Tunc Annibal dixisse fertur".

herself?) we have a dative used as a nominative (or rather as a common case), and that this was formerly the case with *me self* and *us self* (or *us selue, seluen*) as well, which have now been ousted by *myself* and *ourselves*.[1]

191. (134) Sometimes we come across isolated uses of the objective for the nominative case, which are probably to be ascribed to analogical influence exercised by the *self*-combinations. Abbott quotes (§ 214):—

Sh., *John*, iv, 2, 50, "Your safety, for the which my selfe and *them* Bend their best studies"; and says: "Perhaps *them* is attracted by myself," which naturally suggests the objective "myself and (they) them (selves)". That this is the correct explanation seems to be rendered more likely by the parallel passage:—

Marl., *Tamb.*, 433, "Thy selfe and *them* shall neuer part from me,"

and perhaps it is also applicable to these two sentences:—

Sh., *Wint.*, i., 2, 410, "Or both your selfe and *me*

---

[1] It is with some hesitation that I place this use of *him* (*self*) in the section headed "Position," as it neither is nor ever was obligatory to place *himself* after the verb. As this position is, however, the most common, it may have had some influence in determining the form *himself* in preference to *he self*, which was used in O.E., and at any rate the arrangement followed in this section has the advantage of not sundering the two classes of reflexive datives.

Cry lost" | *Cæs.*, i., 3, 76, "No mightier then thy selfe, or *me*" [N.B., than !].

192. (136) In his book *The King's English*, p. viii., Mr. Washington Moon writes:—

"As a specimen of real 'Queen's English,' take the following, which was found written in the second Queen Mary's Bible: 'This book was given the king and *I* at our coronation'."

How is this *I* to be explained? Of course it might be referred to the passive constructions treated above, § 181, though then we should have expected *were* instead of *was* and a different word-order ("The king and I were given this book," or perhaps, "This book the king and I were given"). But I believe that another explanation is possible: *I* was preferred to *me* after *and*, because the group of words *you and I*, *he and I*, etc., in which this particular word-order was required by common politeness, would occur in everyday speech so frequently as to make it practically a sort of stock phrase taken as a whole, the last word of which was therefore not inflected. At all events, it cannot fail to strike one in reading Storm's instances of nominative instead of objective case (*Engl. Philol.*, p. 210 f.) that the great majority of sentences in which *I* stands for *me* present these combinations. (seventeen from Shakespeare,[1] Ben Jonson, Bunyan, Dickens, etc., against two, which are moreover hardly genuine). Abbott says: "*'Tween you and I* seems to

---

[1] Some of these, it is true, may be explained on the principle mentioned in § 156.

have been a regular Elizabethan idiom". It is found for instance in *Macbeth*, iii., 2, 21, and is not yet extinct. I subjoin a few examples to supplement those given by Storm :—

(*Tom Brown*, 3, see § 156) | Goldsmith, *Mist. of a Night*, i., "Won't you give *papa and I* a little of your company?" | S. Pegge, *Anecd.*, 307, "To *you and I*, Sir, who have seen half a hundred years, it is refunding".

It will be seen that, if my explanation is the correct one, we have here an influence of word-position of quite a different order from that pointed out in the rest of this section. Dr. Sweet,[1] while accepting this explanation as far as the Elizabethan idiom is concerned, thinks that when *between you and I* or *he saw John and I* is said now-a-days, it is due to the grammatical reaction against the vulgar use of *me* for *I*.

VI. Phonetic Influences.

193. (137) I now come to the last but by no means the least important of the agencies that have brought about changes in the original relations between the cases of the pronouns. I mean the influence of sound upon sense.

If you glance at the list of pronominal forms printed in § 152 you will see that seven of them rhyme together, the nominatives *we, ye, he, she,* and the accusatives *me, thee*. After the old case-rules had been shaken in different ways, instinctive feeling

[1] See *New Engl. Grammar*, p. 340 f.

seized upon this similarity, and likeness in form has partly led to likeness in function.

As evidence of this tendency I shall first mention Malory's use of the impersonal verbs that in his times were ceasing to have an impersonal and adopting a personal construction (§ 173 ff.). Malory has a manifest predilection for the *e*-forms with these verbs without any regard to their original case-values, I note all the instances found in some hundred pages :—

Malory, 115, "now *me* lacketh an hors" | 127, "*ye* shalle lacke none" | 71, 90, 148, "*me* lyst(e)" | 61, 114, 146, "*ye* lyst" | 76, "*ye* nede not to pulle half so hard" | 115, "*ye* shalle not nede" | 153, "*he* shalle repente . . . *me* sore repenteth" | 59, 82, 83, 84, 96, 106, 107, 117, 133, "*me* repenteth" | 78, 80, "*ye* shalle repente hit" | 117, "*ye* ouȝt sore to repente it" | 79, 82, 118, "*me* forthynketh" (= "I repent") | 121, "it were *me* leuer" | 46, "*ye* were better for to stynte" | 62, "*ye* were better to gyue" | 87, "whether is *me* better to treate" | 69, "that is *me* loth" | 90, "that were *me* loth to doo" | 100, "*he* wylle be lothe to returne" | 105, "*we* wolde be loth to haue adoo with yow" | 115, "*he* is ful loth to do wronge".

The following are the only exceptions :—

131, "though *I* lacke wepen, *I* shalle lacke no worship" | 101, "*hym* nedeth none" | 82, "els wold *I* haue ben lothe" | 112, 131, "*I* am loth".[1]

[1] *Thynke* and *lyke* are always impersonal in Malory; cf. above, § 176.

A century later the same holds good with the verb *lust* in *Roister Doister*: *ye* (pp. 12 and 51), *me* (12), *he* (42), *she* (87); there are two exceptions: *hym* (43), *I* (44).

The phonetic similarity is used to mark the contrast in Sh., *Macb.*, iii., 4, 14 (1035), "'Tis better thee without then he within"; see W. A. Wright's note: "It [Banquo's blood] is better outside thee than inside him. In spite of the defective grammar, this must be the meaning."

194. (138) We now see the reason why *me* is very often used as a nominative even by educated speakers, who in the same positions would never think of using *him* or *her*. Thus after *it is*, see above, § 185, and compare the following utterances:—

LATHAM (see Alford, p. 115): "the present writer ... finds nothing worse in it [*it is me*] than a Frenchman finds in *c'est moi*. ... At the same time it must be observed that the expression *it is me = it is I*, will not justify the use of *it is him, it is her = it is he*, and *it is she. Me, ye, you* are what may be called *indifferent forms*, i.e., nominative as much as accusative, and accusative as much as nominative."

ELLIS (*ibid.*): "*it's me* is good English."

ALFORD: "'It is *me*' ... is an expression which every one uses. Grammarians (of the smaller order) protest: schoolmasters (of the lower kind) prohibit and chastise;

but English men, women and children go on saying it."

SWEET (*Words, Log. and Gr.*, 26): "it is only the influence of ignorant grammarians that prevents such phrases as 'it is me' from being adopted into the written language, and acknowledged in the grammars. ... The real difference between 'I' and 'me' is that 'I' is an inseparable prefix used to form finite verbs [also a 'suffix': am I, etc.], while 'me' is an independent or absolute pronoun, which can be used without a verb to follow. These distinctions are carried out in vulgar English as strictly as in French, where the distinction between the conjoint 'je' and the absolute 'moi' is rigidly enforced."

SWEET (*Primer of Spoken Engl.*, 36): "The nom. *I* is only used in immediate agreement with a verb; when used absolutely, *me* is substituted for it by the formal analogy of *he, we, she*, which are used absolutely as well as dependently: *it's he, it's me; who's there? me*."

195. I shall give here a few quotations to show the parallelism of *me* and *he* as unconnected subjects (see § 164):—

Thack., *Pend.*, ii, 325, "Why the devil are you to be rolling in riches, and *me* to have none? Why should you have a house and a table covered with plate, and *me* be in a garret?" | Black, *Princess of Thule*, ii, 89, "What do you think of a man who would give up his best gun to you, even though you couldn't shoot a bit, and *he* particularly proud of his shooting?" | *ibid.*, ii., 141, "I am not going to be talked out of my commonsense, and *me* on my death-bed!"[1]

The common answer which was formerly always *Not I!* (thus in Shakespeare, see Al. Schmidt, *Sh. Lex.*, p. 565 a, bottom of the page) is now often heard as *Not me!* while the corresponding form in the third person does not seem to be *Not him!* even in vulgar speech, but always *Not he!* At least, I find in the Cockney Stories, *Thenks awf'lly*, London, 1890, p. 82, "Not 'e!"[2]

[1] Compare Thack, *Pend.*, i., 295, "'*Me* again at Oxbridge,' Pen: thought, 'after such a humiliation as that!'" Flügel quotes in his Dictionary, Sterne's *Sent. Journ.*, 314: "my pen governs me, not *me* my pen".

[2] To avoid the natural use of *me*, stamped as incorrect in the schools, and the unnatural use of *I* standing alone, English people add a superfluous verb more frequently than other nations in such sentences as: "he is older than *I am*". Mr. G. C. Moore Smith writes to me: "I do not feel convinced that there is a difference between the vulgar (or natural) English, 'It's me—it's him'; 'not me—and not him'. I think the chief reason of *him* being less common is that while *me* is distinctive, in the third person it is generally necessary to mention the name. It seems to me very familiar English, 'Is he goin'? Not *him*.' Of course such usages may differ in different parts of the country."

196. (139) *Me* thus to a certain extent has become a common case under the influence of *he*, etc., and we find some traces of a development in the same direction beginning in the case of the other pronouns in *e*, only that it is here the nominative that has been generalised:—

Sh, *Wives*, iii, 2, 26, "There is such a league betweene my goodman and *he*" | *Wint. T.*, ii, 3, 6, "But *shee* I can hooke to me" (compare § 162 f.) | *Oth.*, iv., 2, 3, "You haue seene Cassio and *she* together" | (*Love's L.*, iv., 2, 30, "Those parts that doe fructife in vs more then *he*" = in him) | Fielding, *T. Jones*, i., 200 (Squire Western), "It will do'n [do him] no harm with *he*" | *ibid.*, ii, 50 (*idem*), "Between your nephew and *she*" | Cowper, *John Gilpin*, "On horseback after *we*" | (? *Art. Ward, his Book*, 95, "I've promist *she* whose name shall be nameless..").

P. Greenwood, *Grammatica Anglicana*,[1] mentions among errors committed by plerosque haud mediocri eruditione præditos: "He spake it to *shee* whose fountaines is dried up," and he adds: "Non mirum si vulgus barbarè omnino loquatur, cum qui docti, sunt, et habentur, tam inscite, et impure scribunt".

197. (140) Phonetic influences may have been at

[1] This is the oldest English grammar (printed at Cambridge, 1594); on the title-page are the initials P. G.; I give the author's name from a written note in the unique copy belonging to the British Museum.

work in various other ways. If the vowel of the nominative þu was weakened when the word was unstressed the result would be þe [ðə], exactly like a weakened form of the accusative þe. This is, I take it, the explanation of the nominative þe found so often in the *Ayenbite of Inwit* (A.D. 1340) in such combinations as *þe wylt*, *þe miȝt*, *þe ssoldest*. As *u* is undoubtedly weakened into *e* in *Huannes comste*, "whence comest thou" (*Ayenb.*, 268), as *te* stands certainly for *þu* in Robert of Gloucester, 10792 *seiste*, 3150 *zwoste*, 4917 *ȝifst us*,[1] and as similarly *to* is weakened into *te* in the *Ayenbite* as well as in (parts at least of) the *Ancren Riwle*, this phonetic explanation seems to me, as it did to Mätzner,[2] more probable than the two other explanations given by Gummere[3] and Morris.[4]

As, however, this use of *þe* for *þu* is only found in a few texts (also in Sir Beues of Hamtoun, see *Engl. Studien*, xix., 264), we cannot ascribe to it any great influence on the later development.

198. (170) Similarly a *you* pronounced with weak

[1] F. Pabst, *Anglia*, xiii., 290.
[2] *Sprachproben*, ii., 76.
[3] *American Journal of Philol.*, iv., 286; according to him *þe* is here a dative that has become a nominative, as some centuries later *you* became a nominative.
[4] *þe* is a reflexive dative with the subject understood; this is also the view of Voges (*l. c.*, 336 ff.), who is then not able to offer any acceptable explanation of the reflexive dative being used in this text with quite other classes of verbs than elsewhere.

sentence-stress will be reduced to *ye* or even to the short vowel *i*, written *y*. This is especially the case in stock phrases like *thank you* (*thanky*), *God be with you* (*Good-bye*,[1] the *oo*-vowel is probably introduced from the other forms of salutation: *good-morrow, good-night*, etc., the naming of *God* being thus avoided; in Shakespeare it is also written *God buy you*), *God give you good even* (in Shakespeare *Godgigoden, Godigoden, God dig you den*). *Harky* (*hark'ee*) and *look'ee* may contain *ye*, weakened for *you* (§ 188), or the nominative *ye*. I am inclined to think that this phonetic weakening of *you* is the cause of the unstressed *ye* after verbs, which is found so very frequently from the beginning of the sixteenth century, although it is impossible in each single instance to distinguish the *ye* which originates in this way from *ye's* called forth by the other circumstances dealt with in this chapter.

199. (171) Further, we have here to take into account the elision of a final unstressed vowel before a word beginning with a vowel, which was formerly extremely common in English. As early as the thirteenth century we find in Orrm *þarrke* for *þe arrke, tunnderrgan* for *to unnderrgan*;[2] in Chaucer the phenomenon is very frequent indeed: *sitt(e) on hors, t(o) entende, m(e) endyte*, etc.;[3] in more recent

[1] Comp. Skeat, *Principles of Engl. Etymology*, i., 423.
[2] See Klüge in Paul's *Grundriss*, i., 885. Comp. also Old English contractions: *b(e)æftan, b(e)ufan, b(e)utan, n(e)habban*, etc., Sievers, *Ags. Gr.*, § 110 n.
[3] See Ten Brink, *Chaucers Sprache*, § 269.

periods too you will often find *thold* written for *the old*, and so on. In the Elizabethan period there is plenty of evidence to show that elisions of this kind were of everyday occurrence. The phonetician Hart mentions them expressly, and in his *Orthographie* (1569) he constantly writes, *e.g.*, ð*e* (the one), ð*uðer* (the other), ð' -*ius* (the use), *t' ani man* (to any man), *t' ius* (to use), *d' understand* (do understand), *tu b' aspir'd* (to be aspired; the dot as a mark of a long vowel is in Hart under the *i*), *houb' it* (how be it), ð*' ius* (they use), etc. And everybody who is at all familiar with Shakespeare or his contemporaries will know that this elision was in those times of very frequent occurrence, and was very often indicated in the old editions where the modern editors do not choose to mark it. The words *don* for *do on*, *doff* for *do off*, *dup* for *do up*, show the same tendency, and *do* is also curtailed in the formula *much good do it you*, of which the pronunciations "*muskiditti*" and "*mychgoditio*" are expressly mentioned;[1] Similarly where the following word begins with an *h*: *he has became has*, written in the old editions *has*, *h'as* or *ha's* (see, for instance, *Tw. N*., v., 178, 201, 293; *Cor*., iii., 1, 161, 162); so also *he had* became *h'had* (so

[1] See Ellis, *Early Engl. Pronunciation*, i., 165; and iii., 744. Prof. Skeat explains Shak., *Tim*., i., 2, 73, "Much good dich thy good heart," by the frequent use of this *d*(*o*)*it* before *ye* and *you*; the *t* was there naturally palatalised and assibilated, and as the phrase was taken as an unanalysed whole, the *ch* sound was introduced before *thee* as well; see *Transact. Philol. Soc*., 1885-7, p. 695.

Marlowe, *Jew*, 25); *they have* became *th' haue* (*Cor*., i., 2, 30). Now this elision seems to have disappeared from all forms of the language except (the artificially archaic language of the poets and) vulgar speech. In the Cockney Stories, *Thenks awf'lly*, I find among others the following instances:—

the: th'air, th'ether (other), th'id (head), etc. |
to: t'enlearn, t'enimels | *my*: m'arm | *so*: s'help me | *you* (ye): ee y'are (here you are), w'ere y'are (where . . .), y'observe, the mowst crool menner y'ivver see.

200. (142) It will be noticed that these phonetic tendencies cannot possibly have had any influence on the case-relations of most pronouns; weaken the vowel of *me* as you like or drop it altogether, the remaining *m'* is not brought one bit the nearer to the nom. *I*. But in the pronouns of the second person there is this peculiarity, that the cases are distinguished by the vowel only; if the vowel is left out it becomes impossible to tell whether the nominative or the accusative is meant—one more reason for the old distinction to become forgotten.

In Chaucer *thee* is elided, see *Cant. T*, *B*, 1660, *in thalighte*. In Greene's *Friar Bacon*, 12, 78, "For ere thou hast fitted all things for her state," we must certainly read *th'hast* (see also the same play, 13, 37). In countless passages, where modern editions of Shakespeare read *you're* the old folio has *y'are*, which must no doubt be interpreted *ye are*. But when we find *th'art* (for instance, *Cor*., iv., 5, 17 and 100, mod.

edd. *thou'rt*), is this to be explained as *thou art* (*thu art*) or as *thee art*? Similarly *th'hast* (mod. edd. *thou'st*), *th'hadst* (mod. edd. *thou hadst*); in *Macb.*, iv., 1, 62 (1312), "Say if th'hadst rather heare it from our mouthes," it is specially difficult to decide in favour of one or the other form on account of the peculiar constructions of *had rather* (see above, § 180).

201. (143) There is one more thing to be noticed. Where the pronouns are combined with the verbal forms commencing with *w*, those forms are preferred that contain rounded vowels. The past subjunctive of *y'are* is in Shakespeare *you're* (*Cymb.*, iii., 2, 76, "Madam, you're best consider"); the second person, corresponding to *I'le* for *I will*,[1] is not *ye'le*,[1] but *you'le* (Marlowe, *Jew*, 708), or more frequently *you'll*. Now I take it to be highly probable that these forms were heard in the spoken language at a much earlier period than they are recorded in literature, that is, at a time when *you* was not yet used as a nom., and that they are contracted not from *you were, you will*, but from *ye were, ye will* (? *ye wol*), the vowel *u* being thus a representative of the *w* of the verb.[2] If this is so,

[1] According to Al. Schmidt's *Lexicon*, *ye'le* is found only once, in the first quarto of *Love's L.*, i., 2, 54, where, however, the second quarto and the folios have *you'll*.

[2] Prof. Herm. Möller, in his review of my Danish edition, accepts this theory, and explains the phonetic connexion somewhat more explicitly than I had done. I beg leave to translate his words: "The vowel *ĕ* of *ye* combined with the following

we have here yet another reason for the confusion of *ye* and *you*, as the contracted forms *you'll* and *you're* would be felt instinctively as compounds of *you* and *will* or *were*. For *thou wert* we find *thou'rt*,[1] for *thou wilt* similarly *thou'lt* (e.g., Marl., *Jew*, 1144; often in Shakespeare, who also, though rarely, writes *thou't*).

202. (144) We have not yet finished our consideration of those phonetic peculiarities which favour the case-shifting of the pronouns of the second person. The pronouns in question were pronounced by Chaucer and his contemporaries as follows:—

nom. ðu· je·
acc.   ðe· ju·

Side by side with the long vowel forms we must suppose the existence of shortened forms whenever the pronouns were unstressed or half-stressed; we should accordingly write ðu(·) and ju(·) with wavering vowel quantity. A regular phonetic development of consonantal *u* or *w* to form the diphthong *iu*. This group of sounds (which might in those times be written *iu, iw, eu, ew, u*, etc.) was at a later period changed into *ju* (*juw*), the accent being here, as in the Norse diphthong, shifted from the first on to the second element, which was lengthened; the consonant *y* + *iu*, too, could give no other result than *ju* (*juw*), written in the case before us *you*."

[1] The Shakesperian difference between *thou*'*rt* and *th'art* (as well as that between *y'are* and *you're*) is totally obscured in modern editions, which give *thou*'*rt*, *you're* indiscriminately. It is true that *thou'rt* = *thou art* is found in the original editions of some of Shakespeare's plays. *Thou'rt* stands perhaps for *thee wert* in *Temp*, i., 2, 367, "and be quicke thou'rt best".

CASE-SHIFTINGS IN THE PRONOUNS. 259

these pronunciations would have given the following modern forms (compare mod. *cow* [kau], in Chaucerian English pronounced [ku·], etc.):—

nom. ðau, †ðu   ji· (ji)
acc. ði· (ðï)   †jau, ju

Now it will be noticed that the forms marked with a cross are no longer heard, but their former existence is directly evidenced by the works of the old phoneticians. Bullokar (*Booke at large for the Amendment of Orthographie*, 1580, and *Æsopus*, 1585) always, even when the word is emphatic, writes *thu* with a diacritical stroke under the *u*, meaning the short [u] sound; the same sign is used in *full, suffer, thumb, luck, but, us, put*, etc., all of which were then pronounced with the vowel which has been preserved in the present-day pronunciation of *full*.[1] The spelling *thu* is by no means rare in the sixteenth century; it is used consistently, for instance, by Bale. On the other hand, the following passage in Gil's *Logonomia* (1621, p. 41) shows that a pronunciation of *you* rhyming with *how* and *now* was found in his times; it should be noticed that Gil writes phonetically, that *ou* is found in his book in such words as *hou, out*, etc., and that *ü* denotes long [u] (as in Germ. *du*, or perhaps as in Mod. Engl. *do*; Ellis transcribes it *uu*):—

"Observa, primo *you*] sic scribi solere, et ab aliquibus pronunciari; at plerisque *yü*: tamen

[1] It is accordingly not correct when Ellis, iii, 902, gives Bullokar as an authority for the pronunciation [dhuu] with long *u*.

---

260 PROGRESS IN LANGUAGE.

quia hoc nondum vbique obtinuit, paulisper in medio relinquetur".[1]

It is in accord with this that in *Roister Doister* (printed 1566) *you* rhymes with *thou* (pp. 31 and 32), with *now* (pp. 15, 43, 48, 53, 60, 63 and 70), and with *inow* (p. 18).

Now the [au] form of *you* is extinct; the current pronunciation [ju·] or [juw] must be due to a natural lengthening of the originally unstressed form [ju], when it was used with stress.[2] The existence of the form [ju·] at the time of Shakespeare may be concluded from the pun in *Love's Labour*, v., 1, 60.

203. (145) In *thou*, on the other hand, it is the fuller form with [au] that is now heard solely: this

[1] On p. 44, in the scheme of pronominal forms, Gil writes *you*, but elsewhere in his phonetic transcriptions he regularly writes *yü*.

[2] Herm. Möller (*l.c.*, p. 308) explains the modern pronunciation [ju·, juw] differently; it is according to him the regular West-Saxon continuation of O. E. *eow*, in First Middle Engl. *ēw, ēu*, which became first *iu* and at last *jū*, just as O. E. *iw, eow*, Middle Engl. *ēw, ēu* becomes mod. *yew*; the lengthening of *u* in the group *iu* cannot have taken place till after the long *u* in *hūs, cū*, etc., had been diphthongised into *ou* [au]. Mod. Engl. *you* therefore is a combination of the spoken form belonging to the South-west, and the written form belonging to the North and East and denoting properly the pronunciation [jau]. Prof. Möller's explanation and mine do not exclude one another: each accounts for the rise of the prevailing pronunciation in one province, and the concurrence of the two identical though independently developed forms would contribute largely to the rejection of the pronunciation [jau].

is quite natural because the word is now never found in colloquial language, so that only the emphatic pronunciation of solemn or ceremonial speech has survived. But when the two pronouns *thou* and *you* were used *pari passu* in ordinary conversation, their sounds were alike; *you* and *thou* formed correct rhymes, exactly as *thee* and *ye* did.[1] But to the formal likeness corresponded a functional unlikeness: *you* is not the same case as *thou*, but as *thee*, and *ye* has the same case-function as *thou*. Are not these cross-associations between sound and sense likely to have exerted some influence on the mutual relations of the forms?

204. (146) This supposition becomes the more probable when it is remembered that the pronouns of the second person are different from the other pronouns in that the singular and plural are synonymous. *I* and *we* cannot be used in the same signification, except in the case of the "royal" and "editorial" *we*; but the plural *ye, you* begins very early to be used as a courteous form of addressing a single person. The use of these two manners of address in the Middle English and Early Modern English periods has been treated so exhaustively by Skeat, Abbott, Al. Schmidt, and other scholars, that I need only sum up the chief results of their investigations: The use of

[1] The feeling of *you* and *thou* as parallel forms is manifest in the rhymed dialogue in *Roister Doister*, p. 31: "I would take a gay riche husbande, and I were *you*.— In good sooth, Madge, e'en so would I, if I were *thou*."

the singular and the plural pronouns from Chaucer's times till Shakespeare's, and even till about the middle of the last century (*The Spectator*, Fielding), corresponded pretty nearly to that of the French *tu* and *vous*; but it was looser, as very frequently one person addressed the same other person now with *thou* and now with *ye*, according as the mood or the tone of the conversation changed ever so little. This will be seen in many passages quoted by the scholars just named; compare also:—

Malory, 94, "Fair lady, why haue *ye* broken my promyse, for *thow* promysest me to mete me here by none, and I maye curse *the* that euer *ye* gaf me this swerd" | Sh., 1 *H. IV.*, ii., 3, 99, "Do *ye* not loue me? Do *ye* not indeed? Well, do not then. For since *you* loue me not I will not loue my selfe. Do *you* not loue me? Nay, tell me, if *thou* speak'st in iest or no."

When matters stand thus, and when the feeling for case-distinctions is shaken in a multiplicity of ways, must not countless confusions and blendings take place in ordinary careless conversation? The speaker begins to pronounce a *ye*, but, half-way through, he falls into the more familiar manner of address, and thus he brings about the compromise *you*, which is accordingly in many instances to be considered a sort of cross between *ye* and *thou*; *you* = *y*(e) + (th)*ou*. Such blendings of two synonyms, where the resulting word consists of the beginning of one and the end of the other word, are by no means rare in language; Shakespeare has *rebuse* = *rebu*(ke) + (a)*buse* (*Shrew*, i, 2, 7), and Tennyson: *be dang'd* = *da*(mned) + (h)*anged* (*Works*, p. 618); but the nearest parallel to our case, that I know of, is the Scottish pronoun *thon* = *th*(at) + (y)*on* (see Murray, *Dial. South. Counties*, p. 186), where in two synonymous pronouns the very same two sounds are interchanged as in the case before us.[1] In *you* there are, as we have seen, many more inducements at work,[2] which all of them concur in causing the cross to be rapidly recognised and accepted by everybody.

205. (147) If I am not mistaken, then, *thou* had some share in the rise of the *you* nominative: and I find a corroboration of this theory in the fact that, as far as I know, the earliest known instances of *you* as a nominative (fifteenth century) are found in addressing single individuals. This is the case of the four certain instances pointed out by Zupitza in the *Romance of Guy of Warwick*,[3] where *you* is not yet

---

[1] An evident blending is seen in *Roister Doister*, 76, "What *sayst you* ?" In the same play I find an interesting piece of evidence of the extent to which the feeling for the cases was already weakened; the same sentence in a letter is once read aloud with *ye* (p. 51), and another time with *you* (p. 57): "to take *you* as *ye* (*you*) are".

[2] To those mentioned in the text might be added the influence of the possessive *your*, the vowel of which form would naturally favour *you* and not *ye*.

[3] Namely, ll. 4192, 7053, 7217-8 (where *thou* is used in the lines immediately preceding), and 9847. Prof. Zupitza's fifth

---

found as a nom. plural. Some of the old grammarians expressly make this distinction:—

Wallis (1653, p. 87): "Notandum item apud nos morem obtinuisse (sicut apud Gallos aliosque nunc dierum) dum quis alium alloquitur, singularem licèt, numerum tamen pluralem adhibendi; verum tunc *you* dicitur, non *yee*".

Cooper (1685, p. 122): "Pro *thou*, *thee*, et *ye* dicimus *you* in communi sermone, nisi emphaticè, fastidiosè, vel blandè dicimus *thou*".

So, p. 139:—

Sum	*es*	*est* . . .	*estis* . . .
I am	{thou art / *you* are	he is	*ye* are

206. (148) But that distinction could not remain stable; even before the utterances just quoted were written, *you* had in the spoken language found its way to the nominative plural; Latimer (1549) uses *you* in addressing those whom he has just called *ye lords*, and Shakespeare and Marlowe use *you* and *ye* indiscriminately without any distinction of case or number. If any difference is made it is that of using *you* in emphasis, and *ye* as an unstressed form (comp. above, § 197).

example seems to me to be doubtful: "Y prey yow here A [MS. And] gode councill þat *yow* lere". (l. 6352); it appears more natural to take *lere* = doceat and *yow* as the object. The four certain instances are interesting, in so far as *you* is in all of them found after the verb, cf. above, § 184 ff., in the last of them after *hyt were* and after a *but*, which may have had some influence, cf. § 158.

Marl., *Tamb.*, 3988, "*you, you, ye* slaves" | 687, "*you* will not sell it, will *ye* ?"

See also Abbott, who gives some instances of the use of *you* and *ye* being sometimes the directly opposite of the original case one, *e.g.*,

Cæs., iii, 1, 157, "I do beseech *yee*, if *you* beare me hard".

In some of the last plays Shakespeare wrote, *you* is practically the only form used,[1] and not long after his death *ye* must be considered completely extinct in spoken Standard English. But *ye* is not entirely forgotten; the Bible and the old literature keep up the memory of it, and cause it to be felt as a form belonging to a more solemn and poetic sphere than the prosaic *you*. The consequence is that many poets make constant use of *ye* in preference to *you*. While in ordinary language the paradigm is:—

nom. sg. *you.*
acc. sg. *you*
nom. pl. *you*
acc. pl. *you,*

[1] As there is a marked difference in the frequency of *ye* and *you* in Shakespeare's plays (and perhaps also in the use of the contracted forms *th'art, thou'rt,* etc.), I once thought it possible to supplement the already existing tests, metrical and others, by which the chronology of his writings is determined, with a *you*-test; but want of time prevented me from undertaking the necessary statistical investigations— which might, after all, have led to no results of any value.

[2] If Thackeray's representation of the dialect spoken by the Irish is to be trusted, *ye* seems to belong to their everyday language.

in Byron's *Cain* (to take a poetical work at random) everything is so entirely different that, to look only at this pronoun, one would scarcely believe it to be the same language :—

nom. sg. *thou*
acc. sg. *thee*
nom. pl. *ye*
acc. pl. *ye.*

You is practically non-existent in that work; I find it only on p. 252 (*Works*, ed. Tauchnitz, vol. iv.), "And *you, ye* new And scarce-born mortals," and p. 224, where it is used in the indefinite signification of the French *on*.

The old *ye* has yet another refuge, namely, in grammars, where it renders the separate plural forms of other languages, Latin *vos*, German *Ihr*, etc. If this small domain is excepted, the English seem never to feel any inconvenience from their language having the same form for the singular and the plural in this pronoun; if a separate form is now and then required for distinction's sake the want is easily remedied—after the Chinese fashion, see § 66—by the addition of some noun : *you people, you gentlemen, you girls, you chaps, you fellows,* etc.

207. (149) To return to the original singular of the second person. As an early instance of vacillation between *thou* and *thee* I shall mention :—

Chauc., *A. B. C.* (= *M. P.*, 1), 107, "O tresorere of bounte to mankynde, *The* whom God ches to moder for humblesse !"

where the *the* is probably caused by relative attraction; but one MS. has *yee*, and another *þou*.[1] The double reading *thou* (Ellesm. MS.) and *thee* in :—

Chauc., *H.*, 40, "Fy, stinking swyn, fy! foule mot *thee* falle!"

is, I take it, owing to a vacillation between the personal and impersonal constructions.

In the Elizabethan literature *thee* is not rare as a nominative, though it is on the other hand far less frequent than *you* ; we have already seen the explanation of some instances of *thee*, among others 2 *H. VI.*, i, 2, 69, "Here's none but thee and I," where *thee* is placed side by side with *I* ; *Haml.*, v., 2, 63, "Thinkst thee", and several instances of *thee* after *it is*. But these explanations do not hold good in the following quotations :—

Marlowe, *Jew*, 1056, "What hast *thee* done?" | Sh., 1 *H. IV.*, i., 2, 127, "How agrees the diuell and *thee* about thy soule, that *thou* soldest him?" | Dryden, *Poems*, ii., 220, "Scotland and *Thee* did each in other live"

[1] In some passages of the old authors *thee* and *yee* may have been confounded on account of the þ-letter, which has often been mistaken for a *y*, especially in the article (*Roister Doister*, 23, "What is *ye* matter?"). This is perhaps the explanation of Chaucer, *E.*, 508, "Ne I (ne) desyre no thing for to haue, Ne drede for to lese, saue only *ye*," where two MSS. have "*thee* vel *yee*," two *ye* and three *thee*. As Grisildis generally addresses her husband as *ye*, not *thou*, *ye* is probably the correct reading, and then the sentence comes under the category dealt with in § 159.

| Lewis Morris, *Poet. Works*, 74, "What I worship is not wholly *thee*".

208. (149) Here we have really a *thee* nominative, and this nominative is also often found where the use of the old singular pronoun is in living use, irrespective of literary or ecclesiastical tradition. Thus *thee* has ousted *thou* in most of those dialects where *you* has not become the only form used ; see, for instance, Elworthy, *Grammar of West Somerset*, p. 35; Lowsley, *Berkshire Words and Phrases*, p. 6; Mrs. Parker, *Glossary of Words used in Oxfordshire* (*E. Dial. Soc.*, c. 5 [1]). We must here also mention the Quakers (or Society of Friends) ; in the last century their usage does not seem to have been fully settled: witness the following quotations, where Quakers are introduced as speaking :—

Spectator, 132 (Aug. 1, 1711), "*Thee* and I are to part by-and-by. . . . When two such as *thee* and I meet . . . *thou* should'st rejoice" (in what follows he also sometimes says *thou*) | Fielding, *Tom Jones*, ii., 127, "Perhaps, *thou* hast lost a friend. If so,

[1] Here we read about a pronunciation "with a very obscure vowel sound"; is this a continuation of the form *thu* with short [u], mentioned above, § 201? In Mid-Yorkshire *thou* seems still to be used, even as an accusative, according to Mr. Robinson, whose words are not, however, completely clear; see *E. Dial. Soc.*, v., p. xxiii. In the dialect of Windhill in the West Riding of Yorkshire, as described by Dr. J. Wright (*E. Dial. Soc.*, 1892, p. 116), the old case-distinction is preserved, except when the pronouns are used absolutely.

thou must consider we are all mortal. And why should'st *thou* grieve when *thou* knowest. . . . I myself have my sorrow as well as *thee*."[1]

In this century the prevalence of *thee* is shown by the following statements :—[2]

H. Christmas, in Pegge's *Anecd.*, 3rd ed., 131, a Quaker rarely says, "I hope thou art well; wilt thou come and dine with me?"—but, "I hope *thee* are well; will *thee* come and dine with me?"

Gummere, *l. c.*, 285, "In point of fact, few members of the Society of Friends use *thou* in familiar speech. They use the singular in familiar speech, but . . . it is the dat.-nom. *thee*, not *thou*. . . . I have seen a familiar letter of an educated Friend, written in the early part of the eighteenth century, where the *thee* is used as nom., though any solemn passage calls out a formal *thou*. . . . The most remarkable case I ever observed was where a lady, not a Friend, extended to several visitors, who were of that sect, an invitation as follows : 'Won't *thee* all walk into this room ?'"

[1] In the same book, Squire Western also occasionally uses *thee* as a nom.; see iv, 309, "I know her better than *thee* dost".
[2] See also Abbott, *Shaksp. Gramm.*, § 205 ; Storm, *Engl. Philol.*, p. 209 (from *Uncle Tom's Cabin*); Wash. Moon, *Ecclesiast. English*, p. 170.

In Miss Muloch's *John Halifax, Gentleman*, the Friends constantly use this *thee* :—

I, 1, "*Thee* need not go into the wet" | 3, "Unless *thee* wilt go with me" | 4, "Where dost *thee* come from? Hast *thee* any parents living? How old might *thee* be? *Thee* art used to work" | 5, "*Thee* shall take my son home . . . art *thee* . . ." | 11, "*Thee* be . . . has *thou* . . . *thee*'rt" | 15, "*Thee* works . . . *thee* hast never been" | 23, "Didn't *thee* say *thee* wanted work? . . . *thee* need'st not be ashamed . . . Hast *thee* any money ?" | 24, "Canst *thee*" | 26, "Canst *thee* drive? . . . *thee* can drive the cart . . . *thee* hasn't" | 28, "*Thee* said *thee* had no money" | 49, "*Thee* doesn't,"[1] etc., etc.

209. (150) Here I end my survey of the various case-shifting agencies and of their operations. As already mentioned, it extremely often happens that in the same sentence two or more causes co-operate to make the speaker use a different case from what we should expect, or rather from what the grammar of an earlier stage of the language would require. The more frequently such concurrences occur, the greater the vitality of the new manner of using the

[1] I do not know whether the inconsistencies in the use of the different persons of the verbs must be ascribed to the authoress, or if they really occur (or occurred) in the language as actually spoken by the Quakers.

case in question. We saw in § 178 that two separate tendencies, whose effects do not appear properly till some two hundred years later, were powerful enough when co-operating to bring about a visible (that is, an audible) result. And on reading again the quotations used to illustrate the first sections of this chapter you will find that the forms in *e* supply a comparatively greater contingent than the other forms, showing thus the concurrence of the associations treated in § 193. The facts which have been brought to light will, moreover, have made it clear that with the pronouns of the second person more shifting agencies were at work than with the rest (§§ 188, 189, 193-204), the result being that the original case-relations have been completely revolutionised in these pronouns. In the case of *I* and *me*, too, some special causes of changes in the case-relations have been pointed out (§§ 192, 193); but they proved to be much less powerful than those seen in the second person, and operated besides in opposite directions, so that the same simplicity as that found in *you* was here impossible. Finally, we have seen that the invariable position of *who* before the verb has caused it to become a common case, *whom* being relegated to a very limited province which it did not properly belong to.

210. (151) There is one factor I have not taken into account, though it is nearly everywhere given as explaining the majority of case-shiftings in a great many languages,—I mean the *tendency to let the objective case prevail over the subjective case.* My reason is simply that this tendency cannot be considered as a cause of case-shiftings; it does not show us how these are called forth in the mind of the speaker; it *indicates the direction of change and the final result, but not its why and wherefore.* Nay, in English, at least, it does not even exhaustively indicate the direction of change, as will be gathered from some points in the above exposition: the nominative carries the day in the absolute construction, in *who* and in the (vulgar) combination *between you and I*; note also the change of the case used with the old impersonal verbs. Still, it must be granted that the nominative generally has the worst of it; this is a consequence of the majority of the case-shifting agencies operating in favour of the accusative; thus, while it is only the position immediately before the verb that supports the nominative, the accusative is always the most natural case in any other position; see, for instance, the treatment of *than* as a preposition.

211. (152) This will afford an explanation of the fact that wherever we see the development of special emphatic or "absolute" pronouns as opposed to conjoint pronouns (used in direct conjunction with the verb), the former will as a rule be taken from the originally oblique cases, while the nominative is restricted to some sort of unstressed affix to the verb. Such a development is not carried through in Standard English, which has formed the principal subject of our investigations. But if we turn to the dialects now existing in England, we shall find this *distinction of absolute and conjoint pronouns* made very frequently. A thorough examination of the case-relations of living dialects would present very great interest, although it would rather show the results of similar developments to those found in the literary language—with many deviations, it is true —than throw any fresh light on the agencies at work or the causes of the changes effected. These are best investigated in the literary language, because we there have materials from so many succeeding centuries that we are often enabled to discover the first germs of what living dialects would only present to us as a development brought to a definite (or preliminary) conclusion. For this reason, as well as for the obvious one that the dialects of our own days have not been so fully and reliably treated, especially with regard to syntax, as to render a satisfactory exposition possible, I shall content myself with a few remarks only on the pronouns in the dialects.

212. (153) In the dialect of the southern counties of Scotland, so admirably treated by Dr. Murray an emphatic form, originating in the old accusative, is used very much as the corresponding forms in French, *e.g., Thaim* 'at hæs, aye geates mair; *mey, aa canna gang* (moi je ne peux pas aller); *yuw* an' *mey*'ll gang ower the feild. "He gave it to you" = hey gæ *ye'd*; "he gave it to YOU" = hey gæ *yuw'd*; "he gave IT to you" = hey gæ *ye hyt*; "he gave IT to YOU" = hey gæ *yuw hyt*.

For the dialect of West Somerset, Elworthy gives no less than six series of forms, *viz.*, for the *nominative*: (1) "full" forms, used when the nominative stands before its verb with emphasis; among these forms we notice the old objective forms *dhee* and *yùe*; perhaps also *uur*, "her," if Dr. Murray is not right in considering it as the old nom. *heo*; (2) unemphatic forms used before the verb, generally the same forms as in the first series, only weakened [*ee* = ye?]; (3) interrogative enclitic forms, among which [*ees*] *us* is noticeable as being used exactly as the Shakesperian *us* in *shalls*, see above, § 186; in the third person pl. *um* = O. E. *heom* is used in the same manner; and (4) unconnected forms, all of them old accusatives, except *he* (*ee*), compare § 196, and *dhai*. Then for the *objective* case we have two series of forms: (1) the unemphatic, of which we note the second person pl. *ee* = ye and the third person sg. masc., *un, n* = O. E. *hine*, see §§ 151; and (2) emphatic or prepositional, among these *aay* concurrently with *mee*, and *wee* with *uus* (§ 196), and on the same principle also *ee* (he) and *shee*; finally *dhai. Whom* has here as well as in Scotch been completely superseded by *who*.

In the vulgar dialects of the town populations (especially of the London Cockney) the accusative has been victorious, except when the pronoun is used in immediate conjunction with the verb as its subject; a point of special interest is the use of *them* as an attribute adjective before a noun. As examples abound everywhere, I shall give only a few, of which the first and third are peculiarly instructive for the distinction of absolute and conjoint forms:—[1]

Dickens, *M. Ch.*, 352, "Don't *they* expect you then?' inquired the driver.— 'Who?' said Tom. 'Why, *them*,' returned the driver" | *Orig. Engl.*, 140, "*Him* and mother and baby and *me* could all go with him" | 123, "*Them* paddling steamers is the ones for goin'. *They* just begin to puff a bit first." Compare, however, 90, "*Them's* the two I see".

213. (154) To return to Standard English. We see that the phenomena dealt with in this chapter bear on *accidence* (*you, who*), on *syntax* (*himself* as the subject, the absolute nominative, the subject of passive verbs, etc.) and finally on *word signification* (the meaning of some of the old impersonal verbs now being changed; the old *like* = "to be pleasant," the modern *like* = "to be pleased with"). I shall here call special attention to the latent though complete change which has taken place in the grammatical construction of more than one phrase while seemingly handed down unchanged from generation to generation. I am thinking of such phrases as:—

if *you*   *like*,
if *you*   *please*,
formerly : dat. (pl.)   3rd pers. sg. subjunct.
now : nom. (sg.)   2nd pers. (sg. or pl.) indic.

See also Miss Muloch, *J. Halifax*, 207; "Let us talk of something else. Of Miss March? *She* has been greatly better all day? *She*? No, not *her* to-day."

Compare also *you were better do it*, where *you* was a dative and is now the subject in the nominative, and where simultaneously *were* has changed imperceptibly from the third person singular (*it* being understood) to the second person pl. or sg. In handing something to some one you will often say, "*Here you are!*" meaning, "Here is something for you, here is what you want". I think that this phrase too contains an old dative; and perhaps, some centuries ago, in handing only one thing, people would say, "Here you is!"[1]

214. (155) A scheme of the pronominal forms treated in the present chapter according to their values in the every-day language of the close of the nineteenth century would look something like this:—

Subject, joined to the verb:	Nominative, when not joined to the verb:	Everywhere else:
I, we	me, we	me, us
you	you	you
he, she, they	he, she, they	him, her, them
(himself, herself, themselves)	himself, herself, themselves	himself, herself, themselves
who	whom, who	who

215. If now finally we ask: Are the changes described in this chapter on the whole progressive?

[1] Another case in point is perhaps the obsolete combination with *force*; Chaucer has "no force" (*fors*) with the meaning "no matter, it does not matter": *force* is here the noun, Fr. *force*. If this was used with a dative (Sh., *Love's L*, v, 2, 440, "*you force* not to forsweare") it would look like a verb, and the next step would then be to use it as in Sh., *Lucr.*, 1021, "*I force* not argument a straw".

the answer must be an affirmative one. Although for obvious reasons (see § 64) pronouns are more apt to preserve old irregularities than other classes of words, we find instead of the old four irregular forms, *thou, thee, ye* and *you*, one form carried through uniformly; the same uniformity is, as far as case is concerned, observable in the *self*-forms as compared with the old *he self, hine self,* etc., and *who* shows almost the same indifference to cases. Then there is some progress in syntax which does not appear from the scheme just given. Many of the uncertainties in the choice of case exemplified in the early sections of the chapter are owing to a want of correspondence between the logical and grammatical categories; for instance, when a word might be logically, but not grammatically, the subject. Sometimes, also, one grammatical rule would require one case, and another equally applicable rule a different one. The inconsistency was particularly glaring where the logical (and psychological) subject was to be put in quite another case than that generally used to denote the subject; and here, with the old impersonal verbs and in the absolute construction, logic has completely conquered the old grammar. The rule which is entirely incompatible with the old state of things, that the word immediately preceding the verb is logically and grammatically the subject of the sentence, has been carried through on the whole with great consistency. And in the great facility which the English have now acquired of making the real psychological subject grammatically the subject of a passive sentence, the language has gained a decided advantage over the kindred languages, an advantage which Danish is even now struggling to acquire, in spite of the protests of the schoolmaster grammarians. Thus we see that many phenomena, which by most grammarians would be considered as more or less gross blunders or "bad grammar," but which are rather to be taken as natural reactions against the imperfections of traditional language, are really, when viewed in their historical connexion, conducive to progress in language.

CHAPTER VIII.

THE ENGLISH GROUP GENITIVE.

216. To a mind trained exclusively in Latin (or German) grammar such English constructions as "the Queen of England's power," or "he took somebody else's hat," must seem very preposterous; the word that ought to be in the genitive case (*Queen, somebody*) is put in the nominative or accusative, while in the one instance *England*, whose power is not meant, and in the other even an adverb, is put in the genitive case. Similarly, in the case of "words in apposition," where it might be expected that each would be put in the genitive, as in "King Henry the Eighth's reign," only one of them takes the genitive ending.

217. In an interesting and suggestive article, "Die genetische erklärung der sprachlichen ausdrucksformen" (*Englische Studien*, xiv, 99), H. KLINGHARDT makes an attempt to explain this as well as other peculiarities of English grammar (the passive, in "the request was complied with," "he was taken no notice of," "with one another," etc.), by the power of the accent. "In English," he says, "unstressed vowels are weaker than in German; and the distinction between stressed and unstressed syllables greater. So it is with the stressed words of a sentence in relation to the unstressed words surrounding them; the action of stress therefore reaches farther than in German; emphatic words are capable of gathering around them a greater number of weak words than in German.... The [German] pupil will now understand how easily and conveniently in English small groups of words, such as *King Henry the Eighth*, are joined together under one accent, and are inflected, put in the Saxon genitive, etc, exactly in the same manner as single words."

218. I do not think that this theory is the correct one, and I shall state my objections. In the first place, we are not told which word in the group is invested with that powerful accent that is said to keep the group together. Nothing hinders us from pronouncing a group like "King Richard the Second's reign" at one moment with strong stress on Richard (as opposed to, say, *Edward* II.) and at the next with great emphasis on the numeral (as opposed to Richard the *Third*); we may also pronounce the two words with even stress; yet in all of these cases the grammatical construction is the same. Next, if we adopt Dr. Klinghardt's theory, we must assume an historical change in English accent which seems to be supported by no other fact. And thirdly, the theory fails completely to account for the difference between the final *s* in genitives like *Queen of England's* or *sister-in-*

law's, and the *internal s* in plurals like *the queens of England* or *sisters-in-law*.

Before venturing to propose a new explanation it will be well to look somewhat closely at the historical development of the several phenomena with which we are here concerned. I shall group my examples under six heads.

I.

219. Attributive words (adjectives, articles) were in Old English and in the first period of Middle English inflected equally with the substantives to which they belonged. But as early as the beginning of the thirteenth century we find the modern construction used alongside with the old one: thus in the case of the definite article:—

Ancren Riwle, 82, "*þes* deofles bearn, *þes* deofles bles" | 84, "*þes* deofles corbin" | 142, "*tes* deofles puffes" | 188, "*tes* deofles bettles," etc. | | 210, "*iðe* deofles seruise" | 212 and 216, "*iðe* deofles kurt" | 212, "*iðe* deofles berme" | 134, "of *þe* deofles gronen," etc.

I have not examined the matter closely enough to be positive, but it seems as if the uninflected form was chiefly used after prepositions, and it is not entirely improbable that the uninflected genitive of the article originates in those cases where the article belongs as properly or more properly to the noun following than to the genitive: *in the* (devil's) *service*, or *in the devils-service*.[1] Examples of adjectives from the same text:—

402, "of *reades* monnes blod" | 110, "his moderes wop & þe oðres Maries" | 406, "*mines federes* luue" | 48, "*eueriches* limes uelunge" | 180, "*eueriches* flesches eise" | 194, "*pisses* worldes figelunge" | 198, "*pisses* hweolpes nurice" | | 94, "*euerich* ones mede" | 112, "*euerich* monnes flescsh" | 6, "efter *euch* ones manere" | 134, "efter *euerich* ones efne".

220. In Chaucer we find no single trace of an inflected genitive of any attributive adjective; the rapid disappearance of the *s* in the gen. may to a great extent be due to the analogical influence of the weak forms of the adjective, in which after the loss of the final *n* the endings were the same for the genitive as for all the other cases.

In present-day English most adjectives are placed before their nouns, and then are never inflected; an adjective put after its noun is only capable of assuming the genitive *s* in cases like *Henry the Eighth's*; it is impossible to say, for example, *the women present's opinions*. Comp. Marlowe, *Jew*, 242, "That you will needs haue *ten years* [genitive!] tribute *past*," (= the tr. of ten years past).

II.

221. Two or more **words in apposition.** Examples of the old full inflexion:—

[1] The same explanation holds good for the adj. in *A. R.*, 190, "Mor *al þe* worldes golde".

A. S. Chron., E., 853, "Æðelwulfes dohtor West Seaxna cininges" | ibid., A., 918, "Of Eadweardes cyninges anwalde" | ibid., D., 903, "Aþulf ealdorman, Ealhswyðe broðor, Eadweardes moder cynges (brother of Ealhswyðe, the mother of King Edward)" | Ælfric, Sweet's A. S. Reader, 14 b, 7, "On Herodes dagum cyninges" | ibid., 136, "Iacobes wif ðæs heahfædres" | ibid., 15, 231, "Aidanes sawle þæs halgan bisceopes" | A. R., 312, "We beoð alle Godes sunen þe kinges of heouene" | Ch., M., ii., 349 (1021), "By my modres Ceres soule".

It will be observed that the two words in apposition are frequently separated by the governing word; in the following two instances we cannot decide by the form whether the last words are in the nominative or in the genitive case, as neither of them formed the genitive in s at that period:—

A. R., 146, "Hesteres bone þe cwene" | ibid., 412, "Seinte Marie dei Magdalene".

222. But in a great many cases, where we have this word-order—and it is, indeed, the order most frequently used throughout the M. E. period [1]—there can be no doubt that the last word is put in the nominative (or common) case. The leaving out of the case-sign is rare in Old English, but extremely

[1] Cf. Zupitza's note to *Guy of Warwick*, l. 687, where many examples are collected ("on þe maydenys halfe Blanchflowe," etc.), and Kellner, *Blanchardyn*, cvii.

common in Middle English; in Modern English it is getting rarer again. The phenomenon is to be classed with those mentioned above, § 163.

A. S. Chron., E., 855, "To Karles dohtor Francna cining" | A. R., 148, "Moiseses hond, Godes prophete" | ibid., 244, "þuruh Iulianes heste þe amperur" | 352, "Ine Jesu Cristes rode, mi louerd" | Ch., Hous of F., 142, "Seys body the king" | 282, "The kinges meting Pharao" | Ch., B., 431, "Kenulphus sone, the noble king of Mercenrike" | F., 672, "The god Mercurius hous the slye" | L. G. W., 1468, "Isiphilee the shene, That whylom Thoas doghter was, the king" | Malory, 70, "By my faders soule Vtherpendragon" | 91, "Gaweyn shalle reuenge his faders deth kynge Loth" | 126, "In his wynes armes Morgan le fay" | Marl., Tamburl., 193, "In the circle of your fathers armes, The mightie Souldan of Egyptia" | Greene, Friar B., 2, 10, "To Bacon's secret cell, A friar newly stall'd in Brazennose" | Sh., 1 H. IV., ii., 4, 114, "I am not yet of Percies mind, the Hotspurre of the North, he that killes me some sixe or seauen dozen of Scots" | Matt., xiv., 3 (Auth. V.), "For Herodias' sake, his brother Philip's wife" | Wycherley (Mermaid Ser.), 24, "He has now pitched his nets for Gripe's daughter, the rich scrivener" | Tennyson, 322, "Merlin's hand, the *Mage at Arthur's court*" | Mth. Arnold, *Poems*, i., 191, "Doubtless thou fearest to meet *Balder's voice, Thy brother*, whom through folly thou didst slay".[1]

223. In Middle English the opposite word-order, with the whole genitival group before the governing word, is sometimes found; and in course of time it becomes more frequent; the genitive sign is only added to the last word. This construction is especially frequent when a proper name is preceded by a title, while it is generally avoided when the proper name is followed by a somewhat lengthy apposition. I have not thought it necessary to give many modern examples:—

O. E. *Homilies*, ii, 3, "*After ure lauerd ihesu cristes tocume*" | Ch., *L. G.*, 2247, "*King Pandiones faire doghter*" | F., 672, "*The god Mercurius hous*" | Zupitza's *Guy*, 1956, "*The dewke Segwyns cosyn*" | *ibid.*, 8706, "*The kynge Harkes lande*" | Malory, 232, "*My lady my susters name is dame Lyonesse*" | Roister, 67, "*For my friende Goodluck's sake*" | Marl., *Tamb.*, 1168, "*By Mahomet my kinsmans sepulcher*" | Thack., *P.*, i., 18, "*Miss Hunkle, of Lilybank, old Hunkle the Attorney's daughter*".

[1] Mth. Arnold, *Poems*, i., 152, we have a closely connected phenomenon, namely, the repetition of a genitive in the common case, in order to tack on to it a relative clause: "And straight he will come down to *Ocean's* strand, *Ocean* whose watery ring enfolds the world".

224. When the governing word is not expressed, the *s*-ending is—or was—often added to the first noun exclusively; Lindley Murray says (*Grammar*, 8th edit, p. 262) that of the three forms, "I left the parcel at Smith's, the bookseller": or "at Smith, the bookseller's": or "at Smith's, the bookseller's,"—the first is most agreeable to the English idiom; and if the addition consists of two or more nouns, the case seems to be less dubious; as, "I left the parcel at Smith's, the bookseller and stationer". This does not now apply to a group consisting of a title and a proper name, as it did formerly, witness the first two of the following quotations, which would in modern speech be *King Alexander's* and *Admiral Presane's*. Even the last example does not seem to be now very natural; and custom is perhaps more and more in favour of saying "at Smith, the bookseller's," or "at Smith's, the bookseller's," unless "the bookseller" is only part of a phrase, *e.g.*, "at Smith's, the bookseller in Trinity Street". At least, this is the opinion of Mr. G. C. Moore Smith.

Guy of Warw., 7921, "Hyt [the helme] was *Alysaundurs the kynge*" | *ibid.*, 8714, "Hyt [the cuntre] ys *admyrals Presane*" | Sh., *H. V.*, i., 2, 105, "Inuoke his warlike spirit, and *your great vnckles, Edward the Black Prince*" | | Thack., *P.*, i., 259, "He managed to run up a fine bill *at Nine's, the livery stablekeeper*" | *ibid.*, ii, 199, "I remember *at poor Rawdon Crawley's*, Sir Pitt Crawley's "brother" | Beaconsf., *Loth.*, 16, "Villas like my cousin's, the Duke of Luton".

225. When **one of the words in apposition is a personal pronoun** a special difficulty arises from the genitive proper being here replaced by a possessive pronoun. What is the genitive of "we, the tribunes"? It would be a little awkward to say "our, the tribunes' power," and so most people would probably say with Shakespeare (*Cor.*, iii, 3, 100), "the power of vs the tribunes".

The want of a comprehensive genitive is most frequently felt when *all* or *both* is subjoined to *we, you,* or *they*. Here O. E. had a fully inflected form, *heora begra* lufu, "the love of them both"; *heora begra* eagan, "the eyes of them both" (in M. E. often with the gen. form, *bather, bother*), *ealra ura*. A few examples will show this combination in M. E.:—

Lay., 5283 (quoted by Koch, ii., 240), "Heore beire nome ich þe wulle telle" | *Leg. St. Kath.,* 1790, "Hare baðre luue" | Perc., 31, "At the *botheres* wille" | *A. R.,* 52, "Eue vre alre moder" | Ch., *A.*, 799, "At *our aller* cost" | *ibid.,* 823, "Up roos our hoste, and was *our aller* cok" | *M. P.,* i., 84, "*Oure alder* foo" | *L. G. W.,* 298, "*Our alder* pris" | Mal., 134, "Kynge Arthur, *our alther* liege lord" | James I, King's Q., "ȝoure *alleris* frende" (in NED, *all* D. ii., 4, cf. *ibid., both* 4 b, and see also Mätzner, *Wb.,* "*all* a 4, and *beȝen*").

Note the excrescent *-es* in *botheres* and *alleris*, showing that the value of the old genitive ending had been forgotten. In a few cases we find the common gen. ending added to *both*.:—

Ch., *M. P.*, 1, 83, "But, for *your bothes* peynes, I you preye" | Mal., 98, "To *our bothes* destruction"; but in the great majority of cases *both* and *all* are used without any ending; the possessive is generally placed after the adjective, but the two first examples will show the opposite order:—

Ch., *B.*, 221, "Diversitee bitwene *her bothe* lawes" | *M. P.,* 4, 52, "by *her bothe* assent" | Mal., 71, "*Both her* swerdys met euen to gyders" | 79, "I haue *both their* hedes" | 151, "Layd the naked swerd ouerthwart *bothe their* throtes" | *Roister*, 31, "To *both our* heartes ease" | Marl., *Tamb.*, 4644, "*Both their* worths" | Greene, *F. B.*, 8, 110, "*Both our* carcases" | Sh., *W. T.*, v., 3, 147, "*Both your* pardons" | *R. II.*, iii., 3, 107, "By the royalties of *both your* bloods" | *Cor.*, i., 6, 8, "*Both our* powers" | *ibid.*, iii., 1, 103, "*Both your* voices" | *R. III.*, i., 2, 191, "To *both their* deaths" | *T. S.*, v., 2, 15, "For *both our* sakes" | Milton, *P. L.*, vi., 170, "As *both their* deeds compared this day shall prove" | Thack., *V. F.*, 258, "*Both their* husbands were safe" | *ibid.*, 507, "*Both their* lives" | *Pend.*, i., 304, "That warmth belonged to *both their* natures" | R. Browning, iii., 306, "For *both their* sakes".

226. It will be noticed that in most cases it is perfectly immaterial to the meaning of the passage whether we take *both* as qualifying the pronoun or the following substantive, as each of us has only one head, one throat, one life, etc. But in other instances the same consideration does not hold good; when we read, for instance, in *John Halifax, Gent*, ii, 76, "the name set *both our thoughts* anxiously wandering," the meaning cannot be that each of them had only got one wandering thought, so that *both* must certainly here be taken as a genitive case. But the tendency goes undoubtedly in the direction of taking *both* as a nominative, the construction being avoided whenever that would be obviously impossible: I suppose it would be fruitless to search through the whole of the English literature for a connexion like "*both our four eyes*," although, indeed, Fielding writes (*Tom Jones*, iii, 45): "*Both their several talents* were excessive" (each had several talents); compare *ibid*., iii, 66, "The two ladies who were riding side by side, looking steadfastly at each other; at the same moment *both their eyes* became fixed; both their horses stopt," etc.

On the other hand, "the sb. often improperly took the plural form by attraction of the pronoun;[1] this idiom is still in vulgar use, as 'It is *both your faults*,' 'she is *both their mothers*'" (Murray, *N.E.D.*). This I take to be the reason of the pl. *hopes* in Marl., *Jew*, 879, "He loues my daughter, and she holds him dear. But I have sworn to frustrate *both their hopes*." (They have one and the same hope.) So also in :—

Sh., *All's*, i., 3, 169, "You are my mother, Madam; would you were (So that my Lord your sonne were not my brother) indeed my mother, or were you *both our mothers* ..." | *Ro*., ii, 3, 51, "*Both our remedies* Within thy helpe and holy physicke lies (note the sg. of the verb) | Fielding, *T.J.*, iii, 82, "It was visible enough from *both our behaviours*."[1]

Examples of the group genitive with *all* preceding a possessive pronoun :—

[1] The same sort of attraction may occasionally be found where there is no such word as *both* to assist in occasioning it; see Thack., *Ballads*, 80, "The ladies took the hint, And all day were scraping lint, As became their softer *genders*".

[1] Mr. G. C. Moore Smith criticises the view expressed in the text, writing as follows : "I think you are right on 'both your faults'. But in 'both our mothers' and 'both their hopes' I think the notion is plural, as well as the expression. She is—both our—mothers. That is, the mind conceives the two persons for a moment as having each a mother (or a hope of his own)—and then identifies these mothers and hopes. Even if you and I hope for the same end, there are two hopes. If you lost yours, I might keep mine. Of course it may be true, as you say, that the use of the plural is due to attraction from *both*: still it carries with it a sense of plurality, which is present to the speaker's mind. So with 'genders'=as became the sex of each one, sex being looked on as an individual attribute like her name."

Ch., *M. P.*, 5, 618, "I have herd *al youre* opinion" | *F.*, 396, "*Alle her* hertes" | *B.*, 4562, "Hir housbondes losten *alle hir* lyves" | Mal., 134, "*All their* harneis" | Marl., *Tamb.*, 1877, "*All our* bloods" | Sh., *Cor.*, iv., 6, 35, "*All our* lamentation" | Sheridan, *Dr. W.*, 68, "Tell her 'tis *all our* ways" | Dick., *M. Ch.*, 400, "For *all our* sakes" | Stevenson, *Tr. Isl.*, 283, "It went to *all our* hearts" | Hood, "He had drunk up all the stout to *all their* very good healths" | G. Eliot, *Mill*, ii., 210, "All their hearts are set on Tom's getting back the mill".

227. As the subject of the action expressed by a verbal noun in *-ing* is sometimes put in the genitive (I insist on *your* coming) and sometimes in the common case (I insist on *all* coming), a possibility arises of combining these two expressions; note the different ways in which this is done in the following examples:—

Sheridan, "I insist on *your all* meeting me here" | *ibid.*, *Dram. Works*, 56, "The confusion that might arise from *our both* addressing the same lady" | Fielding, *T. J.*, iii, 71, "It cannot be wondered at that *their* retiring *all* to sleep at so unusual an hour should excite his curiosity" | Dick., quoted by Koch, "*Our all three* coming together was a thing to talk about" | Beaconsf., *Lothair*, 435, "I fancy the famous luncheons at Crecy House will always go on, and be a popular mode of *their all* meeting";

where, perhaps, *of all of them meeting* (or: for them all to meet) would be preferable; but note that the order of the words *all their*, ordinary as it is in other cases, is here inadmissible.

228. Here I finally quote some passages where *of* is used to avoid *all our*:—

Ch., *G.*, 192, "Iesu Crist, herde *of vs alle*" | Malory, 84, "The names *of them bothe*" | Greene, *F. B.*, 10, 17, "The liking fancy *of you both*" | *ibid.*, 10, 25, "To avoid displeasure *of you both*" | Thack., *P.*, ii., 215, "The happiest fortnight in the lives *of both of them*" | *ibid.*, 220, "The characters *of both of you* will be discussed" | *ibid.*, 329, 337, etc. | *Frank Fairl.*, i., 337, "She was the life and soul *of us all*" | Troll., *Duke's Ch.*, i., 254, "For the happiness *of them all*".

For the genitive of *both of you*, *some of you*, etc., cf. below, § 232.

229. For the genitive of *we two*, etc., I am able to give four quotations: showing, first, the old genitive of *two*; then the unchanged form; thirdly, the rare *s*-gen.; and finally an evasion of the difficulty by an appositional construction:—

A. R., 406, "I *pisse tweire* monglunge" | Mal., 110, "What be *your ii* names?" | Bullokar, *Æsop*, 90, "*Our twoos chanc*" | Miss Muloch, *Halifax*, ii., 209, "You must let me go . . .

anywhere—out of *their* sight—*those two*" (= out of the sight of those two).

III.

230. Two nouns are **connected by a preposition,** e.g., *father-in-law*, *the Queen of England.* In old times such word-groups were not felt as inseparable units, as they are now ; witness Chaucer, *B.*, 3870, "Ageyn Pompeius, *fader* thyn *in lawe*". Consequently, when they were to be used in the genitive, they were separated by the governing word; this was the universal practice up to the end of the fifteenth century.

Ch., *B.*, 3442, "of *kinges* blood *Of Perse* is she descended" | *B.*, 3846, "*Philippes* sone *of Macedoyne*" | *E.*, 1170, "for the *wynes* loue *of Bathe*" | *M.*, iv, 108, "That was the *kynge Priamus* sone *of Troye*" | Malory, 45, "The *dukes* wyf *of Tyntagail*" | 127, "I am the *lordes* doughter *of this castel*" | 141, "The *kynges* sone *of Ireland*," etc.

The same construction is resorted to even in more recent times whenever the ordinary construction would present special difficulties. It is possible to denote a lady as "she in the cap," but how about the genitive case of such a group? Shakespeare says : "*What's her name in the cap?*" (*L.L.L.*, ii, 209)—"For *honour of former deeds*' sake", would be rather heavy ; so Milton puts it (*Sams. Ag.*, 372). "For *honour's* sake *of former deeds*". Compare also Sh., 1 *H.IV.*, iii, 2,

119, "*The Archbishops* grace *of York*" = the Archbishop of York's grace = his Grace the Archbishop of York.

231. But as early as Chaucer we find occasional traces of the modern construction creeping in : at least, I venture to interpret the following passages as containing it:—

M.P., 3, 168, "Morpheus, and Eclympasteyre, That was *the god of slepes* heyre" (heir of the god of sleep) | *Hous of Fame*, 399, "Ovide, That hath ysowen wonder wide *The grete god of loves* name" (one MS. has "the god of loue bys") | *L.G.W.*, 206, "For *deyntee of the newe someres* sake I bad hem strawen floures on my bed".[1]

From the Elizabethan period the modern usage may be considered as settled and universal ; Ben Jonson mentions in his *Grammar* (printed 1640, p. 72) the construction "for the *Duke's* men of *Mysia*" as existing beside that of "*the Duke of Mysia's* men"; but this may be the ordinary conservatism of grammarians, for the former construction seems to be practically never used at that time; in Wallis's *Gramm. Lingua Anglicana*, 1653, p. 81, the only form mentioned is "*The King of Spain's Court*". I add here a few examples from the three last

---

[1] In Malory, 108, I find, "My name is Gauayne, the kyng Lott of Orkeney sone"; *s* seems here left out by a misprint (Lots ? Orkeneys ?); immediately after that passage the ordinary way of putting it is found : "Kyng Lots sone of Orkeney".

centuries to show the extent of the use of the modern construction:—

Marl., *Tamb*, 645, "*The King of Perseas* crowne" | *ibid*, 3298, "Blood is *the God of Wars* rich liuery" | Sh., *R. III.*, i., 4, 131, "*The Duke of Glousters* purse" | Swift, *Gull*, 133, "To any village or *person of quality's* house" | Field., *T. J.*, iv, 291, "Signed with the *son of a whore's* own name" | Thc., *P.*, i., 20, "Mrs. Wapshot, *as a doctor of divinity's* lady" | *ibid.*, i., 164, "*The member of Parliament's* lady" | Carlyle, *Her.*, 2, "A man's religion is the chief fact with regard to him. A man's or *a nation of men's*" | *ibid.*, 87, "*The man of business's* faculty" | Pattison, *Milton*, 44, "Agar, who was in *the Clerk of the Crown's* office" | G. Eliot, *Life and L.*, ii., 190, "I had *a quarter of an hour's* chat with him" | Ruskin, *Select.*, i., 133, "In some *quarter of a mile's* walk" | Co. Doyle, *Study in Sc.*, 88, "I endeavoured to get *a couple of hours'* sleep" | Christina Rossetti, *Verses*, "Lo, *the King of Kings'* daughter, a high princess".

Sometimes, but very rarely indeed, an ambiguity may arise from this sort of construction, as in the well-known puzzle: "The son of Pharaoh's daughter was the daughter of Pharaoh's son".

In ordinary language the construction is found only with the preposition *of* and in the words *son-in-*

law,[1] etc., so also *the Commander-in-Chief's* levees (Thack., *Esmond*, i., 345) and perhaps: "for *God in Heaven's* sake". But in dialects it is used with other prepositions as well; Murray gives as Scotch (*Dial of the Southern Counties*, p. 166): "*the màn-wui-the-quheyte-cuot's* horse"; and Elworthy quotes from Somersetshire (*Gramm. of the Dial. of W. Soms.*, p. 157): *Jan Snèok wvt tu Langvurds duung kee*, "John Snook out of Langford's donkey"; *Mr. Buurj tu Shoaldur u Muutuns paig*, "Mr. Bridge of the Shoulder of Mutton's pig".

232. What is the genitive of *some of them, any of you, one of us*? There is some difficulty here, and the reason of it is the same as we met with before, *viz.*, the difference between a genitive proper and a possessive pronoun, cf. § 225. In olden days, when a partitive relation could be expressed by the gen. pl., we occasionally find formations like these: *A. R.*, 204, "*hore summes nome*" (the name of some of them), where the genitive ending is tacked on to the nom., or Orrm, l. 2506, "& all onn ann wise fell till *eȝþer peȝȝress* herrte" (to the heart of either of them), where it is added to the old gen. pl.

From more recent times, where the partitive relation has to be expressed by *of*, I have noted the

---

[1] It is curious to note that the gen. pl. of these words, *son-in-law, daughter-in-law*, etc., is avoided, although it would be one of the few instances in which there would be three different forms for the gen. sg., nom. pl. and gen. pl.: "I know all my *sons-in-law's* friends".

following instances of the possessive pronoun being used where the genitive belongs properly to the whole combination; it will be noticed that in most, though not in all cases, it does not affect the meaning of the clause whether we take the adjective, etc., as referring to the genitive or to the governing word (for "some of the men's heads" means either "some of the heads of the men", or "the heads of some of the men") :—

Malory, 79, "I maye not graunte *neyther of her hedes*" | Sh., *Tw. N.*, iii, 4, 184, "God haue mercie vpon *one of our* soules" (the soul of one of us) | *R. II.*, i., 3, 194, "Had the king permitted vs, *One of our* soules had wandred in the ayre" | 2 *H. IV.*, ii., 4, 16, "They will put on *two of our* ierkins" (the jerkins of two of us) | *T. S.*, v., 2, 171, "My mind has been as big as *one of yours*" (as that of one of you) | Drayton, *Love's Farewell*, "Be it not seen in *either of our* brows That we one jot of former love retain" | Moore, *Ir. Mel.*, "(And doth not a meeting like this) Though haply o'er *some of your* brows, as o'er mine, The snowfall of time may be stealing" | Black, *Fortunatus*, i., 183, "The hopeless resignation that had settled on *some of their* faces" | Thack, *P.*, iii, 383, "A painful circumstance which is attributable to *none of our* faults" (to the fault of none of us) | Co. Doyle, *Study in Sc.*, 141, "Without meaning to hurt *either of your* feelings" | T. Hughes, *T. Brown's Schoold*, 118, "I'm taking the trouble of writing this true history for *all of your* benefits" | Jerrold, *Caudle*, 17, "The brandy you've poured down *both of your* throats" | Stevenson, *Catriona*, 29, "For *all of our* sakes".

Dr. Murray once told me that it would be possible for a Scotchman to add the *s* to the whole of such a combination ("Is this *ony of you's?*"), and that you might even, though rarely, in colloquial English hear "This must be *some of you's*". I have some suspicion that this construction is a little less rare in colloquial language when there is a word added in apposition to *you*: "Is this *any of you children's?*"

IV.

233. In the case of a word **defined by a following adverb**, the old practice was to add the *s* of the genitive to the former word, and this may be found even in our times, especially when there is no governing word immediately following:—

Latroon, *Engl. Rogue*, 1665, i., 53, "I should devote myself to her service, and *nones else*" | Thack, *P.*, i., 79, "They were more in Pendennis's way than in *anybody's else*" | Mark Twain, *Mississ*, 236, "The entire turmoil had been on Lem's account and *nobody's else*".

But in most cases the *s* is tacked on to the end of the whole group:—

"I took *somebody else's* hat" | Dick., *M. Ch.*, 372, "*Everybody else's* rights are my wrongs" | Thack., *V.F.*, 244. "On a day when *everybody else's* countenance wore the appearance of the deepest anxiety" | *Pend.*, i., 41, "Women are always sacrificing themselves or somebody for *somebody else's* sake" | *ibid.*, 304, "*Somebody else's* name" | G. Eliot, *Mill*, ii., 13, "*Somebody else's* tradesman is in pocket by somebody else" | *Fortn. Rev.*, Sept., 1877, 355, "Credulity is belief in *somebody else's* nonsense" | Ibsen, *Master Builder*, tr. by Gosse and Archer, 51, "Yes, *who else's* daughter should I be?"

Instead of the last mentioned form, some people would perhaps prefer "*whose else*"; Dr. Murray told me he would say "*who else's* baby," but "*whose else*" when the substantive was understood. In the following quotations both the pronoun and the adverb are inflected:—

Dick., *Christm. Books*, 59 (*Chr. Carol*), "Don't drop that oil upon the blankets, now". '*His* blankets?' asked Joe. '*Whose else's* do you think?'" | Sketchley, *Cleopatra's Needle*, 27 (vulg.), "As if it was easy for any one to find their own needle, let alone *any one's elses*".

The only adverb besides *else* where the same construction might be expected is *ever*,[1] but the genitive of *whoever* seems generally to be avoided. Mrs. Parr, however, writes (in a short story, *Peter Trotman*):—

"The lovely creatures in my imagination took the form of the Matilda, Julia, Fanny, or *whoever's* image at that moment filled my breast".

But some English friends have corroborated my conjecture that it would be more natural to say, *e.g.*, "It doesn't matter *whose ever* it is," than "*whoever's*," which would indeed, according to some, be impossible in this connexion; and if the elements of the word are separated, *who* of course is inflected, as in Sh., *R. III.*, iv., 4, 224, "*whose* hand *soever*".

V.

234. When one word should properly govern two or more genitives, connected by *and* or some other **conjunction**, it makes some difference whether the governing word is placed after the first or after the last of the genitives.

The former was the usual word-order in O. E., and

[1] In answer to my question: "Is the *s*-genitive of words formed like *a looker-on* ever used?" Mr. Moore Smith writes to me: "It would be possible to say, 'You've got the *chucker-out's* place,' but not 'the chucker's-out place' (*chucker-out* is slang for a man employed to turn noisy people out of a meeting); 'This is the *whipper-in's* chair'. Especially when the connexion is very close."

may still be used, especially when two distinct objects are denoted, while it is rare if the same object is meant, as in the *David Grieve* example below:—

Oros., 18, 18, "þæm sciprapum þe beoð of *hwæles* hyde geworht & of *seoles*" | *Chron. A.*, 888, "*Westseaxna* ælmessan & *Ælfredes cyninges*" | *ibid.*, 901, "Butan ðæs *cyninges* leafe & his *witena*" | Ch., *L. G. W.*, 1086, "Be ye nat *Venus* sone and *Anchises?*" | Thack., *P.*, i., 16, "*Little Arthur's* figure and *his mother's*" | *ibid.*, 159, "The empty goblets and now useless teaspoons which had served to hold and mix *the captain's* liquor and *his friend's*" | *ibid.*, 217, "Affecting *Miss Costigan's* honour and *his own*" | Mrs. Humphrey Ward, *D. Grieve*, iii, 65, "In spite of *her* friendship and *Ancrum's*".

235. As the arrangement of the words is analogous to that mentioned above, § 221 (of *Herodes dagum cyninges*), we cannot wonder at finding here again in M. E. a dropping of the genitive ending in the last word, parallel to that in "*Iuliānes heste the amperūr*". Prof. Zupitza quotes the following instances in his edit. of *Guy of Warwick* (note to l. 688): "*kyngys* doghtur and *emperowre*" (= a king and emperor's daughter); "*dewkys* doghtur and *emperowre*; for *Gyes* sowle and for *hys wyfe*" (for Guy's soul and for that of his wife). From more recent times I have noted the following passages:—

Marl., *Jew*, 278, "How, my Lord! my mony?

Thine and the rest" (= that of the rest) | Sh., *Lear*, iii, 6, 101, "*His* life with *thine, and all that* offer to defend him" (= and that of all) | *L. L. L.*, v., 2, 514, "Tis some policie To have one shew worse then the *kings and his companie*" | Byron, iv, 214, "*Thy sire's Maker, and the earth's. And heaven's and all that in them is*" | Troll., *Duke's Ch.*, i., 82, "It is simply self-protection then? *His own and his class*" (protection of himself and of his class) | Tennyson, *Foresters*, 43, "My mother, for *whose sake and the blessed Queen of heaven* I reverence all women".

236. Very nearly akin to these cases are other cases of leaving out the *s* of the last of two or more genitives; the governing word is here also understood from the first genitive; but this is farther off from the genitive without *s* than in the previous examples. Accordingly, there is more danger of ambiguity, and the construction is, therefore, now avoided. It is found in M. E.:—

Ch, *A.*, 590, "His top was dokked lyk a preest biforn" (like that of a p.) | *Guy of Warw.*, 8054, "Hys necke he made lyke no man".

Al. Schmidt has collected a good many examples of this phenomenon from Shakespeare. He considers it, however, as a rhetorical figure rather than a point of grammar; thus he writes (*Sh. Lex.*, p. 1423): "Shakespeare very frequently uses the name of a person or thing itself for a single particular quality or point of view to be considered, in a manner which has seduced great part of his editors into needless conjectures and emendations". I pick out some of his quotations, and add a few more from my own collections:—

Sh., *Pilgr.*, 198, "*Her* lays were tuned like *the lark*" (like the lays of the lark) | *W. T.*, i., 2, 169, "He makes a *July's* day short as *December*" (as a December's day) | *2 H. VI.*, iv., 2, 29, "*Iniquity's* throat cut like *a calf*" | *John*, iii., 486, "*Her* dowry shall weigh equal with *a queen*" | *2 H. VI.*, iii., 2, 318, "*Mine* hair be fixed on end as *one distract*" | *Cor.*, i., 6, 27, "I know the sound of *Marcius'* tongue from *every meaner man*" | *ibid.*, iii., 2, 114, "My throat of war be turned into a pipe small as *an eunuch*" | Greene, *Friar B.*, 3, 36, "Whence are you, sir ? of Suffolk ? for *your* terms are finer than *the common sort of men*" | *ibid.*, 12, 47, "*Her* beauty passing Mars's *paramour*",[1]

237. We now come to the second possible word-order, *viz.*, that of placing the governing word after all the genitives belonging to it. In most cases the genitive ending is added to each of the genitives:

"She came with Tom's and John's children"; but, as a matter of fact, the *s* not unfrequently is added to the last word only, so that we have the formula $(a + b) \times$ instead of $ax + bx$. The earliest instance I know of is that recorded by Prof. Zupitza, *Guy*, 7715, "For *syr Gye and Harrowdes* sake". From more recent times:—

Malory, 37, "It shal be your *worship & the childis* auaille" | Marlowe, *Tamb.*, 3901, "*My lord and husbands* death" | *ibid.*, 4123, "Is not my life and state as deere to me, *The citie and my natiue countries* weale, As any thing of price with thy conceit ?" (doubtful) | Sh., *Mcb*, v., 7, 16, "*My wife and childrens* ghosts will haunt me still" | *R. II.*, iii., 62, "All *my treasurie* . . . shall be *your loue and labours* recompence" | *Cor.*, v., 3, 118, "*Thy wife and childrens* blood" | *Merch.*, iii., 4, 30, "Vntill *her husband and my lords* returne" | *H. VIII.*, ii., 3, 16, "Sufferance, panging As *soule and bodies* seuering" | *Sonn.*, 21, "*Earth and seas* rich gems" | Milt., *S. A.*, 181, "From *Eshtaol and Zora's* fruitful vale" | *Spectator*, No. 36, p. 60, "A widow gentlewoman, well born both by *father and mother's* side" | "A *ship and a half's* length" | "An *hour and a half's* talk" | Darwin, *Life and L.*, i., 144, "The difference he felt between *a quarter of an hour and ten minutes'* work" | S. Grand, *Twins*, 65,

---

[1] In combinations such as "his capacity as a judge", we have a somewhat similar phenomenon, in so far as the common case "a judge" is referred to the genitive "his"; there is, however, the important difference that "a judge" does not stand for a genitive and cannot be replaced by "a judge's".

"Till the bride and bridegroom's return" | Thack, *V. F.*, 169, "The rain drove into the bride and bridegroom's faces" | *ibid.*, 530, "One of the *Prince and Princess Polonia's* splendid evening entertainments" | "The Prince and Princess of Wales's pets" | G. Eliot, *Mill*, ii, 255, "In aunt and uncle Glegg's presence" | Thack., *P*, i., 242, "Mr. and Lady Poker requested the pleasure of *Major Pendennis and Mr. Arthur Pendennis's* company" | Browning, i., 118, "To *pastor and flock's* contention" | T. Brown's *Sch.*, "The *carpenter and wheelwright's* shop" | Waugh Tennyson, 91, "In Sir *Theodore Martin and Professor Aytoun's* 'Bon Gaultier Ballads'".

In the following quotation the *ands* are left out:—
Byron, *Ch. Har.*, iv, 18, "And *Otway, Radcliffe, Schiller, Shakespeare's* art".

Examples with *or* and *nor* (in the last one we have both *or* and *and*) :—
Ch., *G.*, 812, "Cley maad with *hors or mannes heer*" (perhaps doubtful) | Sh., *Cor.*, v., 3, 130, "Nor *childe nor womans* face" | Byron, *Mazeppa*, 5, "Of *vassal or of knight's* degree" | Thack., *V. F.*, 360, "When I see *A. B. or W. T.'s* insufficient acts of repentance" | Darwin, *L. and L.*, ii, 41, "In a *year or two's* time" | Mrs. Ward, *R. Elsm.*, i., 215, "Returning for *an hour or two's*

rest" | *ibid.*, ii, 287, "In a *week or ten days'* time" | Stedman, *Oxford*, 190, "If only *an hour or an hour and a half's* work is left till after lunch".

In view of all these examples, it will not be easy to lay down fully definite and comprehensive rules for determining in which cases the group genitive is allowable and in which the *s* has to be affixed to each member; the group construction is, of course, easiest when one and the same name is common to two persons mentioned (*Mr. and Mrs. Brown's* compliments), or when the names form an inseparable group (*Beaumont and Fletcher's* plays; *Macmillan & Co.'s* publications). On the whole, the tendency is towards using the group genitive, wherever no ambiguity is caused by it.

238. With personal (*i.e.*, where the genitive case is spoken of, possessive pronouns) no such group inflexion is possible; but some difficulty arises from the difference between conjoint pronouns like *my* and absolute pronouns like *mine*. I give the sentences I have collected without any commentary:—

a.—(*A. R.*, 406, "Min and mines federes luue") | Sh., *Cor.*, v., 6, 4, "In *theirs* and in the commons eares" | *Tp.*, ii., 1, 253, "In *yours* and my discharge" | *Haml.*, v., 2, 341, "*Mine*[1] and my father's death come not vpon thee" | Milt., *Sams.*, 808, "*Mine* and

[1] Of course *mine* may here and in *Ado*, v., 1, 249, be the old conjoint form before a vowel; so also *thine*, *Cor.*, i., 3, 25.

love's prisoner" | Browning, iii., 36, "*Mine* and her souls" | Thack., *Esmond*, ii., 144, "He was intended to represent *yours* and her very humble servant" | Darwin, *Life and L.*, ii., 308, "Without Lyell's, *yours*, Huxley's, and Carpenter's aid".

b.—Carlyle, *S. R.*, 71, "To cut *your* and each other's throat" | *ibid.*, *Heroes*, 4, "*Our* and all men's sole duty" | G. Eliot, *Life*, iii., 112, "I enter into *your* and Cara's furniture-adjusting labours" | *ibid.*, iv., 18, "I received *your* and your husband's valued letters" | *ibid.*, 167, "I had heard of *your* and the professor's well-being" | *ibid.*, 266, "With a sense of *your* and Emily's trouble" | Sharp, *Browning*, 143, "On the eve of *her* and her aunt's departure" | Hales, *Longer E. Poems*, 289, "One of *their* and Pope's friends".

c.—Carl., *Heroes*, 97, "Turn away *your own* and others' face" | Thack., *P.*, ii., 103, "Trifle with *your own* and others' hearts" | *ibid.*, iii., 34, "I will not forget *my own* or her honour".

d.—Ch., *G.*, 1129, "In *your* purs or *myn*" | Mal., 92, "That knyȝte *your* enemy and *myn*" | Marl., *Jew*, 969, "For *your* sake and *his*

owne" | Thack., *P.*, ii., 229, "As becomes one of *your* name and *my own*" | G. Eliot, *Mill*, ii., 324, "I measured *your* love and *his* by my own".

e.—Ch., *M.*, iii., 194, "The wille of *me and of my wyf*" | Thack., *V. F.*, 372, "For the expenses *of herself and her little boy*" | Mrs. Ward, *R. Elsm.*, ii., 297, "The shortest way to the pockets *of you and me*" | Hardy, *Tess*, 411, "For the sake *of me and my husband*".

VI.

239. Finally the genitive ending may be added to **a relative clause.** Dr. Sweet, in his *New Engl. Gr.*, § 1017, mentions as an example of group-inflexion, "*the man I saw yesterday's* son,"[1] "in which the genitive ending is added to an indeclinable adverb, inflecting really the whole group, *the-man-I-saw-yesterday*". But this is generally avoided, at least in literary language; the only example I have met with in print is from the jocular undergraduate language of *Cambridge Trifles* (London, 1881), p. 140:— "It [a brick] went into *the man who keeps below me*'s saucepan".

In English dialects the phenomenon seems to be very widely spread; thus in Scotland (Murray, p.

[1] In his *Words, Logic, and Grammar*, p. 24, "*the man I saw yesterday at the theatre's father*".

166). "*The-màn-ăt-ye-mæt-yesterday's dowchter*"; in Cheshire (Darlington, *E. D. S.*, xxi, p. 55). "I've just seen *Jim Dutton, him as went to 'Meriky's weife*," = the wife of J. D, the man who went to America; in Somersetshire (Elworthy, *Gr.*, 15). "That's *the woman what was left behind's child*," *i.e.*, that is the child belonging to the woman who was left behind.

240. After thus passing in review all the different kinds of group genitives,[1] it remains for us to find an explanation that will account for all the facts mentioned. It is obvious that the reason of our phenomenon might

[1] In Danish the group genitive is of very frequent occurrence in nearly the same cases where it is found in English (*kongen af Danmarks magt, Adam og Evas börn*, etc.). In literary Swedish "*kungens af Sverge makt*," etc., is written, but the spoken language prefers "*kungen af Sverges makt*". In German only very slight traces of the group genitive are found, even such names as *Wolfram von Eschenbach* being not inflected collectively ("die gedichte Wolframs von Eschenbach"). Still in modern family names, where the combination of *von* and a name is not felt as indicating birth-place or estate, the *s* is often, though not exclusively, tacked on to the latter name; Steinthal, for instance, on one title-page writes: "Die Sprachwissenschaft W. v. Humboldt's und die Hegelsche Philosophie"; but on another, "Die Sprachphilosophischen Werke Wilhelm's von Humboldt". According to Grimm (*Deutsche Gramm.*, ii., 960) the lower classes will sometimes say "des kaiser-von-Oestreich's armee," instead of "des kaisers von Oestreich armee," but it is "rare and ignoble".

be sought either in the nature of the compound group, or in that of the ending and its function.

It might perhaps be urged that the phenomenon was due to the natural instinct taking *the Queen of England* or *King Henry the Eighth* as one inseparable whole, that would allow of no case-ending separating its several elements. The case would then be a parallel to the German treatment of those word-groups which, like *sack und pack, grund und boden*, have been fused together to the extent of making it impossible to inflect the former word and say, *e.g.*, *mit sacke und packe* or *grundes und bodens*; indeed, we here, though very rarely, may find something corresponding to the English group genitive; thus, Wieland has "des zu Abdera gehörigen *grund und bodens*".[1] But an inspection of the above collected examples will show that the explanation does not hold good; for in the majority of cases we have not only group-compounds, but also free groups[2] inflected like single words. This feeling of connectedness may

[1] Paul, *Princ. d. Sprachgesch.*, 2nd edit., p. 280.

[2] For the distinction see Sweet, *N. E. G.*, § 440: "Many word-groups resemble sentences in the freedom with which they allow one word to be substituted for another of like grammatical function, or a new word to be introduced. We call such word-groups *free groups*. Thus the free group *for my sake* can be made into *for his sake*. ... But in such groups as *son-in-law, man-of-war, bread-and-butter, cup-and-saucer*, no such variation is possible, the order of the elements of these groups being as rigidly fixed as in a compound word. We call such combinations *group-compounds*."

have gone for something in the development of the modern word-order where the genitive of *the Queen of England* is placed before the governing noun, instead of the old "the Queen's crown of England"; and it undoubtedly plays some part in the cases mentioned in § 237 (A and B's); but it gives no satisfactory explanation of the difference between the plural *the Queens of England* and the genitive *the Queen of England* s.

241. As the nature of the group fails to give an answer to our question we turn our attention to the ending, and the first thing that strikes us is that we find no trace of the group genitive with any of the O. E. genitive endings -*a*, -*ra*, -*an*, -*e*, -*re*, etc. (cf. § 127), but only with -(*e*)*s*. It is not till this ending has practically superseded all the other ways of forming the genitive that our phenomenon begins to make its appearance. In other words, the first condition of forming genitives of whole groups as if they were single words is that the manner of formation of genitives should be on the whole uniform. Where the genitive is formed irregularly, as is now only the case with the personal pronouns, we have had until the present day only rudimentary and feeble attempts at group genitives.

242. Now, if we were to ask: What is the reason of this regularity in the formation of English noun genitives? then any student that is at all acquainted with modern linguistic theories and methods would be out with the answer: "Why, it is due to analogy;

the *s*-ending has gradually been extended to the whole of the vocabulary, the analogy of those nouns which had an *s*-genitive in O. E. prevailing over the others".

Very good; the answer is obviously correct. And yet it is not entirely satisfactory, for it does not account for the difference observable in many words between the formation of the genitive and that of the plural. In the latter, too, the *s*-ending has been analogically extended in pretty much the same way as in the former; but how is it that we so often see the irregular plural preserved, whereas the genitive is always regular? We have the irregular plurals *men, children, oxen, geese*, etc., as against the regular genitives *man's, child's, ox's, goose's*, etc. In the days of Chaucer and Shakespeare the plural and the genitive of most words ending in *f, e.g., wife* and *life*, were identical, *wives* and *lives* being said in both cases; why has the analogy of the nom. sg. been more powerful in the genitive (modern *wife's, life's*) than in the plural?

The only explanation, as far as I can see, lies in the different function of the two endings; if we put a singular word into the plural, the change affects this word only; its relation to the rest of the proposition remains the same. But if, on the other hand, we put a word in the genitive case which was in the nominative, we change its syntactical relation completely; for the function of a genitive is that of closely connecting two words.

243. There is yet another thing to be noted. The O. E. genitive had many different functions; we may broadly compare its syntax to that of the Latin genitive. We find in Old English possessive, partitive, objective, and descriptive genitives; genitives governed by various adjectives and verbs, etc. And the position of the genitive is nearly as free as it is in Latin. But if you will take the trouble to read a few pages of any Old English prose book, of the Anglo-Saxon chronicle, of King Alfred, or of Ælfric, you will soon observe that where the Old English genitive might be rendered by a genitive in Modern English, it nearly always precedes its noun; where the word-order is different, the old genitive construction has, in the majority of cases, been abandoned. It is a significant fact that the only surviving use of the English genitive is a prepositive one; the word-order "the books my friend's" for "my friend's books" is, and has been for many centuries, as impossible in English as it is frequent in German: "die bücher meines freundes".

244. We are now in a position to draw our conclusions. The *s* is always wedged in between the two words it serves to connect; it is, accordingly, felt as belonging nearly as much to the word following it as to the preceding one. Nay, it is now more important that the *s* should come immediately before the governing word than that it should come immediately after the noun which it turns into a genitive case. It is now partly a suffix as of old, partly a prefix; if we were allowed to coin a new word we should term it an *interposition*.

This peculiar development gives us the clue to the problems mentioned above. If the *s* of the genitive is more loosely connected with the word it belongs to than is the *s* (or other suffix) of the plural, that is the reason why it tolerates no change in the body of the word: the old plural *wives* may remain; but the genitive (originally *wives* also) must be made to agree with the nominative—and so it becomes *wife's*.[1]

And we now see clearly why such groups as *the Queen of England*, when put in the genitive, affix the *s* to the last word of the group, but when put in the plural, to the first.

245. Let us look again at some of the above examples; they will enable us to formulate the following three rules:—

When the governing word follows immediately after the genitive, the *s* is never left out;

But this is very frequently the case when the governing word is placed elsewhere (or is understood);

Whenever the *s* is taken from the word to which it should properly belong (according to the old grammar) and shifted on to some other word, this

---

[1] In the present orthography, too, the gen. is brought nearer to the spelling of the nom. sg. than the nom. pl. is: gen. *lady's*, *church's*, but pl. *ladies*, *churches*; Shakespeare and Addison would write *ladies* and *churches* for both forms.

latter is always followed immediately by the governing word.

Compare, for instance:—

(O. E.) *anes reades monnes blod* ... ... (Mod.) *a red* man's blood
(M. E.) Julianes heste þe *amperur* ... ... (Mod.) the *Emperor* Julian's command
(M. E.) the *kinges* meting Pharao ... ... (Mod.) *King* Pharao's dream
at Smith's the *bookseller*['s] ... at Smith the *bookseller*'s office
(Ch.) for your *bothes* peyne ... for *both* your pains
(Ch.) kinges blood of *Perse* ... (Marlowe) the King of *Perseas* crowne

anybody's else ... ... anybody *else's* hat
(it does not matter *whose* ever it is) ... ... (*whoever*'s image)
(M. E.) *kyngys doghtur and emperowre* ... ... (Mod.) a king and emperor's daughter
(Sh.) Her lays were tuned like *the lark* ... ... they were tuned like *the lark's* lays
(his father is richer than the *man's* we met yesterday[1]) (he is richer than the *man* we met yesterday's father)

246. Now, let us sum up the history of the genitive ending *s*.

In the oldest English it is a case-ending like any other found in flexional languages; it forms together with the body of the noun one indivisible whole, in which it is often impossible to tell where the kernel of the word ends and the ending begins (compare

[1] I have placed those sentences within parentheses which have only a theoretical interest, as neither playing nor having played any noticeable part in natural speech.

endes from *ende* and *heriges* from *here*); the ending is only found in part of the vocabulary, many other genitive endings being found elsewhere.

As to syntax, the meaning and the function of these genitive endings are complicated and rather vague; and there are no fixed rules for the position of the genitive in the proposition.

In course of time we witness a gradual development towards greater regularity and precision. The partitive, objective, descriptive and some other functions of the genitive become obsolete; the genitive is invariably put immediately before the word or words it governs: irregular forms disappear, the *s*-ending only surviving as the fittest, so that at last we have one definite ending with one definite function and one definite position. If the syntactical province of the genitive has been narrowed in course of time, the loss—if such it be—has been compensated, and more than compensated, as far as the *s*-ending is concerned, by its being now the sole and absolute sovereign of that province; its power is no longer limited to some masculine and neuter nouns nor to one number only; it rules irrespective of gender and number.

247. In an Old English genitive the main ("full") word and the case-forming element are mutually dependent on each other, not only in such genitives as *lufe* or *suna* or *bec* or *dohtor*, but also in the more regular formations in *-es*; one part cannot be separated from the other, and in the case of several words belonging together, each of them has to be put in the genitive case: *anes reades mannes | þære godlican lufe | ealra godra ealdra manna weorc*, etc.

In Modern English, on the other hand, the *s* is much more independent: it can be separated from its main word by an adverb such as *else*, by a prepositional clause such as *of England* or even by a relative clause such as *I saw yesterday*; and one *s* is sufficient after such groups as *a red man* or *all good old men*. If, therefore, the definition given above of flexion (§ 92) be accepted, according to which its chief characteristic is inseparableness, it will be seen that the English genitive is in fact no longer a flexional form; the *s* is rather to be compared with those endings in agglutinating languages like Magyar, which cause no change in the words they are added to, and which need only be put once at the end of groups of words (§ 31);[1] or to the empty words of Chinese grammar (§ 66). Our present nineteenth century orthography half indicates the independence of the element by separating it from the body of the preceding noun by an apostrophe; there would be no great harm done if the twentieth century were to go the whole length and write, *e.g.*, *my father's house*,

[1] Professor Vilh. Thomsen, in his lectures on the Science of Language some ten years ago, used to illustrate the principle of agglutination by a comparison with the Danish genitive ending *s*, which is in many respects analogous to the English ending.

the Queen of England's power, somebody else's hat, etc.[1] Compare also Thackeray's lines (*Ballads*, p. 64):—

> He lay his cloak upon a branch,
> To guarantee his Lady Blanche
>   's delicate complexion.

It is important to notice that here historically attested facts show us in the most unequivocal way a development—not, indeed, from an originally self-existent word to an agglutinated suffix and finally to a mere flexional ending, but the exactly opposite development of what was *an inseparable part of a complicated flexional system to greater and greater emancipation and independence.*

APPENDIX TO CHAPTER VIII.

"BILL STUMPS *HIS* MARK," ETC.

248. The tendency to turn the genitive ending into an independent word meets with, and is to a certain degree strengthened by, a phenomenon that has originally nothing to do with it; I mean, the **expression of a genitive relation by a common case plus a possessive pronoun.** The best known instance of this is "for *Jesus Christ his sake*" in the Common Prayer Book.

[1] It is true that this spelling would perhaps in some cases suggest a false pronunciation, for *phonetically* the ending still belongs to the preceding rather than to the following word, as its triple pronunciation [s, z, iz, § 253] is determined by the final sound of the former.

This peculiar idiom is not confined to English: it is extremely common in Danish, Norwegian and Swedish dialects, in Middle and Modern Low German, in High German (Goethe: "Ist doch keine menagerie So bunt wie *meiner Lili ihre!*"), in Magyar, etc. In English the phenomenon has been noticed by many grammarians;[1] and if any one wishes to see other or more instances than those from which I have tried to form an idea of the origin and character of the idiom, it is to their works that I must refer him.

249. In most cases the phenomenon is a form of that anacoluthia which I have already had occasion to mention (see § 162), and which consists in the speaker or writer beginning his sentence without thinking exactly of the proper grammatical construction of the word that first occurs to him, so that he is subsequently obliged to use a correcting pronoun. As this want of forethought is common everywhere and at all times, we find the grammatical irregularity in many languages,[2] and it is naturally very frequent when a lengthy clause is introduced: it is also often

---

[1] Mätzner, *Grammatik*, iii, 236; Fr. Koch, *Gramm.*, ii, 249; Abbott, *Shak. Gr.*, § 217; Storm, *Engl. Philol.*, 1881, 262; Einenkel, *Streifzüge*, 109, and Paul's *Grundriss*, i., 909; Kellner, Blanch., xxxvi., and *Hist. Outl. of Engl. Syntax*, § 308; Franz, *Engl. Studien*, xvii., 388.

[2] One French example from Bourget, *Cruelle Enigme*, 18: "*Elles* qui vivaient dans une simplicité de veuves sans espérance, et qui n'auraient pour rien au monde modifié quoique ce fût à l'antique mobilier de l'hôtel, *leur* sentiment pour Hubert leur avait soudain révélé le luxe et le confort moderne".

---

resorted to where a foreign name is introduced that does not conform to the native declensions.

The possessive pronoun is often, for some reason or other, separated from its antecedent:—

A. R., 82, "*þe þet* swuch fulðe speteð ut in eni ancre eare me schulde dutten *his* muð" | Ch., *L. G. W.*, 2180, "*Thise false lovers*, poison be *hir* bane!" | *M. P.*, v., 99, "*The wery hunter*, sleping in his bed, To wode again *his* mynde goth anon" | Sh., *R. III*., iii., 2, 58, and *Wint. T.*, iii., 2, 98, quoted in § 162 | *R. III.*, i., 4, 217, "Alas! for whose sake did I that ill deed? For *Edward*, for *my brother*, for *his* sake."

But we are here chiefly concerned with those cases in which the possessive pronoun followed immediately on its antecedent:—

Oros., 8, "*Asia & Europe hiera* landgemircu togædre licgað . . . *Affrica & Asia hiera* landgemircu onginnað of Alexandria". *ibid.*, 12, "*Nilus seo éa hire* æwielme is neh þæm clife þære Readan Sæs" | Malory, 126, "This lord of this castel his name is syr Damas, and he is the falsest knyght that lyueth" | Sh., *Tp.*, v., 1, 268, "*This mishapen knaue, his* mother was a witch" | Scott, *Lay of the Last Minst.*, i., 7, "But *he, the chieftain of them all, His* sword hangs rusting on the wall" | Rossetti, *Poet. W.*, 164, "For *every man on God's ground*, O King, *His* death grows up from his birth" | Tennyson, 616, "*The great tragedian*, that had quenched herself In that assumption of the bridesmaid, she that loved me, *our true Edith*, *her* brain broke with over acting".[1]

Ch., *M.*, iii, 145, "For sothly *he that precheth to hem that liste not to heere his wordes, his* sermounhem anoyeth" | Num., xvii, 5 (Revised Version), "It shall come to pass, that *the man whom I shall choose, his* rod shall bud" (Auth. Vers. . . . "that the man's rod whom I shall choose, shall blossom'").

The similarity between this sentence from the Revised Version and "the man I saw yesterday's father" is conspicuous.

250. There are, however, other sources from which this genitive construction by means of possessive pronouns may arise. First I shall mention what Einenkel thinks the sole origin of it, *viz.*, the construction after some verbs meaning to *take* or *rob*, where a dative + a possessive pronoun very nearly amounts to the same thing as a gen., as will be seen in the following instances:—

A. R., 286, "þet tu wult . . . reauen *God his* strencðe" | *ibid.*, 300, "Schrift reaueð *þe*

ueonde *his* lond" | Malory, 110, "Syr Tor alyghte and toke *the dwarf his* glayue".

But even if we include in this rule other verbs of a kindred nature, as in:—

A. S. Chron., A., 797, "Her Romane *Leone* bæm papan *his* tungon forcurfon & *his* eagan astungon",

the instances of this particular construction are not numerous enough to account for the frequency of the *his*-genitive. Language is here, as elsewhere, too complex for us to content ourselves with discovering the source of one of the brooklets that go to forming a big river. Looking round for other sources we see that other verbs as well as "rob," etc., may be followed by a dative + *his*, nearly equivalent to a genitive (*to ask a man his pardon* is nearly equivalent to *asking a man's pardon*); compare also the following examples, in none of which a substitution of a genitive for the dative + the possessive pronoun would involve a change in the meaning:—

A. R., 84, "He mid his fikelunge & mid his preisunge heleð & wrihð *mon his* sunne" (he with his flattery and with his praise concealeth and covereth from man (for a man) his sin = concealeth a man's sin) | Byron, v., 260 (*Sardanap.*, iv., 1), "and there at all events secure *My nephews and your sons their* lives" | Hughes, *Tom Br.*, 5, "There is enough of interest and beauty to last *any reasonable man his* life" | Tennyson, 372,

---

[1] A curious example with the pronoun of the first person is Sh, *Tp.*, i., 2, 109, "*Me (poore man) my* Librarie was dukedome large enough"; if we do not here take *me* as a dative = *to me*, we have something like an apology for the missing genitive *a* of "*I poor man*," cf. § 225.

"*Merlin* . . had built *the king his* havens, ships, and halls".

251. In yet other instances it is a nominative that combines with *his* to form our quasi-genitive. When we read in Chaucer manuscripts, for instance :—

"Heer beginnith the *Chanouns yeman his tale*,"

Prof. Skeat finds it necessary to warn us : "The rubric means, 'Here the *Canon's Yeoman* begins his tale'. The word *tale* is not to be taken as a nominative case." But it will be observed that it does not matter much for the understanding of the phrase as a whole whether we take it as a nominative or an accusative; Prof. Skeat may be right in thinking that in these rubrics *begin* was originally a transitive verb; but as in most other mediæval rubrics *begin* was taken intransitively (the subject being the title of the book), an analogous interpretation would naturally present itself in instances like the above, and then *yeman his* would be the equivalent of a genitive before *tale*. That some, at least, of the old scribes were not of Prof. Skeat's opinion, appears from the rubric found in MS. Arch. Seld. B, 114 :—

"Here endith the man of lawe his tale. And next *folwith the shipman his* prolog."

For it is here out of the question to construe, "And next the shipman follows his prologue;" this, then, is undoubtedly an instance of the *his*-genitive.

252. Sprung as it is, then, from various sources, this makeshift genitive now converges with and meets the originally totally different interpositional descendant from the old flexional *s*-genitive, so that the two formations become often practically indistinguishable.[1] The similarity is of a purely phonetic nature; *his* would, of course, be pronounced with weak stress, and in unstressed words in the middle of a sentence *h* is scarcely if at all audible (as in the rapid pronunciation of "he took *his* hat," etc.; compare also *it* for older *hit*, and *'s* for *has*). Thus, *þe bissop his broþer*, etc., in the B-text of Layamon, may be only another way of writing *bissopis* or *bissopes*.[2]

253. When, in the fifteenth century or so, most of the weak *e*'s disappeared in pronunciation, the genitive ending *-es* [-iz] was differentiated into the three forms which it still has :—

[s] after voiceless sounds (bishop's);
[z] after voiced sounds (king's), and
[iz] after hisses (prince's).

But the same change happened with the possessive pronoun, as will be seen very frequently in Shakespeare :—

All's, ii., 2, 10, "Put *off's* cap, *kiss his* hand" | *Cor.*, ii., 2, 160, "May they *perceiue's* intent" | *ibid.*, ii., 3, 160, "*At's* heart" | 171, "*For's*

[1] Compare such accidental convergings of not-related words as that of *sorrow* and *sorry*, § 87.

[2] Perhaps we have *Venus his* written for *Venuses* in Ch., *M. P.*, 4, 31, "The thridde hevenes lord (Mars) . . . hath wonne Venus his love"; or is *his love* = "his beloved one," in apposition to Venus ?

countrey" | v., 3, 159, "*To's* mother" | *Meas.*, i., 4, 74, "*For's* execution," etc. | | Marlowe, *Jew*, 1651, "*on's* nose" (cf. A. Wagner's note to his edit. of the same play, 294).

Compare the treatment of the verbal form *is*: *that's, there's, this is*. In Elizabethan English, *it* was treated similarly. I *saw't, for't, do't, upon't, done't,* etc. So also *us* (comp. mod. *let's*): *upon's, among's, upbraid's, behold's,* etc.

254. Here I add a few examples of the *his*-genitive from Chaucer down to the vulgar speech or burlesque style of our days:—

Ch., *L. G. W.*, 2593, "*Mars his* venim is adoun" | Sh., *Haml.*, ii., 2, 512, "Neuer did the Cyclop hammers fall On *Mars his* armours" | *Tw. N.*, iii., 3, 26, "'Gainst the *Count his* gallies" | 2 *H. IV.*, ii., 4, 308, "Art not thou *Poines his* brother?" | *L.L.L.*, v., 2, 528, "A man of *God his* making" (folio: God's) | Thack, *Pend.*, iii., 6 (a housekeeper says), "In *George the First his* time" | Gilbert, *Bab Ball.*, 36, "Seven years I wandered—Patagonia, China, Norway, Till at last I sank exhausted At a pastrycook *his* doorway".

255. To the popular feeling the two genitives were then identical, or nearly so; and as people could not take the fuller form as originating in the shorter one, they would naturally suppose the *s* to be a shortening of *his*; this is accordingly a view that we often find either adopted or contested, as will appear from the following quotations, which might easily be augmented:—

HUME, *Orthographie*, 1617, ed. by Wheatley, p. 29, "This *s* sum haldes to be a segment of his, and therfoer now almost al wrytes his for it as if it were a corruption. But it is not a segment of his: 1. because his is the masculin gender, and this may be foeminin; as, A mother's love is tender; 2. because his is onelie singular, and this may be plural; as, al men's vertues are not knawen."

MAITTAIRE, *Eng. Gr.*, 1712, p. 28, "The genitive ... is expressed by -s at the end of the word: as, *the childrens bread, the daughters husband, its glory.* The *s*, if it stands for *his*, may be marked by an apostrophus: *e.g.,* for Christ's sake: and sometimes *his* is spoken and written at length, *e.g., for Christ his sake.*"

ADDISON, *Spect.,* No. 135, "The same single letter [s] on many occasions does the office of a whole word, and represents the *his* and *her* of our forefathers. There is no doubt but the ear of a foreigner, which is the best judge in this case, would very much disapprove of such innovations, which indeed we do ourselves in some measure, by retaining the old termination in writing, and in all the solemn offices of our religion."[1]

ENQUIRE WITHIN, 1885, § 208, "The apostrophe (') is used to indicate the combining of two words in one, as *John's book*, instead of *John, his book*".

In its struggle for an independent existence, the *s*-interposition seemed likely to derive great assistance from the concurrence of the *his*-construction. But the coincidence was not to last long. On the one hand, the contraction of the weak *his* seems to have been soon given up, the vowel being reintroduced from the fully stressed form, even where the *h* was dropped (*he took 'is hat*); on the other hand, the limited signification of the possessive pronoun counteracted the complete fusion which would undoubtedly have taken place, if *his* had been common to all genders and to both numbers, instead of being confined to the masc. (and in former centuries the neuter) sg. A formation like "Pallas her glass" (quoted by Abbott from Bacon) does not fit in with the rest of the system of the language, and "Pallas his glass" would jar upon English ears because *his* is too much felt as a pronoun denoting sex.

[1] This remark of Addison's gives us the clue to the retention of "for Jesus Christ his sake" in the Prayer Book; it is no doubt the old syllabic ending *Christès* remained unaltered after the *e* had generally become silent, on account of the accustomed rhythmic enunciation; a better way of spelling it would therefore be *Christès* as in *blessèd*, etc.

CHAPTER IX.

ORIGIN OF LANGUAGE.

I. METHOD.

256. GOETHE, in his *Dichtung und Wahrheit*, relates how in Strasburg he was in constant intercourse with Herder at the time when the latter was engaged in writing his prize essay for the Berlin Academy on the origin of language; and how he read the manuscript, although, as he confesses himself, he was very little prepared to deal with that subject; "I had," he says, "never bestowed much thought on that kind of thing; I was still too much engrossed by present things (zu sehr in der mitte der dinge befangen) to think about their beginning or end".

If it is not presuming too much to compare oneself with Goethe, even in so small a matter, and one, moreover, of so negative a character, I must confess that I too, like Goethe, have given most study to languages as they are now-a-days, to the "middle" of languages; the earlier stages I have studied mainly, if not exclusively, in so far as they are capable of throwing light upon the languages which are still living: I have therefore only an imperfect and sporadic knowledge of the vast literature which deals with the origin of speech; and the impressions left by occasionally reading some book or short paper on the subject have not encouraged me to master that literature more systematically. Under these circumstances I felt greatly relieved to come across the following verdict of WHITNEY'S: "No theme in linguistic science is more often and more voluminously treated than this, and by scholars of every grade and tendency; nor any, it may be added, with less profitable result in proportion to the labour expended; the greater part of what is said and written upon it is mere windy talk, the assertion of subjective views which commend themselves to no mind save the one that produces them, and which are apt to be offered with a confidence, and defended with a tenacity, that are in inverse ratio to their acceptableness. This has given the whole question a bad repute among sober-minded philologists."[1]

257. Although I look upon all previous attempts to penetrate the secret with very much the same feelings as those of the fox in the fable, when he noticed that all the traces led into the den, and not a single one came out, I shall ask my readers to join me in casting a rapid glance at those theories which have hitherto been most generally accepted as containing the clue of our problem. In mentioning them I shall make use of those nicknames by which they

[1] *Oriental and Linguistic Studies*, i., 279.

are familiar to readers of the discussion between Max Müller and Whitney.

First comes the old *bow-wow* theory: Primitive words were imitative of sounds; man copied the barking of dogs and thereby obtained a natural word with the meaning of "dog," or "bark".

The next theory is the *ding-dong* or "nativistic" theory: according to this there is a somewhat mystic harmony between sound and sense; "there is a law which runs through nearly the whole of nature, that everything which is struck rings. Each substance has its peculiar ring. Gold rings differently from tin, wood rings differently from stone; and different sounds are produced according to the nature of each percussion. It was the same with man." Language is the result of an instinct, a "faculty peculiar to man in his primitive state, by which every impression from without received its vocal expression from within". But this "creative faculty which gave to each conception as it thrilled for the first time through the brain a phonetic expression, became extinct when its object was fulfilled" (Max Müller, who has, however, abandoned this theory).

The *pooh-pooh* theory derives language from interjections, instinctive ejaculations called forth by pain or other intense sensations or feelings.

The fourth and last of these theories is the *yo-he-ho*, first propounded by Noiré,[1] and subsequently adopted

[1] Although Herbart seems to have had similar thoughts: "Die naturlaute oder zufälligen äusserungen bei gelegenheit

by Max Müller: under any strong muscular effort it is a relief to the system to let breath come out strongly and repeatedly, and by that process to let the vocal chords vibrate in different ways; when primitive acts were performed in common, they would, therefore, it is said, naturally be accompanied with some sounds which would come to be associated with the idea of the act performed, and stand as a name for it; the first words would accordingly mean something like "heave" or "haul".

258. Now, these theories—which, by the way, it is rather difficult to represent with perfect impartiality in a few lines—denounce and combat each other; thus Noiré and Geiger, in their explanation of the origin of speech, think it perfectly possible to do entirely without sound imitation, or onomatopœia. And yet what would prevent our uniting these several theories and using them concurrently? It would seem to matter not so very much whether the first word uttered by man was *bow-wow* or *pooh-pooh*, for the fact remains that he has said both one and the other. Each one of the theories—save, perhaps, the *ding-dong*, which is hardly anything but a rather misty variation of the interjectional theory—is able to explain *parts of language*, but still only parts, and not even the most important parts—the main body of language they hardly seem even to touch.

des gemeinsamen handelns reproducirten sich bei jedem in wiederkehrender lage," quoted by Marty, *Vierteljahrssch. f. wiss. philosophie*, xiv., 72.

To all the theories, that of Noiré only excepted, it may further be objected that they are too individual; they do not touch language as a means of human intercourse; as Ellis puts it, "The Pooh-pooh! the Bow-wow! and the Ding-dong! theories might serve for Robinson Crusoe. With Man Friday would begin real language—attempted and partially effected interchange of thought by mouth and ear".[1] Moreover, they all tacitly assume that up to the creation of language man had remained mute or silent; but this is most improbable from a physiological point of view. As a rule we do not find an organ already perfected on the first occasion of its use; an organ is only developed by use.

259. As to the *bow-wow* theory in particular, it is in the first place rather an unlucky hit that the dog's cry should have been chosen of all others; for naturalists maintain that dogs did not learn to bark till after their domestication (one might perhaps wish that they had not learned then!). But apart from this— and we might of course just as well use some other animal's cry to name the theory after; there is abundance of choice—it still seems rather absurd, as remarked by Renan, to set up this chronological sequence: first the lower animals are original enough to cry and roar; and then comes man, making a language for himself by imitating his inferiors.

To the advocates of the *pooh-pooh* theory it must be objected that they do not go deep enough when they

[1] *Transactions of the Philol. Soc.*, 1873-74, p. 18.

take interjections for granted, without asking where they originate. This is a question which philologists have entirely disregarded; but natural science has offered an explanation of at least some of our interjections. In DARWIN's interesting work on *The Expression of the Emotions*, which it is not to the credit of the science of language to have overlooked, purely physiological reasons are given for the feeling of contempt or disgust being accompanied by a tendency "to blow out of the mouth or nostrils, and this produces sounds like *pooh* or *pish*". And Darwin goes on to say: "When any one is startled or suddenly astonished, there is an instantaneous tendency, likewise from an intelligible cause, namely, to be ready for prolonged exertion, to open the mouth widely, so as to draw a deep and rapid inspiration. When the next full expiration follows, the mouth is slightly closed, and the lips, from causes hereafter to be discussed, are somewhat protruded; and this form of the mouth, if the voice be at all exerted, produces, according to Helmholtz, the sound of the vowel O. Certainly a deep sound of a prolonged *Oh!* may be heard from a whole crowd of people immediately after witnessing any astonishing spectacle. If, together with surprise, pain be felt, there is a tendency to contract all the muscles of the body, including those of the face, and the lips will then be drawn back; and this will perhaps account for the sound becoming higher and assuming the character of *Ah!* or *Ach!*"

260. It is a common feature of all previous attempts at solving the question that the investigator has conjured up in his imagination a primitive era, and then asked himself: How would it be possible for men or manlike beings, who have hitherto been unable to speak, to acquire speech as a means of communication of thought? Not only is this method followed, so to speak, instinctively by everybody, but we are even positively told (by Marty) that it is the only method possible. In direct opposition to this assertion I should like to advance the view that it is chiefly and principally due to this method and to this manner of putting the question that the result of all attempts to solve the problem has been so very small. Linguistic philosophers have acted very much as the German did in the well-known story, who set about constructing the camel out of the depths of his inner consciousness. Hegel began his philosophy with pure non-existence, and thence took a clean jump to pure existence; and our philosophers make the same jump with regard to language. But jumps are dangerous if you have no firm ground to take off from!

If we are to have any hope of success in our investigation, we must therefore look out for new methods and new ways; and there are, as far as I can see, only two ways which lead us to where we may expect to see new views opened before us over the world of primitive language.

261. One of these has its starting-point in the language of children. On a great many points biologists have utilised the discovery that the development of the individual follows on the whole the same course as that of the race; the embryo, before it arrives at full maturity, will have passed through essentially the same stages of development which in countless generations have led the whole species to its present level. Would it then be surprising if the course of development by mankind at large of the faculty of speech and the mental conceptions therein implied should be humbly mirrored to us in the process by which any child learns to use its vocal organs to communicate its thoughts?

This idea has obviously been present, more or less consciously, to many; and children's language has often been invoked to furnish illustrations and parallels of the process gone through in the formation of primitive language. But I cannot help thinking that philologists have generally been guilty of an erroneous inference in applying this principle; inasmuch as they have taken all their examples from a child's acquisition of an already existing language. The fallacy will be evident if we suppose for a moment some one endeavouring to imagine the evolution of music from the manner in which a child is now-a-days taught to play on the piano. Manifestly the modern learner is in quite a different position to primitive man, and has quite a different task set to him: he has an instrument ready to hand, and melodies already composed for him, and finally a teacher who understands how to draw these tunes forth from the instrument. It is just the same thing with language: the task of the child is to learn an existing language, that is, to connect certain sounds heard from the mouths of its fellow-creatures with the same ideas which the speakers associate with them, but not in the least to frame anything new. No; if we are seeking some parallel to the primitive acquisition of language, we must look elsewhere and go to baby language as it is spoken in the first year of life, before the child has as yet begun to "notice" and to make out what use is made of language by grown-up people. Here, in the child's first purposeless murmuring, crowing, and babbling, we have real nature sounds; here we may expect to find some clue to the infancy of the language of the race.

262. The second way hinted at above is likely to yield more important results; it is exactly the opposite of that followed by the propounders of the usual theories. They make straight for the front of the lion's den; we have seen that this is fruitless (*vestigia terrent!*) and we will therefore try and steal into the den from behind. They think it logically correct, nay necessary, to begin from the beginning; let us, for variety's sake, begin from the "middle" of things, from languages as accessible at the present day, and let us attempt from that starting-point step by step to trace the backward path. Perhaps in this way we may reach the very first beginnings of speech.

The method I recommend is, in other words, to trace our modern nineteenth-century languages as far back in time as history and our materials will allow us; and then, from this comparison of present English with Old English or Anglo-Saxon, of Danish with Old Norse, and of both with "Common Germanic," of French and Italian with Latin, of Modern Persian with Zend, of modern Indian dialects with Sanskrit, etc., to deduce definite laws for the development of languages in general, and to try and find a system of lines which can be lengthened backwards beyond the reach of history. If we should succeed in discovering certain qualities to be generally typical of the earlier as opposed to the later stages of languages,[1] we shall be justified in concluding that the same qualities obtained in a still higher degree in the beginning of all; if we are able within the historical era to demonstrate a definite direction of linguistic evolution, we must be allowed to infer that the direction was the same even in those primeval periods for which we have no documents to guide us. But if the change witnessed in the evolution of modern speech out of older forms of speech is thus on a larger scale projected back into the childhood of mankind, and if by this process we arrive finally at uttered sounds of such a description that we cannot help thinking that this is no longer a real language, but something antecedent to language—why, then the problem will have been solved; for transformation is something we can understand, while a creation out

[1] In some instances we may also take the languages of contemporary savages as typical of more primitive languages than those of civilised nations.

of nothing can never be comprehended by human understanding; it can at best be left to stand as a religious postulate, as a miracle or a *crux*.

This, then, will be the object of the following rapid sketch: to search the several departments of the science of language for general laws of evolution—most of them have already been indicated and discussed at some length in the opening chapters of this volume—then to magnify the changes observed, and thus to form a picture of the outer and inner structure of some sort of speech more primitive than the most primitive language accessible to direct observation.

II. SOUNDS.

263. First, as regards the purely phonetic side of language, we observe everywhere the tendency to make pronunciation more easy, so as to lessen the muscular effort; difficult combinations of sounds are discarded, those only being retained which are pronounced with ease. In most languages therefore only such sounds are used as are produced by expiration, while inbreathed sounds and "clicks" or suction-stops are not found in connected speech. In civilised languages we meet with such sounds only in interjections, as when an inbreathed voiceless *l* (generally with rhythmic variations of the strength of breathing and corresponding small movements of the tongue), is used to express enjoyment, especially the enjoyment caused by eating and drinking, or when a click formed with the tip of the tongue (generally, but rather inadequately spelled *tut* in our alphabet, which is not at all adapted to the writing of such sounds) is used to express impatience; in drivers' shouts to their horses some other clicks occur. In some very primitive South-African languages, on the other hand, these and similar sounds are found as integral portions of words; and Bleek's researches render it probable that in former stages of these languages they were in more extensive use than now. We may perhaps draw the conclusion that primitive languages in general were extremely rich in all such difficult sounds.

264. Of much more far-reaching consequence is the following point. In some languages we find a gradual disappearance of differences of musical accent (or pitch); this has been the case in Danish, whereas Norwegian and Swedish have kept the old tones; so also in Russian as compared with Servo-Croatian. With regard to the tones in use in most early languages it is extremely difficult to state anything with certainty, as written documents scarcely ever indicate such things; still, we are fortunate enough in the works of old Indian, Greek and Latin grammarians to have express statements to the effect that pitch accents played a prominent part in those languages, and that the intervals used must have been comparatively greater than is usual in our modern languages. No doubt the same thing may be asserted with regard to languages spoken now-a-days by savage tribes, though here too our materials are very scanty, as most of the writers who have made a first-hand study of such languages have not had the necessary qualifications for undertaking this kind of investigation; nor can this astonish us, seeing how imperfectly tonic accents have been hitherto studied even in the best-known European languages. Here and there, however, we come across some information about peculiar tonic accents, as, for instance, in the case of some African languages.[1]

265. So much for word-tones; now for the sentence melody. It is a well-known fact that the modulation of sentences is strongly influenced by the effect of intense emotions in causing stronger and more rapid raisings and sinkings of the voice. I may here refer to the excellent introduction to HERBERT SPENCER'S essay on *The Origin and Function of Music*, where the illustrious author examines the

[1] It may not be superfluous expressly to point out that there is no contradiction between what is said here on the disappearance of tones and the remarks made above (§ 69) on Chinese tones. There we had to deal with a change wrought in the meaning of a word by a mere change of its tone; this was explained on the principle that the difference of meaning was at an earlier stage expressed by suffixes, etc., the tone that is now concentrated on one syllable belonging formerly to two syllables or perhaps more. But this evidently presupposes that each syllable had already some tone of its own—and this is what in this chapter is taken to be the primitive state. Word-tones were originally frequent, but meaningless; afterwards they were dropped in some languages, while in others they were utilised for sense-distinguishing purposes.

influence of the feelings on the loudness, quality or timbre, pitch, intervals, and rate of variation of the sounds uttered. "The utterances grow louder as the sensations or emotions, whether pleasurable or painful, grow stronger.... The sounds of common conversation have but little resonance; those of strong feeling have much more. Under rising ill-temper the voice acquires a metallic ring.... Grief, unburdening itself, uses tones approaching in *timbre* to those of chanting; and in his most pathetic passages an eloquent speaker similarly falls into tones more vibratory than those common to him.... While indifference or calmness will use the medium tones, the tones used during excitement will be either above or below them; and will rise higher and higher, or fall lower and lower, as the feelings grow stronger.... Extreme joy and fear are alike accompanied by shrill outcries.... While calm speech is comparatively monotonous, emotion makes use of fifths, octaves, and even wider intervals.... The remaining characteristic of emotional speech which we have to notice is that of variability of pitch.... On a meeting of friends, for instance—as when there arrives a party of much-wished-for visitors—the voices of all will be heard to undergo changes of pitch not only greater but much more numerous than usual."[1]

[1] Cf. also Carlyle, *Heroes*, Lect. 3, p. 78: "Observe too how all passionate language does of itself become musical,—with a finer music than the mere accent; the speech of a man even in zealous anger becomes a chant, a song...."

266. Now, it is a consequence of advancing civilisation that passion, or, at least, the expression of passion, is moderated, and we must therefore conclude that the speech of uncivilised and primitive men was more passionately agitated than ours, more like music or song. And this conclusion is borne out by what we hear about the speech of many savages in our own days. I shall quote a few passages[1] showing this:—

"At Huaheine (Tahiti) several people had the habit of pronouncing whatever they spoke in a very singing manner" (Forster). "At the Friendly Islands, the singing tone of voice, in common conversation, was frequent, especially among the women" (*ibid.*). The Bhils, one of the hill tribes of India, "speak in a drawling sort of recitative" (Heber). "The language spoken by the inhabitants of the mountainous regions of the river Dibáng, east of the Abor country ... is distinguished by its very peculiar tones, and some of its consonants are extremely difficult of enunciation" (Richardson). "The speech of this nation (the Abipones of South America) is very much modulated and resembles singing." The East African's language is "highly artificial and musical" (Burton).

[1] Taken from H. Spencer's *Descriptive Sociology*. I should not give that work as an authority on linguistic facts in general, but here I may be allowed to use its convenient tabulations, as the question is not one of observing or interpreting grammatical facts, but only of the general impression which the speech of savages left on the ear of European travellers.

These facts and considerations all seem to point to the conclusion that there once was a time when all speech was song, or rather when these two actions were not yet differentiated; but I do not think that this inference can be established inductively at the present stage of linguistic science with the same amount of certainty as the statements I am now going to put forth as to the nature of primitive speech.

267. Linguistic evolution seems constantly to display a tendency to shorten words. Besides the shortening processes shown in such instances as *cab* for *cabriolet* and *bus* for *omnibus* (above, § 47), and haplologies, by which one of two succeeding similar sounds or sound-groups is discarded as in the pronunciation [wustə] for *Worcester*, in *England* for *Englaland*, in *simply* for *simplely*, in the familiar or vulgar pronunciations of *library*, *February*, *probably*, *literary*, *mama* as [laibri, Febri, probli, litri, ma'], etc., in Latin *nutrix* for *nutritrix*, *stipendium* for *stipipendium*, *tuli* for *tetuli*, etc., in French *controle* for *contre-rôle*, *idolâtre* for *idololâtre*, *Neuville* for *Neuveville*, colloquial [talɛr] for *tout à l'heure*, in Italian *cosa* for *che cosa*, *qualcosa* for *qualchecosa*, etc., etc.,[1] for *pease*, *adder* for *nadder* (§ 50); besides these more and finally shortenings by subtraction, such as *pea* sporadically-occurring processes we find that a great many of the constant phonetic changes of every

[1] See my remarks on this phenomenon, *Nord. Tidsskrift f. Filol.*, n. r. vii., 216, and ix., 323.

language result in the shortening of words: vowels in weak syllables are pronounced more and more indistinctly and finally disappear altogether; final consonants are dropped (as is perhaps best seen by a comparison of the pronunciation and the spelling of Modern French: the spelling will be found to retain a great many sounds which were formerly pronounced); initial consonants are often as unstable (see, for instance, Engl. *kn*, *gn* and *wr*, where the *k*, *g* and *w*. were formerly sounded), and in the middle of words assimilation and other causes lead to similar results. Every student of historical linguistics is familiar with numerous examples of seemingly violent contractions, which have really been wrought by regular and gradual changes continued through centuries: *lord*, with its three or four sounds, was formerly *laverd*, and in Old English *hlaford*; nay, the Old Germanic form of the same word contained indubitably as many as twelve sounds; Latin *augustus* has in French through *aoust* become *août*, which now consists only of two sounds [au], or, in a very widelyspread pronunciation, of only one sound [u]; Latin *oculus* (*oculum*) has shrunk into four sounds in Italian *occhio*, three in Spanish *ojo*, and two in French *œil*. These are everyday occurrences, while lengthenings of words (as in English *sound* from Fr. *son*, M. E. *son*, *soun*) are extremely rare. The ancient languages of our family, Sanskrit, Zend, etc., abound in very long words; the further back we go, the greater the number of *sesquipedalia*. This fact inspires us with distrust of the current theory, according to which every language started with monosyllabic roots; even the rare agreement on this point of two otherwise such fierce opponents as Professors Max Müller and Whitney cannot make us accept the theory; and the bull of excommunication issued by the latter[1] must not deter us from the heresy of saying: If the development of language took the same course in pre-historic as in historic times—and there is no reason to doubt it—then we must imagine primitive language as consisting (chiefly at least) of very long words, containing many difficult sounds, and sung rather than spoken.

III. GRAMMAR.

268. Can anything be stated about the grammar of primitive language? Yes, I think so, if we continue backwards into the past the lines of evolution resulting from the investigations contained in the preceding chapters. Ancient languages have several forms where modern languages content themselves with fewer; forms originally kept distinct are in course of time confused, either through a phonetic obliteration of differences in the endings, or through analogical extension of the functional sphere of one form; the single form *good* is now used where O. E. used the

[1] "The historically traceable beginnings of speech were simple roots . . . he who does not make that theory the basis of his further inquiries into the origin of language must not expect even to obtain a hearing from scholars" (*Oriental and Ling. St.*, i., 284).

forms *god, godne, gode, godum, godes, godre, godra, goda, godan, godena*; Ital. *uomo* or French *homme* corresponds to Lat. *homo, hominem, homini, homine*. Where the modern language has one or two cases, in an earlier stage it had three or four, and still earlier even seven or eight. The same thing is seen in the flexion of the *verb*: an extreme, but by no means unique example, is the English *cut*, which can serve both as present and past tense, both as singular and plural, both in the first, second and third persons, both in the infinitive, in the imperative, in the indicative, in the subjunctive, and as a past participle; compare with this the old languages with their separate forms for different tenses and moods, for two or three numbers, and in each for three persons; and remember, moreover, that the identical form, without any inconvenience being occasioned, is also used as a noun (*a cut*), and you will admire the economy of the living tongue. A characteristic feature of the structure of languages in their early stages is that each form of a word (whether verb or noun) contains in itself several minor modifications which, in the later stages of the language, are expressed separately, *e.g.*, by auxiliary verbs or prepositions. Such a word as Latin *cantavisset* unites into one inseparable whole the equivalents of six ideas: (1) "sing," (2) pluperfect, (3) that indefinite modification of the verbal idea which we term subjunctive, (4) active, (5) third person, and (6) singular.

269. These general tendencies of the later stages

of language may be properly denoted by the term "analysis". If, however, we accepted "synthesis" as the designation of the earliest stage we should be guilty of inconsistency: for as *synthesis* means composition, putting together, it presupposes that the elements "put together" had at first an independent existence; and this we deny. Therefore, whoever does not share the usual opinion that all flexional forms have originated through independent words gradually coalescing, but sees that we have sometimes to deal with the reverse process of inseparable parts of words gradually gaining independence (§§ 50, 57, 246 ff.), will have to look out for a better or less ambiguous word than *synthesis* for the condition of primitive speech. What in the later stages of language is analysed or dissolved, in the earlier stages was unanalysable or indissoluble; "entangled" or "complicated" would therefore be better renderings of our impression of the first state of things. In Latin *homini* nobody is able to see where the designation of "man" ceases, or which element signifies the dative case and which the singular number.

270. The direction of movement is towards flexionless languages (such as Chinese, or to a certain extent Modern English) with freely combinable elements; the starting-point was flexional languages (such as Latin or Greek); at a still earlier stage we must suppose a language in which a verbal form might indicate not only six things like *cantavisset*,

but a still larger number, in which verbs were perhaps modified according to the gender (or sex) of the subject, as they are in Semitic languages, or according to the object, as they are in some American Indian languages. But that amounts to the same thing as saying that the borderline between word and sentence was not so clearly defined as in more recent times; *cantavisset* is really nothing but a sentence-word, and the same holds true to a still greater extent of the sound-conglomerations of Indian languages. It is, indeed, highly characteristic of the primitive mind, and a subject of constant astonishment to those who study the languages of savage races, that a thing by itself cannot be conceived or spoken of: it is an utter impossibility for a savage to think of "knife," for instance, by itself; his power of abstraction is not sufficiently developed; but he can perfectly well say, "give me that knife," or "he plunged the knife into the hart". It will be noticed that in speaking of "sentence-words" as the original units of language I do not use that expression in exactly the same sense as certain linguistic writers, who exemplify their notion of primitive sentence-words by such modern instances as "Fire!" or "Thief!" In my opinion primitive linguistic units must have been much more complicated in point of meaning, as well as much longer in point of sound.

271. Another point of great importance is this: in early languages we find a far greater number of irregularities, exceptions, anomalies, than in modern ones. It is true that we not unfrequently see new irregularities spring up, where the formations were formerly regular; but these instances are very far from counterbalancing the opposite class in which words once irregularly inflected become regular, or anomalies in syntax, etc., are levelled. The tendency is more and more to denote the same thing by the same means in every case, to extend the ending, or whatever it is, that is used in a large class of words to express a certain modification of the central idea, until it is used in all other words as well.

Primitive language no doubt had a superabundance of irregularities and anomalies, in syntax and word-formation not less than in accidence. It was capricious and fanciful, and displayed a luxuriant growth of forms, entangled one with another like the trees in a primeval forest. Human minds of those times disported themselves in these long and intricate words as in the wildest and most wanton play. Primitive speech was certainly not, as is often supposed,[1] distinguished for logical consistency; nor, so far as we can judge, was it simple and facile: it is much more likely to have been extremely clumsy and unwieldy. Renan rightly reminds us of Turgot's wise saying: "Des hommes grossiers ne font rien de simple. Il faut des hommes perfectionnés pour y arriver."

[1] Cf., for instance, H. Sweet, *A New Engl. Grammar*, § 543, "In primitive languages they [grammatical and logical categories] are generally in harmony".

IV. VOCABULARY.

272. If we turn to the inner side of language, that is, to the meaning connected with the words, we shall find a development parallel to that noticed in grammar; and indeed, if we go deep enough into the question, we shall see that it is really the very same movement that has taken place here. The more advanced a language is, the more developed is its power of expressing abstract things. I use this term "abstract" not in the narrow sense of some logicians, who make it cover only such words as "whiteness" or "love"; but in a wider sense, so as to denote also the so-called general terms. Everywhere language has first attained to expressions for the concrete and special. In accounts of barbaric people's languages we incessantly meet with such phrases as these: "The aborigines of Tasmania had no words representing abstract ideas; for each variety of gum-tree and wattle-tree, etc., etc., they had a name; but they had no equivalent for the expression 'a tree'; neither could they express abstract qualities, such as 'hard, soft, warm, cold, long, short, round'"; or, "The Mohicans have words for cutting various objects, but none to convey *cutting* simply; and the Society Islanders can talk of a dog's tail, a sheep's tail, or a man's tail [?], but not of *tail* itself. The dialect of the Zulus is rich in nouns denoting different objects of the same genus, according to some variety of colour, redundancy, or deficiency of members, or some other peculiarity, such as 'red cow,' 'white cow,' 'brown cow,' etc."[1] Some languages have no word for *brother*, but only for "elder brother" and "younger brother"; others can only express "hand" as being either "my hand" or "your hand" or "his hand," and so on. In Cherokee, instead of one word for "washing," we find different words, according to what is washed : *ku-tuwo*, "I wash myself"; *ku-lestula*, "I wash my head"; *tsestula*, "I wash the head of somebody else"; *kukuswo*, "I wash my face"; *tsekuswo*, "I wash the face of somebody else"; *takasula*, "I wash my hands or feet"; *takunkela*, "I wash my clothes"; *takategra*, "I wash dishes"; *tsejuwu*, "I wash a child"; *kowela*, "I wash meat". Many savage tribes possess specific appellations for a number of shades of relationship which we can only express by a combination of two or three words, etc., etc.

In old Germanic poetry we find an astonishing abundance of words translated in our dictionaries by "sea," "battle," "sword," "hero," and the like: these may certainly be considered as remains of an earlier condition of things, in which each of these words at present only differing in form had its separate shade of meaning, which was subsequently lost.[2] The nomenclature of a remote past was undoubtedly

[1] Sayce, *Introd. Sc. Language*, ii, 5 ; cf. *ibid.*, i., 121.
[2] In Sanskrit dictionaries, according to Max Müller, are found no less than 5 words for "hand," 11 for "light," 15 for "cloud," 20 for "moon," 26 for "snake," 33 for "manslaughter," 35 for "fire," 37 for "sun".

constructed upon similar principles to those which we still come across in a word-group like *horse, mare, stallion, foal, colt*, instead of he-horse, she-horse, young horse, etc. So far, then, primitive speech had a larger vocabulary than later languages.

273. While our words are better adapted to express abstract things and to render concrete things with definite precision, they are comparatively colourless. The old words, on the contrary, spoke more immediately to the senses, they were manifestly more suggestive, more graphic and pictorial ; while to express one single thing we are not unfrequently obliged to piece the image together bit by bit, the old concrete words would at once present it to the hearer's mind as an indissoluble whole; they were, accordingly, better adapted to poetic purposes. Nor is this the only way in which we see a close relationship between primitive words and poetry.

274. If we try mentally to transport ourselves to a period in which language consisted of nothing but such graphic concrete words, we shall discover that, in spite of their number, even if taken all together, they would not suffice to cover everything which needed expression; a wealth in such words is not incompatible with a certain poverty. Words will accordingly often be required to do service outside of their proper sphere of application. That a figurative or metaphorical use of words is a factor of the utmost importance in the life of all languages, is a well-known fact ; but I am probably right in thinking it played a more prominent part in old times than now. In course of time a great many metaphors have become stiffened and worn out, so that nobody feels them to be metaphors any longer. Examine closely such a sentence as this: "He *came* to *look* upon the low *ebb* of morals as an *outcome* of bad *taste*," and you will find that nearly every word is a dead metaphor.[1] But the better stocked a language is with those ex-metaphors which have now become regular expressions for definite ideas, the less need is there for going out of your way to find new metaphors. The expression of thought tends therefore to become more and more mechanical or prosaic.

Primitive man, however, on account of the nature of his language, was constantly reduced to using words and phrases figuratively: he was forced to express his thoughts in the language of poetry. The speech of modern savages is often spoken of as abounding in similes and all kinds of figurative phrases and allegorical expressions. Just as in the traditionally known literature poetry is found in every country to precede prose, so poetic language is on the whole older than prosaic language; lyrics come before science, and Oehlenschläger is right when he sings:—

>   Naturlig er slig drift; af alle munde
>   Klang digtekvad, før prosa tales kunde,

[1] Of course, if instead of *look upon* and *outcome* we had taken the corresponding terms of Latin root, *consider* and *result*, the metaphors would have been still more dead to natural linguistic instinct.

which might be Englished:—

>   Thus Nature drove us; warbling rose
>   Man's voice in verse before he spoke in prose.[1]

V. CONCLUSION.

275. If now we try to sum up what has been inferred about primitive speech, we see that by our backward march we arrived at a language whose units had a very meagre substance of thought, and this as specialised and concrete as possible; but at the same time the phonetic body was ample; and the bigger and longer the words, the thinner the thoughts! Much cry and little sense! No period has seen less taciturn people than the first framers of speech; primitive speakers were not reticent and reserved beings, but youthful men babbling merrily on, without being so very particular about the meaning of each of their words. They did not narrowly weigh every syllable,—what were a couple of syllables more or less to them? They chattered away for the mere pleasure of chattering, resembling therein many a mother of our own times who will chatter away to baby without measuring her words or looking too closely into the meaning of each; nay, who does not care a bit for the consideration that the little deary does not understand a single word of her affectionate eloquence, and perhaps is not even able to hear it. But primitive speech—and we return here to an idea

[1] This translation I owe to the courtesy of the young Danish poet, the translator of Browning and Æschylus, Niels Möller.

thrown out above—still more resembles the speech of little baby himself, before he begins to listen properly to the words of grown-up people and to frame his own language after the pattern of theirs; the language of our remote forefathers was like that ceaseless humming and crooning with which no thoughts are as yet connected, which merely amuses and delights the little one. As Preyer has it, there is a period in the life of a child when his tongue is his dearest toy and best plaything;[1] Language originated as play, and the organs of speech were first trained in this singing sport of idle hours.

276. Primitive language had no great store of ideas, and if we consider it as an instrument for expressing thoughts, it was unwieldy and ineffectual; but what did that matter? Thoughts were not the first things to press forward and crave for expression; emotions and instincts were both much more primitive and far more powerful. Who does not know Schiller's often-quoted lines?—

Einstweilen, bis den bau der welt
Philosophie zusammenhält,
Erhält sie das getriebe
Durch hunger und durch liebe.

Which of the two, hunger or love, was the more powerful in producing germs of speech? To be sure, it was not hunger or that which is connected with hunger: mere individual self-assertion and the struggle for material existence. This prosaic side of life has

[1] *Die Seele des Kindes*, 2te aufl., 1884, p. 348.

only been capable of calling forth short monosyllabic interjections, howls of pain and grunts of satisfaction; but these are isolated and not capable of much further development; they are the most immutable portions of language, and remain now on essentially the same stand-point as thousands of years ago.

277. It is quite otherwise with love; as far as I see, linguistic considerations and generalisations point towards essentially the same source of language as that which Darwin arrived at by other paths: the effort to charm the other sex. To the feeling of love, which has left traces of its vast influence on countless points of the evolution of organic nature, are due not only the magnificent colours of birds and flowers: it inspired the first songs, and through them gave birth to human language as well.

278. If after spending some time over the deep metaphysical speculations of German linguistic philosophers you turn to men like Madvig or Whitney, you are at once agreeably impressed by the sobriety of their reasoning and their superior clearness of thought; but if you look more closely, you cannot help thinking that they imagine our primitive ancestors after their own image as serious and well-meaning men endowed with a large share of common-sense. By their laying such great stress on the communication of thought as the end of language and on the usefulness to primitive man of being able to speak to his fellow-creatures about matters of vital importance, they leave you with the impression that these "first framers of speech" were sedate, alderman-like citizens, with a prominent sense for the purely business and matter-of-fact side of life; indeed, according to Madvig, women had no share in the creating of language. Speech seems chiefly to have been instituted as a vehicle of important communications and judicious reasonings.

279. In opposition to this rationalistic view I should like, for once in a way, to bring into the field the opposite view: the genesis of language is not to be sought in the prosaic, but in the poetic side of life; the source of speech is not gloomy seriousness, but merry play and youthful hilarity: in primitive speech I hear the laughing cries of exultation when lads and lasses vied with one another to attract the attention of the other sex, when everybody sang his merriest and danced his bravest to lure a pair of eyes to throw admiring glances in his direction. Language was born in the courting days of mankind: the first utterance of speech I fancy to myself like something between the nightly love lyrics of puss upon the tiles and the melodious love songs of the nightingale.

280. Strong, however, as must have been the influence of love, it was not the only feeling which tended to call forth primitive songs.[1] Any strong emotion, and, more particularly, any pleasurable excitement, will result in song. Singing, like any other sort of play, is due to an overflow of energy, which is discharged in "unusual vivacity of every kind, including vocal vivacity". Out of the full heart the mouth sings! Mr. Spencer has a good many quotations to the effect that savages will sing whenever they are excited: exploits of war or of the chase, the deeds of their ancestors, the coming of a fat dog, any incident, "from the arrival of a stranger to an earthquake," is turned into a song; and most of these songs are composed extempore. "When rowing, the Coast-negroes sing either a description of some love intrigue or the praise of some woman celebrated for her beauty. In Loango the women as they till the field make it echo with their rustic songs." Park says of the Bambarran: "They lightened their labours by songs, one of which was composed extempore, for I was myself the subject of it". In some parts of Africa nothing is done except to the sound of music. They are very expert in adapting the subjects of these songs to current events. The difference between them is not so great as would appear from Mr. Spencer's words. Only I must take exception to Mr. Spencer's expression that song or chant is derived from "emotional speech in general," if it is implied therein that speech is older than song. On the contrary, I hold that our comparatively monotonous spoken language and our highly developed vocal music are differentiations of primitive utterances, which had, however, more in them of the latter than of the former.

[1] See Mr. Herbert Spencer's criticism of Darwin's view in the *Postscript* to the *Essay on the Origin of Music*, in the library ed. of his *Essays*, vol. ii., 1891, p. 426 ff. As I feel utterly incompetent to decide when two such eminent doctors disagree, I have tried to combine their views; perhaps the

Malays amuse all their leisure hours with the repetition of songs, etc. One of Mr. Spencer's quotations aptly illustrates the way in which primitive men, as I fancy, struck up their songs long before language was developed for the communication of ideas: "In singing, the East African contents himself with improvising a few words without sense or rhyme and repeats them till they nauseate".

Nor is this sort of singing on every and any occasion confined to savages; it is found wherever the in-door life of civilisation has not killed out open-air hilarity; formerly in our Western Europe people sang much more than they do now. The Swedish peasant Jonas Stolt, writing about 1820, says: "I have lived in a time when young people were singing from morning till eve. Then they were carolling both out- and in-doors, behind the plough as well as at the threshing-floor and at the spinning-wheel. This is all over long ago: now-a-days there is silence everywhere; if some one were to try and sing in our days as we did of old, people would term it bawling."[1]

281. The first things that were thus expressed in song were, to be sure, neither deep nor wise; how could you expect it? Even now the thoughts associated with singing are generally neither very clear nor very clever; like humming or whistling, singing is often nothing more than an almost automatic expression of a mood; "and what is not worth saying can be sung". Besides, it has been the case at all times that things transient and trivial have been readier to find expression than Socratic wisdom. But the frivolous use ground the instrument, and rendered it little by little more serviceable to a multiplicity of purposes, so that it became more and more fitted to express everything that touched human souls.

282. Men sang out their feelings long before they were able to speak their thoughts. But they did not originally sing in order to communicate their ideas or feelings; in fact, they had not the slightest notion that such a thing was possible. They "sang but as the linnet sings"—this word is truer of primitive men and women than ever it was of the late poet laureate. They little suspected that in singing as nature prompted them, they were paving the way for a language capable of rendering minute shades of thought; just as they could not suspect that out of their coarse pictures of men and animals there should one day grow an art enabling men of distant countries to speak to each other. As is the art of writing to primitive painting, so is the art of speaking to primitive singing. And the development of the two vehicles of communication of thought present other curious and instructive parallels. In primitive picture-writing, each sign meant a whole sentence or even more—the image of a situation or of an incident being given as a whole—; this developed into an ideographic writing of each word by itself; this system was

[1] Jonas Stolt's *Optegnelser*, udg. af R. Mejborg, Copenh., 1890, p. 111.

succeeded by syllabic methods, which had in their turn to give place to alphabetic writing, in which each letter stands for, or is meant to stand for, one sound. Just as here the advance is due to a further analysis of language, smaller and smaller units of speech being progressively represented by single signs, in an exactly similar way, though not quite so unmistakably, the history of language shows us a progressive tendency towards analysing into smaller and smaller units that which in the earlier stages was taken as an inseparable whole.

283. While an onomatopoetic or echo-word like *bow-wow* and an interjection like *pooh-pooh* were at once employed and understood as signs for the corresponding idea, this was not the case with the great bulk of language. Just as we have seen above with regard to many details of grammatical structure[1] that by indirect and round-about ways they acquired other meanings than they had had originally, or acquired meanings where they had originally had none, so it was also with language at large. Originally a jingle of empty sounds without meaning, it came to be an instrument of thought. If man is, as Humboldt has somewhere defined him, "a singing creature, only associating thoughts with the tones," we must answer the question: How did this association of sense and sound come about? I think we can arrive at forming some idea of that process by remembering what has been said above on the signification of primitive words. This we must imagine to have been concrete and special in the highest degree. There are, however, no words whose signification is so concrete and special as proper names,—not such proper names as our modern *John* or *Jones* or *Smith*, which have become so common as to be scarcely proper names any longer; but proper names of the good old kind, borne by and denoting only one single individual. How easily might not such names spring up in a primitive state such as that described above! In the songs of a particular individual there would be a constant recurrence of a particular series of sounds sung with a particular cadence; no one can doubt the possibility of such individual habits being contracted in olden as well as in present times. Suppose, then, that "In the spring time, the only pretty ring time," a lover was in the habit of addressing his lass "With a hey and a ho, and a hey nonino!" his comrades and rivals would not fail to remark this, and would occasionally banter him by imitating and repeating his "hey-and-a-ho-and-a-hey-nonino". But when once this had been recognised as what Wagner would term a person's "leitmotiv," it would be no far cry from mimicking it to using the "hey-and-a-ho-and-a-hey-nonino" as a sort of nick-name for the man concerned; it might be employed, for instance, to signal his arrival. But when once proper names were given, common names (or nouns) would not be slow in following;

---

[1] Endings §§ 57, 60, 62, French negative *pas* § 58, tones § 69, interrogative particles §§ 73, 74, word-order § 85, vowel-changes § 91.

we see the transition from one to the other class constantly going on, names originally used exclusively to denote an individual being used metaphorically to connote that individual's most characteristic peculiarities, as when we say of one man that he is "a Croesus" or "a Vanderbilt," and of another that he is "no Bismarck". We may also remind the reader of the German schoolboy who stated in his history lesson that Hannibal swore he would always be a *Frenchman* to the Romans.[1] This is, at least, one of the ways by which language arrives at designations for such ideas as "rich," "statesman," and "enemy". Names of tools are in some cases proper names, used originally as some term of endearment, as when in thieves' slang a crowbar or lever is called a *betty* or *jemmy*; English *derrick*, as well as the German and Scandinavian word for a picklock (German, *dietrich*; Dan., *dirk*; Swed., *dyrk*), is nothing but the proper name *Dietrich* (*Derrick*, *Theodoricus*); compare also the history of the words *bluchers*, *jack* (boot-jack, jack for turning a spit, a pike, etc., also *jacket*), *pantaloon*, *hansom*, *to burke*, to name only a few examples.

284. Again, we saw above that the further back we went, the more the sentence was one indissoluble whole, in which those elements which we are accustomed to think of as single words were not yet separated. But it is just sentences of this sort whose genesis we can imagine with greatest ease on the supposition of a primitive period of meaningless

Polle, *Wie denkt das Volk*, 1889, p. 43.

singing. If a certain number of people have together witnessed some incident and have accompanied it with some sort of impromptu song or refrain, the two ideas are associated, and later on the song will tend to call forth in the memory of those who were present the idea of the whole situation. Suppose some dreaded enemy has been defeated and slain; the troop will dance round the dead body and strike up a chant of triumph, say something like "Tarara-boom-de-ay!" This combination of sounds, sung to a certain melody, will now easily become what might be called a proper name for that particular event; it might be roughly translated, "The terrible foe from beyond the river is slain," or "We have killed the dreadful man from beyond the river," or "Do you remember when we killed him?," or something of the same sort. Under slightly altered circumstances it may become the proper name of the man who slew the enemy. The development can now proceed further by a metaphorical transference of the expression to similar situations ("There is another man of the same tribe: let us slay him as we did the other!"); or by a blending of two or more of these proper-name melodies. I can give nothing but hints; but does not the reader begin now dimly to see ways by which primitive "lieder ohne worte" may have become, first, indissoluble sentences, and then gradually combinations of words more and more capable of being analysed? And does not this theory explain better than most others the great part

ORIGIN OF LANGUAGE.   365

which chance and fortuitous coincidence always seem to play in languages?

285. Language, then, began with half-musical unanalysed expressions for individual beings and events. Languages composed of such words and sentences are clumsy and insufficient instruments of thought, being intricate, capricious and difficult. But from the beginning the tendency has been one of progress, slow and fitful progress, but still progress towards greater and greater clearness, regularity, ease and pliancy. No one language has arrived at perfection; an ideal language would always express the same thing by the same, and similar things by similar means; any irregularity and ambiguity would be banished; sound and sense would be in perfect harmony; any number of delicate shades of meaning could be expressed with equal ease: poetry and prose, beauty and truth, thinking and feeling would be equally provided for: the human spirit would have found a garment combining freedom and gracefulness, fitting it closely and yet allowing full play to any movement.

But however far our present languages are from that ideal, we must be thankful for what has been achieved; seeing that—

Language is a perpetual orphic song,
Which rules with Dædal harmony a throng
Of thoughts and forms, which else senseless and shapeless were.

THE END.

INDEX.

The references are to the numbers of the paragraphs.

-a of the fem., 52, 53, 60, 61; of the pl. neuter, 62.
ablaut, 58, 91.
absolute construction, 165, 183; absolute pronouns, 57, 211.
abstract forms and words, 22 ff., 270, 272 ff.
accent, 46, 69.
accidence and syntax, 101, 103, 106.
accusative, ch. vii.; acc. with infinitive, 155.
adder, 108.
adverbial connexions, 233 ff.
after-correction, 162.
agglutinating languages, 4, 88.
agglutination theory, 54 ff.
ah, 179.
albeit, 45.
Alford, 26 note, 28, 194.
all our, 225 ff.
amalgamation, 94.
American languages, 90.
anacoluthia, 162 ff.
analogy, 144 ff.
analysis, 23, 92, 269.
anatomy, 50.
anomaly, *see* irregularity.
aoul, 267.
apposition, 163, 221.
Arian languages, 2, etc.
arrangement of grammar, 103 ff. article, in Bantu, 50; in Scandinavian, 54.
as, 160.
atomy, 50.
attraction, relative, 154, 162.
attributive words, 219 f.
auxiliaries, 22.

back-formations, 50.
Bantu languages, 34 ff.
Basque, 88, 89.
better, had better, 180, 213.
between you and I, 192.
Bleek, 34 ff.
blendings, 65, 155 ff., 177, 204.
Boney, 47.
Bopp, 4 note, 7, 63.
both our, 225 ff.
bow-wow theory, 257, 259, 283.
Bréal, 87.
Brincker, 38.
Brugmann, 55, 60, 91, 104.
but, 158.

cantlaveram, 22, 63, 268.
case-systems, ch. vi.; case-shiftings, ch. vii.
cherry, 50.
children's language, 261, 275.
Chinese, 4, 5, 66-72.
clicks, 263.
coalescence of cases, 81, 125, 134.
concord, 27-32, in Bantu, 34 ff.; in English, 219 ff., 247.
concrete words and forms, 22 ff.
conjoint pronouns, 211.
conjunctions and prepositions, 158 ff.; gen. of words connected by conjunctions, 234 f.
contaminations, *see* blendings.
contractions, 47.
controle, 267.
cosa for *che cosa*, 267.
curtailings of words. 47, 267.
'*cute*, 50.

(366)